BH9424

WILKES

'A FRIEND TO LIBERTY'

by the same author

Thomas Paine: His Life, Work and Times
Bernard Shaw: Man and Writer
etc.

WILKES

'A FRIEND TO LIBERTY'

by AUDREY WILLIAMSON

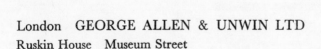

London   GEORGE ALLEN & UNWIN LTD
Ruskin House   Museum Street

First published in 1974

© Audrey Williamson 1974

ISBN 0 04 923064 6

Printed in Great Britain
in 11pt. Baskerville type
by The Aldine Press, Letchworth

ACKNOWLEDGMENTS

All biographers owe a debt to previous writers in the same field, both biographers as such and historians of political and social history. I hope I have indicated this both in the text and bibliography.

In addition, I must specially thank Sir Francis Dashwood, Bart, for driving me around his estate at West Wycombe and freely providing access to many private papers, and the cellar books of the 'Monks of Medmenham', at his beautiful Buckinghamshire house, West Wycombe Park, now preserved by the National Trust. The attached museum at West Wycombe, and the 'Hell-Fire' caves still preserved and open to the public there, also provided interesting material. I must also thank Sir Humphrey Sherston-Baker, Bart., for kind permission to reproduce the Zoffany painting of Wilkes and his daughter in his possession.

The Guildhall Library, the Westminster City Library, the National Portrait Gallery, Mr Christopher Brunel and various photographers have also helped with illustrations and other information; and the complete sets of that excellent paper, *The Sussex Weekly Advertiser or Lewes Journal* (1770–8), in Brighton Reference Library proved a mine of information, some of it quite new, in connection with Wilkes and local elections and also Wilkes' many tours of Sussex and the East and South of England.

I have also used material from a number of books on or by contemporaries of Wilkes, and research into the period by recent social historians, not referred to by previous biographers. These sources throw a new light on the nature of certain social manifestations of the time and also on some of Wilkes' associates.

AUDREY WILLIAMSON
October, 1973

CONTENTS

ILLUSTRATIONS

I

THE POLISH OF A GENTLEMAN

He was born with a squint and an ugliness which, if it did not merit the satanic cartoon drawn by his enemy William Hogarth, was remarkable enough to have impressed itself on everyone who met him. How much the squint, like the crippled foot of Lord Byron, accounted psychologically for the drive behind his voracious appetite for women, we cannot truly tell. If John Wilkes had any initial sense of inadequacy, he was, unlike Byron, a master at concealing it. He boasted he could talk away his face in thirty minutes; and although as he grew older he tended to expand the time allowance for the feat, to a fortnight and even, near the end, a month, he never gave any indication of his spirits being dashed by the experience. It was a challenge, never an inhibition.

'Gay Wilkes,' wrote his young acquaintance James Boswell from Pietole, the supposed birthplace of Virgil, 'congratulate with me: an hour of felicity is invaluable to a man whom melancholy clouds so much . . .' Wilkes' hours of felicity seemed untouched by adversity: his sunny resilience survived everything from a decamping cherished mistress to successive expulsions from Parliament and imprisonment. Women, on the whole, were the happier for their association with him: he left behind him no savage epitaphs of being 'mad, bad and dangerous to know', no shattered Caroline Lambs or murderous, child-bereaved Claire Clairmonts. 'A merry, cock-eyed, curious looking sprite', as Byron called him,[1] he made his mark on his century but left no wounds on it; only a tradition of audacity and courage, in the cause of liberty, which was to be grasped like a torch by younger hands, both in his own lifetime and later.

He was educated to be a gentleman, but not born one: a fact which may have accounted for his only occasional

[1] *The Vision of Judgement.*

13

inconsistency through life, when he seemed uncertainly poised between the classes, neither an enlightened aristocrat nor (as he is once said to have remarked to his late enemy, King George III) quite 'a Wilkeite'. But generally he had the engaging talent of mixing without self-consciousness with people from most social strata, men as well as women, and although towards the end of his life, his battles mainly past, he settled into something like parliamentary conformity, he never openly sank to the snobbery of Byron's 'I am and have been for reform always, but not for the reformers. I saw enough of them at the Hampden Club; Burdett [1] is the only one of them in whose company a gentleman would be seen . . .'

There were few, throughout his life, in whose company John Wilkes would not be seen, whatever quip he may have made about their education or manners in private: in this sense at least parental urge to turn him into a gentleman did not spoil him. He was born, most probably, on 17 October, 1725, although he himself gave the year as 1727 and duly celebrated his forty-fifth climacteric birthday some two years late. The matter has been scholastically discussed at some length, probably to the amusement of Wilkes' ghost if (as has been maintained) it still haunts his burial place in Grosvenor Chapel. He may have had a sudden whiplash of vanity about his age, a kind of rare rebellion against his face; if not, the onslaught of puberty, in such a character, must surely have occasioned some doubts or surprise at the time. The adoption by England of the new calendar, two centuries after the rest of Europe – thus very belatedly following the recommendation of John Dee, the Elizabethan astronomer royal – in any case complicates the dating of many men born in the eighteenth century. It took place as from 1 January 1752, and in addition the day after 2nd September that year became the 14th. Wilkes would not have been the only man

---

[1] Sir Francis Burdett: friend and admirer of Thomas Paine, who in 1798, according to the Diary of Thomas Holcroft, was 'inquiring into the number of persons imprisoned on suspicion, and their treatment, meaning to state the particulars to Parliament'. In 1810 he was himself imprisoned in the Tower, for political reasons, after a conflict in Parliament.

or woman to welcome or manufacture an unexpected age
bonus (the actor, David Garrick, had a feverish correspondence with his sister on the entries in the family Bible,
resulting in the happy conclusion that he was now only
thirty-five, not thirty-six years of age).

Wilkes' birthplace was Clerkenwell, where his father,
Israel, carried on a lucrative business as a malt distiller. He
was a descendant of a Staffordshire yeoman farmer, Richard
Wilkes of Auderly, who died in 1655. Wilkes' contemporary
biographer, Almon, quite wrongly claimed he was descended
from Edward Wilkes of Leighton Buzzard, a Yeoman of the
Removing Wardrobe of Charles II whose son Luke, said to
be John Wilkes' great-grandfather, was childless according to
the parish records and his own Will. This was probably a
confusion with Edward Wilkes of Albrighton, Shropshire, the
son of Richard Wilkes of Auderly, Staffordshire. John
Wilkes in later life used the arms of the Wilkes family of
Wolverhampton, Staffordshire. The family, in any case, was
inescapably middle class, but ready to take advantage of the
social rise, through wealth and marriage, which was to bring
tradesmen a growing influence and position in the coming
Industrial Revolution and beyond.

Wilkes was born in St John's Square, in the vicinity of
Clerkenwell Green, now not inaptly a centre of left-wing
politics and the venue of the Karl Marx Library. The house
not far away in St James's Square, where Wilkes was brought
up, was already an affluent one. Israel Wilkes, grandson of
Richard Wilkes, had arrived in London almost penniless, and
started his path to fortune driving a brewer's dray. But these
were times later to be immortalized in Hogarth's ferocious
'Gin Lane' cartoon, and gin, the cheapest of drinks on the
market, was to be 'mother's milk' to many before the aunt of
Shaw's Eliza Doolittle. Every fourth house in St Giles was
said to be a dramshop, and as Henry Fielding was to write in
the *Enquiry*: 'A new kind of drunkenness, unknown to our
ancestors, is lately sprung up amongst us, and which if not
put a stop to, will infallibly destroy a great part of the
inferior people. The drunkenness I hear intend is . . . by this
poison called Gin . . .' Every generation has its drug against

the pain of living, or to stimulate the nerves of experience: gin and port, the eighteenth-century escape routes for the poor and oppressed on the one hand, or the rich and powerful on the other, were merely the forerunners of opium and laudanum in the nineteenth century, and the cocktail or cannabis in the twentieth.

The acute Israel Wilkes became an apprentice to a distiller and in 1690 gained official recognition as a member of the Distillers' Company. When he died in 1745, the year before Culloden and the last Stuart bid to return to the English throne, he left his son, another Israel, considerable wealth. This Israel, John Wilkes' father, married Sarah Heaton, the daughter of a Bermondsey tanner, and through her he gained in addition a property in Hoxton Square. In religion she was a Dissenter, meaning she belonged to one of the non-Conformist groups now tolerated by the State outside the Anglican Church; and her husband, although he did not share her religion, drove her to chapel (as himself to church) in a coach-and-six. She was, nevertheless, buried, according to her Will, in the Church of St James, Clerkenwell.

Some writers on Wilkes, entirely without warrant or evidence, have assumed from the dissenting religion that she was, in fact, an unamicable puritan and a repressive force on her son. On the contrary, she must have been a woman of reasonable education and tolerant views, for on her death she left an art collection of some taste, including two items (resignedly classic-pagan in style) to her errant son. One of them, most inappropriately, was a bronze statuette of Antinous, the Emperor Hadrian's beautiful, homosexual cup-bearer. In her Will she left the residue of her estate to her less successful son Heaton, but added: 'my dear son John Wilkes in the most frank and liberal manner assured me my request in favour of his brother Heaton Wilkes should be strictly performed, and also added that he would lose no opportunity to render all the services in his power to his brother'. In the event, the services proved interchangeable, but the spirit of John's promise was kept.

John was the second of three sons, the others being Israel (who later emigrated to America) and Heaton, who eventually succeeded to the distillery but was for some time associated with his brother in his politics and finance, both equally hazardous and involved. There were two sisters, Sarah, who remained an eccentric recluse, and Mary, the younger, who was to be three times married and reflect more than a touch of her brother John's voluptuous tastes. John was educated at a private school in Hertford, where he established a reputation for quickness. He was then, after five years, sent to the Reverend Matthew Leeson, a dissenting minister of Aylesbury, Buckinghamshire, a town and county which were later to be much tossed by the tempest of Wilkesian electioneering. Leeson found in him an aptitude for the classics and a 'tincture of heretical theology' which he thought suggested a possible future as a freethinker. In fact, although a supporter of religious toleration, Wilkes as an Alderman and Lord Mayor of London made no bones about toeing the line of established churchgoing: his instincts were rational but he was not one to think it worth rebelling against this particular demand of office.

The question then arose as to the university most suited to a rich tradesman's son with pretensions to gentility. His father was a Whig in politics, and Oxford had a Jacobite reputation. (It would be interesting to see what it would have made of the later anti-Scottish Editor of *The North Briton*. Its reputation for learning was not encouraging: of Edward Gibbon, author of the monumental *Decline and Fall of the Roman Empire*, it was said 'he arrived at Oxford hungering for knowledge, and went away unsatisfied'.) Cambridge was considered by the unsuspecting father to be dangerous morally, so Leyden University was eventually chosen, perhaps, as has been suggested, in tribute to King William and the 'Glorious' Revolution of 1688 (it was also, long ago, the scene of another type of revolutionary, John of Leyden).

Leeson went with the boy, but his influence proved morally imperceptible. Boswell's notes made in Italy over twenty years later record Wilkes as declaring: 'at school and college I never read: I was always among women. At Leyden my father gave me as much money as I pleased. I had three or four whores, and was drunk every night. I had a sore head the morning after and then I read. I'm capable of sitting thirty hours over a table to study'. It was probably not an idle boast, on all counts. 'Men of wit and fancy', wrote Mary Wollstonecraft, the feminist, with surprising perspicacity, 'are often rakes; and fancy is the food of love.' In spite of his conscientious profligacy Wilkes was a widely-read man, with a fine library whose partial disposal, in times of economic crisis, hurt him more than almost anything in his buoyantly danger-prone life. Later in life he drank abstemiously, perhaps instinctively aware of family trade profits.

He entered Leyden on 8 September 1744, and was a contemporary there of Alexander Carlyle, William Dowdeswell and Charles Townshend. Altogether Leyden at this time had twenty-two British students. Dowdeswell was subsequently Chancellor of the Exchequer in the first Rockingham administration and the leader of the Rockingham Whigs in the House of Commons. He was, however, no political match for Charles Townshend, 'that splendid shuttlecock' as he was described by Richard Rigby in a letter to the Duke of Bedford. Townshend's brilliance was to be flawed by the eighteenth-century vice *in excelsis*, a shifting of focus that tended to follow, like a magnet, the lure of ambition and high office; and his posthumous reputation was to sink under the weight of his eloquent support of the doomed American Stamp Bill, and disastrous part, on the side of the King's party, in the preliminary attitudes of despotism that sparked off the American Revolution. But his ability was unquestioned and his support of Wilkes in Parliament and by pamphlet in the matter of general warrants was to sustain at least one loyalty formed in student days at Leyden.

The Reverend Dr Alexander Carlyle left an Autobiography in which he made an interesting comparison of the young Wilkes and Townshend. 'In the art of shining', he wrote, Wilkes 'was much outdone by Charles Townshend.' Townshend's person and manners were more engaging. 'He had more wit and humour, and a turn for mimicry.' Wilkes, in spite of his 'ugly countenance', was however in conversation a 'sprightly and entertaining fellow'. He adds the interesting remark (in view of the virulently anti-Scottish tone of Wilkes' later paper, *The North Briton*) that in those days at least Wilkes liked the Scots. But at university Wilkes was not yet engaged in combating a trend of government appointments, and Carlyle was no more than a congenial companion.

They were to have a common link in years to come in an admiration of David Garrick. Carlyle, who loved the theatre, in February, 1746, befriended on the packet for Harwich, on stormy seas, 'a young person of about sixteen, very handsome indeed, whom we took for a Hanoverian baron coming to pay his court at St James's'. The youthful gallant's fears and voice soon betrayed her sex; she was a young Viennese dancer named Violetti, thus protected *en travesti* by her party, and on her way to England to appear at the Opera at the Haymarket. Carlyle not unnaturally went twice to see her there, and found she performed exquisitely. He was not the only one of her audience to be entranced. A few years later she married the enraptured David Garrick, a love match that survived till Garrick's death in 1779, and on her side far beyond. The little dancer Violetti, now known by her real name, Eva Maria, died in 1822 at the age of almost one hundred years, outliving whole generations of her husband's eighteenth-century friends and admirers, while his name, and that of Wilkes who knew them both, passed into legend.

When Wilkes left Leyden he moved on to Utrecht, and travelled in the Rhinelands. As intended, he returned to England with the 'tone and bearing of a scholar and a gentleman'. Another university companion, Baron d'Holbach, the atheist later prominent in the Paris of the *philosophes*, supports this description with his lament that when Wilkes left Leyden 'the enchantment ceases, the delightful image vanishes, and nothing is left to me but the friendship which is of all my possessions the firmest and truest'. It was one of Wilkes' engaging qualities that, face or no face, he could charm a bird off a tree, and he seems to have aroused little of the resentment, among other men, often experienced by the conspicuously successful 'lady's man'.

In spite of his youth, marriage plans, in the way of the time, were ready for him on his arrival back in England. Parental choice had fixed on Mary Mead, the spinster daughter of Leeson's wealthy patron at Aylesbury, a retired merchant. She was ten years older than Wilkes, and possibly it was considered her last chance. Wilkes had imbibed enough of the gentleman's spirit to have no objection to marrying for money, and as the girl was not unhandsome he may even have had a few additional stirrings of susceptibility. There is no ground for the assumption, as has sometimes been made in works on Wilkes, that she was particularly ugly or as Calvinist as her mother. It was simply a doomed match between a young rake and a rather dull girl brought up as a Dissenter, with a mother whose character and influence carried with them all the religious inhibitions that implied.

The marriage, in 1747, was accompanied by hopeful horticultural tributes from d'Holbach concerning 'paths of love spread over with flowers': but the flowers withered as quickly as might have been expected. The couple settled in Mary's house at Aylesbury but with regular visits to the mother-in-law in Red Lion Court, close to John's parents' home in St James's Square, Clerkenwell. Calvinism threatened to envelop the reluctant bridegroom, who loved London, 'this charming, warm, wicked town' as he called it, but hankered after a more fashionable district and expensive way of life. The marital string began to stretch like elastic, and soon it inevitably snapped.

Wilkes was well content, and indeed he had compensations. His father, on his marriage, had settled on him properties in East Anglia worth £350 a year; he had a daughter, Polly, born in 1750, on whom he was to dote all his life, who stood to inherit an immense sum on her grandmother's death, and whom his wife, at least Wilkes gives us to assume, had no compunction about abandoning to him; and he was attracting around himself a wild but congenial band of boon companions with possibilities of a political future. 'I hated my wife but was the civilest husband to her', he confessed later, according to Boswell. It is probably true: his manners remained pleasant and elegant, and his temper equable, to the end of his life. Wit was his saving straw, whenever the tides of misfortune threatened to drown him. But below the surface there lay the tart polemics and political lampooning of the journalist, too, and the marriage rankled more than he admitted. One of his few really discreditable actions, a few years later, was his attempt to gain the support of the King's Bench in making his wife surrender her allowance. This was the annuity of £200 a year which, by mutual agreement, was arranged on the breaking up of the marriage in return for his wife's surrender of her jointure, including the estate at Aylesbury and house and demesne worth £700 a year. Under eighteenth-century law, the wife had no rights in her own property, once married. Even so, Wilkes well knew his wife was living in luxury with her wealthy mother, and, with his natural extravagance and political expenses, her annuity became a burden to him on more than one occasion. The King's Bench, in 1758, dismissed his petition.

Freedom, however, was worth the price, and indeed considering all things the price was little. Although he once referred to 'the miserable monotony of those who are more interested in the death of a calf or the capture of a poacher than by the decease of a great statesman or the conquest of a whole nation', Wilkes was busying himself with his Aylesbury estate, in constant touch with people who were later to be valuable in parliamentary elections: John Stevens, the vicar; John Dell, gentleman farmer and surveyor; Edward and Richard Terry, brewers; Henry Sheriff, the proprietor of the George Inn; and John Perkins, merchant and landowner. And as a country gentleman he certainly enjoyed riding, although he did not hunt or shoot.

He was already making a slight but noticeable imprint on the pattine of English society. In April, 1749, he had been elected a Fellow of the Royal Society: a startling tribute for so young a man, especially one who did not share the contemporary passion for amateur scientific experiment, like Benjamin Franklin and others so distinguished by the Society. It would seem, however, that the Society needed members whose learning or interest in philosophic enquiries (the reasons given for the election of Wilkes' brother Israel later) acted as helpful ballast to its income and reputation, and Wilkes' sponsors included the physician Dr Mead and the Reverend Thomas Birch, a friend of Dr Johnson. Johnson was not known to Wilkes, but passages of arms were due in the future. More entertainingly, he was on 19 January 1754 admitted to the Sublime Society of the Beefsteaks, where Boswell, dining himself with Lord Eglinton, first saw him. Wilkes on that occasion was with his friends, the satirical poet Charles Churchill, and the randy Lord Sandwich: a few years later, Dr Johnson's indefatigable biographer and diarist saw Wilkes there again, dining now in full political glory beneath a canopy inscribed 'Beef and Liberty'.[1] The Sublime Society of Beefsteaks was one of the many clubs of the time with a special attraction for the dilettante of the arts and the young gentleman of rather raffish tastes.

In 1751 and 1752 he had made his first trips to Bath, fashionable haven of eighteenth-century society, most conveniently without his wife who had (perhaps perceptively) refused to accompany him. Here he first met Thomas Potter, an association which was to burgeon in the future. Potter was already middle-aged, a good-looking rake whom Wilkes found easily attractive as a companion, in spite of his incongruous ancestry (Potter was the son of a former Archbishop of Canterbury). Wilkes having so long and early lost his innocence it would hardly be accurate to say that Potter was an instrument in his degradation; but he certainly made sure that his young friend continued along the path lined with primroses. He set himself up as useful pimp-about-town. 'May Venus be propitious to you at Tonbridge. Should you meet a goddess there under the vulgar appellation of Miss Betty Spooner, offer incense to her for my sake. You will find in her liveliness and lechery', he wrote (Wilkes' marriage was still officially operating). And later: 'If you prefer young women and whores to old women and wives, if you prefer toying away hours with little Sattin Back to the evening conferences with your mother-in-law . . . but above all if the divinely inspired passion called lust has not deserted you, hasten to town to take a place in my post-chaise for Bath . . .'

Wilkes followed the beckoning hand; and found himself for good enmeshed in a less desirable attachment of Potter's, the money-lender Isaac Fernandes Silva. The Beefsteak Club was at least more catholic, including actors and writers as well as simple roisterers. Its chairman was the Earl of Sandwich, whose snacks at the gaming table were to gain him an immortality his disreputable career could not have attained, although he was later a not totally incompetent First Lord of the Admiralty. Wilkes was learning one of the first qualities of an eighteenth-century gentleman and man of fashion: the ability to live above his means.

But the contacts were not only raffish: they were also political. Potter was a friend of William Pitt, as far as anyone could be a friend of that lonely man of dark moods and surging ambition; and also of the related Grenville family, extremely influential in the politics of the time. Lord Temple, for long Wilkes' faithful and (financially) long-suffering friend on the political scene, was Pitt's brother-in-law; George Grenville was Temple's brother; and although Pitt had not yet achieved the fame and eminence that he did later, he was already a force in politics and a flattering acquaintance for a young country squire like Wilkes. Wilkes through Potter, in fact, was moving into the orbit of a rising political faction: and the faction was an almost indispensable feature of the parliamentary system of the age. 'Factions', as Professor J. H. Plumb has written, 'were groups of politicians tied to each other by family or territorial loyalties; men who had decided to strive for power together.'[1]

It was the age, too, of the 'rotten borough', expensively and corruptly, but quite safely, in the gift of local squirearchy, and Aylesbury was one of the most expensive. Nevertheless, Wilkes already was thinking in terms of becoming its representative in Parliament. In the General

[1] *Chatham* (Collins, 1953; 'Makers of History' series, 1965).

Election of 1754, however, he bided his time; partly out of necessity, partly because he had scraped a rather whore-masterly acquaintance with Aylesbury's present MP, Jack Willes. But with the help of Potter and the Grenvilles he was appointed High Sheriff of Buckinghamshire, and unsuccessfully stood as parliamentary candidate for Berwick-on-Tweed (the neighbouring Scots probably later looked on this as a lucky escape). Wilkes polled less than half the votes of his opponent, Delavel, whom he later accused in a petition to Parliament of using 'most flagrant bribery'. The petition was withdrawn, and probably Wilkes was in no position to pursue it. He had himself been forced to distribute some £3,000 in election 'expenses', notwithstanding his boast to his intended constituents: 'I come here uncorrupting, and promise you I shall ever be uncorrupted. As I shall never take a bribe, so I will never offer one.'

As a Parliamentarian, later, he was to a large extent to keep to this ideal, although the passage to this suave independence was not to be totally smooth or unsullied. Wilkes always tended to be virtuous by accident. At Berwick, however, he made one declaration which was more prophetic than he probably realized at the time: he announced a 'steady attachment to the cause of Liberty'.

In 1757 there was another election at Aylesbury, and Wilkes decided to stand. It was still expensive, for it had, in comparison with many 'rotten boroughs', quite a large number of voters: over three hundred. (The growing industrial town of Manchester, population 60,000, Thomas Paine was to write in *Rights of Man* thirty years later, was unrepresented in the House of Commons, while two members were sent by the tiny non-village of Old Sarum, which had been William Pitt's first constituency, and only the same number by the whole county of Yorkshire, with one million inhabitants.) The small town of Aylesbury also sent two members, one of whom, after a false alarm in which it was supposed he was giving up his seat, was still Willes. On this rumour, Wilkes had already paid out a good deal of the expected bribery of voters. In the end, however, Wilkes was elected to the other seat; it had been held by Potter, who was able to abandon it when Pitt offered him his seat at Okehampton (Pitt was now candidate for Bath). Until the Reform Bill of 1832, this was the procedure by which Parliament got most of its elected members. The kind of democratic franchise Wilkes later (rather irresolutely) suggested, and which became the standard demand of the radical fringe from the 1790s right through to the Chartists in the middle of the next century, was unheard of. The Whig Government was as corrupt as the King's party became later: government was a matter of birth, land and property, the 'rotten boroughs' and large towns alike had only a small proportion of inhabitants eligible to vote, and those votes were bought regularly by the highest bidder. Sometimes the candidates, fairly evenly matched in their ability to buy votes, clashed on the hustings and riot was a regular feature of elections, including sometimes actual murder. Hogarth at this time loosed on a delighted and cynically appreciative world his series of 'Election' cartoons: as savage and grotesque a picture of the English social scene as his 'Gin Lane' several years before.

In comparison, Wilkes had a fairly uneventful election at Aylesbury, although his later conflicts of this kind were not to be so bloodless. On 6 July 1757 he was returned unopposed. His stormy career in and out of Parliament had begun.

II

THE SATANIC MONKS

The elections at Berwick and Aylesbury had cost Wilkes some £11,000. Perhaps the knowledge weighed on him, for in Parliament he remained a silent member. Wilkes did not set out as a rebel against the system of contemporary politics, or what we today would call 'the Establishment'. He had been educated to accept the political pattern of his time, and to fit into it as a Whig careerist while moving in the top social circles as a gentleman of pleasure. Pitt was the coming man: 'You will doubtless', wrote Potter, 'wish to leave your name at Mr Pitt's door.' Grenville wished to be 'the first to embrace his new brother member'. There seemed every inducement to Wilkes to pursue these obvious advantages, and indeed at first he did so, writing how greatly he wished 'to be numbered among those who had the highest esteem and veneration for Mr Pitt'. It would seem Pitt reciprocated in some measure, for Wilkes later 'was not a little mortified to lose the pleasure of seeing you when you was so good as to call at my house'.

There was apparently encouragement, too, on the purely social side: had not Potter, on a visit to Pitt, written to his crony: 'At dinner yesterday we read over your parody. He bade me tell you he found with great concern you was as wicked and agreable as ever?' It may have been true: Wilkes certainly believed it, although Pitt's natural bent was far from rakish and later he was to dissociate himself in public from Wilkes' particular brand of immorality, even though stoutly maintaining his cause in the matter of parliamentary privilege and general warrants. Wilkes promptly accused him of hypocrisy, but the fact is we, and apparently Wilkes himself, have no word for Pitt's earlier appreciation of his randy wit than that of Thomas Potter.

In 1757, when Wilkes entered the House of Commons,

King George II was still on the throne, and Pitt was in office for the first time. In April, hardly three months before Wilkes was returned unopposed, but expensively, as MP for Aylesbury, there had been a crisis and the King had dismissed Pitt from office. But the governmental crack had been pasted over with a new kind of wallpaper, leaving the dismissed minister in control of the Seven Years' War and foreign policy. It was indeed in foreign affairs that Pitt was primarily to make his mark, and the war was a matter of popular support in London. In 1755, the discontent at the failure of the Government to attack the French had resulted in virtual riots at Drury Lane Theatre, where the young Noverre, a great choreographer and philosopher of ballet in the making, had been brought over from the continent by Garrick to stage an elaborate *Chinese Festival* at great expense. The belief that 'all the leading French dancers were enemy agents in disguise' had sparked off a prolonged pandemonium, and Garrick had been forced to capitulate, at enormous financial loss.

The war finally came in 1756, and by 1757 was in full popular flood. Ballads sold on the streets, ballad operas at Sadler's Wells, recruited for the navy; and the press gangs operated, in their usual desperate bid to man the fleet (the ill pay and known shocking conditions had small attraction without coercion), to public acclaim or indifference, apart from the unfortunate pressed victims. The twenty-year-old Tom Paine, mysteriously escaped or released from a spell as a runaway at sea, was in London for the first time: uninterested (or so he later claimed) in the 'jockeyship' that passed for politics, and busy buying globes to attend lectures on Newtonian science. William Blake, in the same city, was equally busy getting himself born. The radicals were alive, but not yet kicking, apart from the little Blake in his cradle, and Nelson, who was to turn the British fleet into the most formidable weapon the country possessed, was not even in his cradle. He was born in Norfolk, Paine's home county, the following year, 1758. One year later still, in 1759, his ship the *Victory* was launched and radicalism gained its most formidable feminist, Mary Wollstonecraft, who was born, defiantly red-haired, to a dissipated father with a family fortune rapidly on the down grade.

The laws were savage and as the century aged were to get more so. Petty theft was a crime punishable by hanging, and public executions (notably of well-known highwaymen, in some cases the 'pop-stars' of the day) took place with military honours and full entertainment rites. Bedlam, the madhouse, was open to fascinated audiences, jail fever picked off victims in the prisons and on the Bench, and the undeserving poor soaked themselves in gin to produce a kind of miasma against depressing circumstances. Nevertheless, the better parts of London had attractions often envied by visitors from the continent: fine glass shop-fronts, a thriving if undistinguished theatre (apart from the great actor David Garrick), coffee houses that were a haunt of the *literati* and those seeking political argument or to read the newspapers, and pleasure gardens like Vauxhall which had everything from enticing women and tormented bears to fireworks. The entrance fee was one shilling, and since 1735 a London workman had been able to earn about two shillings a day, and a London craftsman at least one shilling more. Tailors earned 2s 7d a day, working from six in the morning to seven or eight at night, and similar long hours were a feature of most other professions and crafts. When the tailors complained of the hours and the strain on their eyesight, they were accused of 'impudence'. Bookbinders until 1785 worked an even longer day, from 6 a.m. to 9 p.m. [1]

A surprising number of workers, nevertheless, found the money and time to go to the Vauxhall Gardens; but Vauxhall was very much a night entertainment. A cup of coffee in a coffee house cost one penny, and talk was free. The middle class chattered as much as the rich, and servant girls were better and more cleanly dressed than anywhere in Europe. Already there was Thomas Coram's foundling hospital, and three years after Wilkes entered Parliament, in 1760, a letter in the *Public Advertiser* was to provoke the movement for the protection of the child chimney-sweeps,

---

[1] George Rudé: *Wilkes and Liberty: A Social Study of 1763 to 1774* (Clarendon Press, 1962).

one of the worst scandals of the eighteenth century. It was probably written by the philanthropist, Jonas Hanway, who in 1767 succeeded in getting through Parliament an act attempting to improve the appalling conditions of children in parish workhouses. It had some effect; although many as a result were sent in batches to work in the factories in the North, thus creating a pool of cheap child labour which was to cause even more suffering and scandal as the Industrial Revolution progressed.

In 1757 this had scarcely begun. Cottage industries continued in towns and villages lapped by rural woods, hill and river; stage coaches ploughed across the country, undeterred by mud-traps in winter; and even London, now spreading rapidly beyond the City, though it had its sewage problems, was easily accessible to outlying countryside activities beyond Mayfair, a fashionable centre for the aristocracy and the wealthy. Kensington, Chelsea and Knightsbridge were still country villages, well outside the London radius. The rich, then as now, had their country estates or houses, and their private coaches plied vigorously to and fro from London and the surrounding counties of Surrey, Middlesex and Buckinghamshire. The exclusive London clubs and gaming tables were not the only delights life had to offer the young gentleman of fashion, and one need not travel as far as Bath to plunge into dissipation and illicit pleasure. This Wilkes had early discovered. Among London's thriving brothels were Mrs Goadby's 'nunnery' and Charlotte Hayes's bagnio in King Street, sometimes referred to as the 'Abbey of Santa Carlotta'. The 'nunnery' and similar types of description, perhaps originally meant to mislead, went back to Elizabethan times: at least one Shakespearean scholar has pointed out the possible bitter double-meaning of Hamlet's advice to Ophelia, at a moment of suspicion, 'Get thee to a nunnery'. 'Santa Carlotta', forever seeking recruits among the young girls up from the country, advertised her wares, by private invitation card, with gusto, presenting her 'most respectful compliments' with the information that tomorrow evening, at 7 p.m., 'Twelve Beautiful Nymphs, unsullied and untainted' would perform 'the celebrated rites of Venus'. Her nymphs were reputed to be used extensively at Medmenham Abbey.

It is historically uncertain when Sir Francis Dashwood founded the group known as the 'Monks of Medmenham', often referred to more notoriously later as the Hell-Fire Club. One recent historian has even boldly declared it to be a myth.[1] Even without the specific correspondence and records still preserved by the Dashwood family and in the Bodleian Library, it is, however, too recent in history for legend, and its hold on contemporary imagination too explicit, even though the details and membership are somewhat questionable. One source of material on its activities is a work called *Chrysal* by Charles Johnstone, a picaresque novel published in 1760, to which in 1765 the author added two volumes describing orgies and black magic ritual presumed to give a picture of the Monks of Medmenham. Even allowing for a strong fictional element, Johnstone quite obviously had a genuine source of information. It is said that when on the Grand Tour (he was a noted traveller), Dashwood entered the Sistine Chapel during flagellation ceremonies which he considered ludicrously feeble, and, in the dark, enlivened the proceedings by attacking those present in good earnest with a horse-whip, so that they fled with terrified cries of '*Il Diavolo!*' Horace Walpole, whose Diaries are entertaining and informative but often unreliable, noted that Dashwood then had himself painted in the costume of a Franciscan monk, kneeling before a statue of the Venus of Medici. In fact he was painted thus in 1742, before the conversion of Medmenham Abbey, but the fact that he holds in one hand a 'Holy Ghost Pye' (a symbol of a certain branch of Satanism) is possibly significant. The painting is still preserved at West Wycombe.

Dashwood has been dismissed by Wilkes' biographers as a dull-witted and undistinguished mediocrity, but this on the evidence is not true. As Dashwood's belated and scholastic biographer makes clear, he was not only interested and active in building experiments, of which the rehabilitation of

[1] Betty Kemp: *Sir Francis Dashwood* (Macmillan, London; St Martin's Press, New York, 1967).

Medmenham Abbey formed a part, but he was, in the House of Commons, member 'of a notably long series of committees to discuss bills and petitions for the repair of roads and the establishment of Turnpikes in all parts of the country, the building of bridges, and the improvement especially of London but also of other cities and boroughs. He was prominent in the movement to drain the fens and improve the navigation of the river Witham, which finally led to the Witham Drainage Act of 1762, and he sat on a number of Commons committees for bills concerned with draining and navigation.' In 1747 he had introduced a poor-relief Bill, aimed to relieve the unemployed, and three years later put theory into practice by employing the poor of West Wycombe to build a new road outside the village. In 1744 he had pressed in Parliament for double taxation of government 'place men and pensioners', presumably to constrict corruption, and the following year urged the freeing of the House of Commons from 'undue influence'. He had also with compassionate generosity opposed the execution of Admiral Byng, scapegoat for the loss of Minorca.

As Chancellor of the Exchequer, hastily appointed by Lord Bute in 1762 after the downfall of Newcastle and Pitt, he was undistinguished and indeed quickly extinguished: he was a man, said his second-in-command, 'to whom a sum of five figures was an impenetrable mystery'. 'From puzzling all his life over tavern bills', wrote Wilkes with more malice, 'he was called by Lord Bute to administer the finances of a Kingdom over a hundred millions in debt.' (Wilkes, certainly a member of the Medmenham fraternity, was by then as a journalist in bitter opposition to Bute.)

In December, 1766, the returning Pitt, now Earl of Chatham, made him Joint Postmaster-General, a post Dashwood held until his death in 1781. He was also shifted from the House of Commons to the House of Lords under the title of Lord le Despencer. In the Post Office he was by no means unopen to innovation: his régime saw the establishment of the penny post in Dublin and experiments with mail carts, long before the first official mail coach of 1784. It was part of the general corruption of the times that John Walcot,

Dashwood's brother-in-law, was appointed Accountant-General in the Post Office in 1767 and in 1771 became Comptroller to the Post Office in Ireland. Three other Walcots also obtained good positions in the postal services. Dashwood by now was certainly not averse to propagating family interest from 'undue influence'.

More interestingly, Dashwood used the position in 1774 to befriend Benjamin Franklin, who was that year dismissed from his office of Postmaster-General for America. It was not his only association with Franklin, as will be seen. In an age devoted to party interests he sat for some time in the House as an Independent, although to Wilkes' disgust he allowed the chance of office to divert him solidly into the King's party later. He encouraged archaeological exploration and the measurement of Greek ruins, and was a Fellow both of the Royal Society and of the Society of Antiquaries.

The immediate background to his formation of the Monks of Medmenham was his architectural and landscaping interests and his founding, in 1732, of the Society of Dilettanti, which acted as a more legitimate encouragement of the arts, although later rumour saw in it slight hints of the altogether more ribald society of 'monks'. In the early 1750s Dashwood extensively improved his house at West Wycombe and began to repair and restore Medmenham Abbey, partly from architectural zeal but also with a more sinister purpose. Medmenham lay on the River Thames near Marlow, and was a converted Cistercian abbey. In beautiful country, the river between Henley and Marlow was a centre for boating and fishing, and Dashwood's biographer Betty Kemp is doubtless right that the country club he established there was in part a form of pleasure gardens with river activities attached. A letter-poem in rather curious Latin from Wilkes to Dashwood, dated 27 July 1761 and written in answer to an invitation to Medmenham, refers to sailing 'the Thames's waves' and gathering up 'great fish in a net'. From its other references to wine and sexual union, and jocular comments on Sir Francis' 'broad smile' and 'riddles' (for which his host was well known), it is obvious there is a deliberate double-meaning, not unconnected with the fishing of girls.

Thomas de Greys, listed among records of the 'monks' and believed to be Sir Thomas Stapleton, is mentioned as an expected companion in these delights.

Boating was certainly a feature of West Wycombe Park itself at this time. A Thomas Phillibrown noted in his Diary in 1752 that on the afternoon of 5th October he and others rode to Sir Francis Dashwood's seat at West Wycombe, 'which is exceedingly fine and pleasantly situated and from the road you have a charming view of a large piece of water which he caused to be made, also his walks, alcoves, canals, parks, etc. on the large piece of water are several vessels, the largest of which is called a Snow, is completely rigged and carries several brass guns . . . There is also another smaller 2 mast vessel, a little in the Venetian manner, also a 1 mast vessel like a sloop and also a barge which little Fleet makes a beautiful appearance.' Arthur Young, the agricultural expert and traveller, a few years later, in 1767, also described the charm of the West Wycombe lake 'on which floats a ship, completely rigged, with a long-boat, and another lying alongside; her masts rising above the adjoining trees in a manner which adds greatly to the landscape'.

Phillibrown's party with 'a little fear' also inspected the Church of St Lawrence, the tower of which 'Sir Francis (at his own expense) for the sake of a prospect to his House and Gardens, raised to twice the height it was before and on the top of the said tower is building a spire of timber, on the top of which is built of wood a very large hollow globe, the diameter of which is 8 feet and the outside of it is to be covered with gilt . . .' He also refers to the 'good new broad road, by the side of his park to High Wycombe', then in course of construction. 'Sir Francis has a very great character both at High and West Wycombe for a very public spirited and generous man.'

The golden ball on the church, still its most prominent feature, was used according to Wilkes for card parties and drinking ('the best Globe Tavern I ever was in'): an adjunct to the Medmenham activities which later became a subject of local superstitious rumour, somewhat damaging to the 'public spirited' reputation of the West Wycombe squire.

33

Architecturally, the golden ball, which held up to eight people in cramped conditions, was inspired by churches Dashwood had seen abroad, particularly in Venice. The ball of St Lawrence Church on West Wycombe Hill is 646 feet above sea level, and whatever its purpose an imposing feature of eighteenth-century landscaping effect.

Wilkes' Latin response to Dashwood's invitation in 1761 is signed 'Monachus' (The Monk) and from other letters of the kind in the museum now connected with West Wycombe Park, and those records that survive, it is clear that the fiction of a religious body known as 'Franciscans' (named after the Father Superior, Sir Francis) was always used and the 'monks' took their own Christian name with a disguised addition (Wilkes was 'John of Aylesbury'). All the letters to Sir Francis preserved ecclesiastical phrasing, though with a strong *soupçon* of the *double entendre*.

This was doubtless in part because the first Hell-Fire type societies had been legally suppressed by a royal proclamation of 28 April 1721; but the whole nature of the Medmenham club was to some extent a blasphemous religious deviation. Although the body of members (the original number was twelve, equivalent to the twelve apostles, one of whom was yearly elected 'Abbot', with Dashwood as the Christ-figure Superior, the thirteenth) were undoubtedly mainly frivolous seekers after sensation, with the cellar book, which is still preserved, and the unidentified ladies called 'the nuns' as the two primary attractions, Dashwood's own extensive library, not only of pornography but of satanic and liturgical literature, shows that the apparently genial host had a more serious and in its way scholarly side to his creative impulse. Sir Richard Burton, the nineteenth-century explorer of the source of the Nile, whose own pornographic library was extensive, even suggested that Sir Henry Vansittart, a member, introduced the teachings of the most famous Sanscrit work of the kind, *Kama Sutra*, to Medmenham, together with its strange rites. Vansittart had been Governor of Bengal, and although he was in India between 1755 and 1763, when the club was particularly active, he was painted by William Hogarth in the habit of a Monk of Medmenham in 1753. Among the private papers left by Dashwood's illegitimate daughter, the beautiful and eccentric Rachel Antonina Lee, was a copy of the *Kama Sutra* in translation, inscribed from 'Henry Vansittart to the Founder'.

Much has been made by Miss Kemp, Dashwood's biographer, of *An Abridgement of the Book of Common Prayer* that he published, with a Preface written by Benjamin Franklin, in 1773, but although Franklin managed to get it introduced quite successfully into American use (it was largely ignored in England), it is naïve to suggest on all the evidence that this proves Dashwood's innocence of either libertinism or satanism. An interesting suggestion has been made by H. T. F. Rhodes [1] that certain elements in this abridgement, such as the omission of the canon and consecration of the bread and wine, reach back to the 'dual' religion of the Knights Templars, Cathars and other Satanists, for long the subject of attack as heretical by the Catholic Church. By this time, it is true, the Medmenham Monks as such had been disbanded and Sir Francis had settled down, after the death of his wife, to a more domesticated existence with an ex-actress named (confusingly, for she was not the famous actress of that name in Garrick's company) Mrs Barry; but there is some indication that sideline activities of the same nature continued in the caves excavated under West Wycombe Hill (the excavations are surmised in part to have been made to provide the materials for the building of the West Wycombe road). They are still open to the public under the direction of the present Sir Francis Dashwood, with entertaining wax models of the 'monks' and commentary attached, but although they are loosely labelled 'the Hell-Fire Caves' it must be emphasized that in fact the description 'Hell-Fire' was never used in Dashwood's time but became attached later from comparison with similar 'Hell-Fire' clubs.

Although Dashwood's original imagination, fermented on his travels on the Continent and in Russia, gave to everything he was involved in, from architecture and

[1] *The Satanic Mass* (Rider, 1954; Arrow paperback, 1964-73).

decoration to satanism, a flavour of highly personal eccentricity, he was in no sense an originator of the secret society movement, as the earlier proclamation shows. It was a flourishing part of eighteenth-century rakedom and the 'enlightenment', questioning traditional beliefs, and the Monks of Medmenham themselves bred offsprings, such as John Hall-Stevenson's Demoniacs of Skelton Castle in Yorkshire. Hall-Stevenson knew both Dashwood and Wilkes and had probably been a member of the Medmenham Monks. One of his letters to Wilkes, dated 5 July, 1762, complains 'I am now suffering amongst the Damned that are Bathing in Sulphur at Harrogate for not believing that there was anything miraculous in the Shrine of St Francis: say a Mass for me . . .' (Harrogate was already thriving on the eighteenth-century passion for sea-bathing cures.) It was Stevenson's *Confessions of Sir F . . . of Medmenham* which first viciously put forward a hint of Dashwood's using the nuns' masks (which they are said to have worn to conceal their identity) to facilitate incest:

> Like a Hotspur young cock, he began with his mother,
> Cheer'd three of his sisters one after another;

It was scandalous fiction, as Sir Francis' own mother died when he was two years old: though his latest stepmother could have been suggested. But Stevenson bore a grudge against Dashwood, and his writings, published after Dashwood's death, were too malicious for serious consideration. [1] Wilkes, however, it would seem from his rather equivocal correspondence with Stevenson, suspected some mystery relative to Dashwood and West Wycombe of which he believed Stevenson, on his hints, might have the key. It could have been connected with the satanic rites, or something more personal: Dashwood to this day is a slightly enigmatic figure, Pan-like in mischief but by no means only the pranksome fool history has tried to paint him. Whatever the mystery, Wilkes never unravelled it, and Stevenson's

[1] *The Works of John Hall Stevenson* (3 vols, 1795). See also Donald McCormick: *The Hell-Fire Club* (Jarrolds, 1958; reprint West Wycombe Caves Ltd, paperback, 1964).

scurrilities, written to cash in on prurient contemporary curiosity, are not likely to provide any real clue. His own connection with Medmenham was certainly less extensive than Wilkes'.

Hall-Stevenson was the dilettante author of *Crazy Tales* and *Monkish Epitaphs*, and an amateur of erotic prose and verse: 'the possessor of a certain small original literary gift, which he expended in vaguer rhyming on facetious and satiric themes'.[1] Laurence Sterne, the novelist, notwithstanding his parsonic profession, was a member of Hall-Stevenson's club, and known there by the ritual name of 'The Blackbird' because of his ecclesiastical clothes. Like the Monks of Medmenham, the Demoniacs had a country club 'cover' when, as Quennell writes, they 'shot, fished, engaged in disputation or raced their chaises wildly along Saltburn sands . . .' The influence spread right on into the Romantic Movement of the next century, when Byron at Newstead Abbey formed such a society in which the members drank wine from human skulls. This was supposed by the romantics to derive from activities of the Monks of Medmenham, but in fact there is no evidence for this: it was probably a macabre twist emanating from the young Byron's fertile brain.

The secret activities of the Monks of Medmenham took place at night, and indeed secrecy had been enjoined on the workmen when reconstructing the Abbey with its hidden chapel, a fact which alone suggests some black magic or blasphemous intentions. The motto over the door, 'Fay ce que voudras', is from Rabelais, and one may take it that Walpole was right in his view that 'Whatever their doctrines were, their practice was rigorously pagan.' Witchcraft lingered on in Buckinghamshire and the Black Mass and devil worship are not unknown even today in the home counties. But as so often in such practices, the main object was not so much blasphemous as sexual. Within the garden, according to Wilkes who obviously enjoyed the experience, was a naked statue of Venus, pulling a thorn from

[1] Peter Quennell: *Four Portraits. Studies of the Eighteenth Century* (Collins, 1945).

her foot and exposing a full and voluptuous rear to those who approached her. There was also a statue with a grotesque phallus, inscribed:

> Peni tento,
> non
> Penitenti

which emphasized, according to Wilkes, 'that the favourite doctrine of the Abbey is certainly not penitence'.

What kind of women came to provide entertainment and more for the initiates is not surely known, apart from Charlotte Hayes' prostitutes already mentioned. There is certainly indication that ladies of quality, with depraved tastes, came on occasion, and the masks were meant to protect them from identification. The lines of the young poet Charles Churchill, Wilkes' closest friend, emphasize the costume often chosen:

> Whilst womanhood in habit of a nun
> At Medmenham lies, by backward monks undone.

'If there was, indeed, any possibility of a woman coming to Medmenham not "undone"', as Wilkes' biographer, Raymond Postgate, wrote, 'it was quite certain that she would not leave it again in the same condition.'[1] It would seem the 'monks' themselves wore white robes, and the procedure was normally for them to retire with their chosen mate into private cells. Whatever the rituals and whatever the form of the lecheries, there is no real indication either of 'group sex' or of perversions such as homosexuality, although these have been claimed by some purely sensational writers. Eighteenth-century vice tended to be heartily heterosexual, and the Marquis de Sade's excesses in France were only widely read and disseminated later. In his time, he was treated as an undisputable mental case.

'Churchill's immorality was not incompatible with much generosity and manliness', Johnstone suggests in *Chrysal*, and this was certainly true. In fact Churchill's libertinism was strangely combined with something closely allied to

[1] *That Devil Wilkes* (Constable, 1930; revised edn, Dobson, 1956).

romantic idealism. Extreme libertinism is not necessarily divorced from humane attributes and also good political works and thinking, as seems the case with Dashwood, Churchill and Wilkes if not all of those who have been named (rather loosely) as members of the Medmenham society. They included Lord Sandwich, who was from 1768 to 1770 Joint Postmaster-General with Dashwood; Churchill's and Wilkes' friend, the poet Robert Lloyd; Thomas Potter; Lord March, later the notoriously vicious Marquess of Queensberry, known as 'Old Q'; and another poet, Paul Whitehead, who was secretary of the society and like Dashwood a man of advancing middle age. He is reputed to have burned the club's minute books before his death. Whitehead's most interesting attribute had nothing to do with the Monks of Medmenham: he was owner of a chair belonging to Shakespeare, which Garrick in vain tried to borrow from him for use in his rained-out Shakespeare Jubilee at Stratford-on-Avon in 1769. On Whitehead's death it was bought by John Bacon of Barnet, who had tried to arrange its loan to Garrick, and in modern times it became a part of the collection of Lord Fairhaven. In 1774 Dashwood organized a ceremony in West Wycombe Park to commemorate Whitehead's death, including a procession with vocal and instrumental music and the performance in the church of an oratorio, Atterbury's *Goliath*, which had been performed at the Haymarket Theatre in 1773. His heart was placed in an urn in the imposing Mausoleum built by Sir Francis, mainly for his wife and family, adjacent to the church: the inscription over the entrance commemorates the notorious rake Bubb-Doddington, Lord Melcombe of Melcombe Regis, who bequeathed to his friend £500 which was used to erect the building. Later, Whitehead's heart was mysteriously stolen and never recovered.

It is, of course, impossible to accept Betty Kemp's strange conclusion that Wilkes and Churchill worked up the Medmenham Abbey myth purely to discredit Dashwood politically. Politicians and aristocrats in the eighteenth century were so widely and openly dissolute that this would be pointless, quite apart from its equal effect in discrediting

Wilkes and Churchill, who admitted to membership of the group with total and buoyant lack of penitence. It was only a century later that society began to take the puritanical view that private morality invalidated a man for public office, and swept Dilke, Parnell and Profumo out of Parliament, quite arguably to Parliament's loss. Even then, the law was 'Thou shalt not be found out': such hypocrisy was rare in the Age of Reason and Enlightenment, although Wilkes was to experience an instance of it in his political life later. That it still persists the fate of John Profumo and Lord Lambton in recent years shows.

Whether the Medmenham orgies took place later in the golden ball Dashwood had erected on West Wycombe Church, or in the caves in his grounds, is perhaps disputable (the caves are uncomfortably dank and chilly). So is the story that Wilkes ended the activities of the Medmenham club around 1763 when he broke up the diabolical revels by letting loose a baboon dressed up as the Devil, thus frightening the praying Earl of Sandwich out of his wits (Sir Henry Vansittart is reputed to have brought back a baboon from Bengal). It is indubitably true that Sandwich became one of Wilkes' bitterest opponents in Parliament, and that Wilkes and Churchill later, in their paper *The North Briton*, attacked Dashwood in print. There were, however, political reasons for this, and indeed diverging politics are reputed to have been the direct cause of the breaking up of the Medmenham brotherhood around 1763.

The suggestion that Benjamin Franklin was a member seems hardly viable, in spite of his association with Dashwood over the *Abridgement to the Book of Common Prayer*. Dashwood had certainly planned this alone in the first case, and if there were undertones in the form of 'dualism' (which was the worship of a God in which both beneficent and diabolical aspects were united) Franklin would probably have been quite innocent of their nature. His Preface, written on behalf of himself and Lord le Despencer (as Dashwood now was), indicates clearly the excisions are made to help those whose 'age or infirmities will not suffer them to remain for hours in a cold church', and to eliminate the length and repetitions which encourage the mind to wander, and fervency of devotion to slacken.

His own youthful phase of what might be termed 'loose talk' and sexual wild oats was long in the past. He was in his sixties when his office brought him in contact with the Joint Postmaster-General, but he certainly visited West Wycombe in the summers of 1772, 1773 and 1774, and was shown over the caves by his host. His description of Dashwood in a letter is enthusiastic and possibly naïve: referring to 'the kind countenance, the facetious and very intelligent conversation of mine host, who, having been for many years engaged in public affairs, seen all parts of Europe, and kept the best company in the world, is himself the best existing'.

In September, 1774, Dashwood accompanied Franklin to the opening of Theophilus Lindsey's Unitarian Chapel, which became a meeting place for liberal reformers (ecclesiastic and political) such as Dr Joseph Priestley, Dr Richard Price, Thomas Hollis and the Duke of Grafton, who as Prime Minister had earlier had rather equivocal associations with Wilkes. Both Franklin and Hollis had connections with Thomas Paine, who at the end of this same month of September, 1774, sailed to America with a warm recommendation by Franklin in his pocket. Hollis, a friend of Pitt and benefactor of Harvard University, was, nearly twenty years later, to help William Godwin and the playwright, Thomas Holcroft, to guide Paine's *Rights of Man* (in his absence in France) through publication. Even Grafton had a tenuous link, being the local squire of the 'rotten borough' of Thetford in Norfolk, where Paine was born. His politics were far more liberal than Wilkes, and possibly Paine, gave him credit for.

If Dashwood turned to more orthodox, if dissenting, theology, it can safely be said that Wilkes was by nature all his life a rationalist in spirit, if not open declaration, and the devil worship or more superstitious aspects of the Monks of Medmenham could have aroused only his disbelieving merriment. The irreverent breaking up of the revels would have been in character, and may have taken place, and aroused resentment, in some form.

In any case the 'worshippers' scattered, and Parliament became the centre of their future clashes: although it is curious to find Wilkes still visiting West Wycombe on friendly terms after the virtual demise of Medmenham. The beautiful house and surroundings, not to count Sir Francis' eclectic tastes in design, doubtless had their own attractions. The dining-room ceiling of the 'Triumph of Bacchus and Ariadne', painted by Giuseppe Borgni from Annibale Caracci's baroque masterpiece in the Palazzo Farnese in Rome, was to find an echo in one of Wilkes' banquets as Lord Mayor of London later. Bacchus (rather surprisingly in view of his reputation for light drinking elsewhere) was not a negligible part of Wilkes' Medmenham activities. In the cellar books from 28 August 1760 to 26 September 1764, 'Brother John of Aylesbury' heads the list with twenty attendances. The bottles of claret he ordered certainly suggest that to him women were not the only attractions in the club. The fact that these cellar books continued until 9 September 1770 seems to indicate that at least some aspects of the Medmenham society were transferred to West Wycombe, either in the ball of the church or in the caves. One of the 'nuns', a curious figure known as 'Saint Agnes' with a virginal type of spirituality, claimed to have operated in the caves as a platonic figurehead. It has even been suggested that her presence was part of the mystery associated with Sir Francis. Later married in France, she died in the middle of the following century, and would certainly have been too young to have been concerned in the earlier Medmenham activities.

Another curious footnote to Medmenham is that the idealistic atheist, Shelley, while living at Marlow in 1816, wrote much of his poetry on an island directly opposite the Abbey. Its ghosts and revels had long been laid to rest, and probably even Shelley's imagination was undisturbed by them.

For Churchill and Wilkes it was to remain a deep and lasting association, dissoluble only by death.

III

THE KING AND THE
'NORTH BRITON'

The Seven Years' War had begun when England was under the weak direction of the last representative of the Pelham family in office, the Duke of Newcastle. Its major cause was the conflict of British and French interests in America and India, and it epitomized a period in which France and England were almost continuously at war. Mismanagement of the war, culminating in the execution of Admiral Byng, blamed for the loss of Minorca, was a cause of widespread criticism and discontent, and the sacrifice of the unfortunate scapegoat, Byng, did little to still the outcry. Robert Clive in India was in the midst of further disaster: the Nawab of Bengal had declared war in June 1756, captured Calcutta and caused the deaths of 146 persons – merchants, officials and women as well as soldiers – in what was to become known, with horror, as the 'Black Hole of Calcutta'. In America in 1754 a party of Virginian militia, headed by a Major George Washington, had been beaten and forced to surrender after a dash on Fort Duquesne and a skirmish at Great Meadows. The colonists had demanded reinforcements, and a force of 2,200 men, partly British regulars, repeated the attack the next year under General Braddock, only to be ambushed by an inferior force of French and Indians. The General's force was routed, and he himself killed.

Altogether when the war in Europe finally broke out in 1756, the English public were in no mood for further catastrophes, and when these came Newcastle's fall was inevitable. The King summoned the opposition Whigs to form a cabinet, and William Pitt and the Duke of Devonshire came to power. Pitt at least had the confidence of the nation at large, its being widely believed that he was one

43

of the few politicians of the time free from political corruption.

It is true Newcastle continued undermining tactics and the King disliked him, but his temporary dismissal only ended, as we have seen, in Pitt's being reinstated with a free hand in foreign policy and the management of the War. Wilkes, therefore, when he entered the House in 1757 had an enviable connection with persons in the highest places. Although also a friend of George Grenville, his closest association was with Grenville's brother and Pitt's brother-in-law, Lord Temple, and Temple, until a disagreement many years later, was to remain Wilkes' most constant political ally and friend. The fact remains that Wilkes made little attempt to advance his career during the three years remaining of the current government, and one reason may have been his surprising (for a man with so ready a wit) inarticulacy as an orator. Temple thought this laziness, which in view of Wilkes' athletic activities among the ladies and the 'monks' outside the House may have had some foundation. 'Give yourself up to parliamentary labours', he wrote to his unsatisfactory protégé in 1762, 'and let applauding senates give testimony to the excellent talents of the gallant gay Lothario. I wish you had been, and were, deprived of pen, ink, and paper for some time, that all your ideas might concentre in the great object of eloquence.'

The gallant gay Lothario never did master eloquence, to the end of his eventful career; but pen, ink and paper were to become transformed into steel, a sword that was to thrust through the whole tradition of parliamentary procedure, and establish an individual liberty which is part of our democratic inheritance today.

The Aylesbury election of 1757 had in any case coincided with a private crisis for Wilkes of particular distress. His seven-year-old daughter Polly, soon after the separation from his wife, developed smallpox, and Wilkes had appealed in vain to her mother to visit the child. According to Wilkes and his male biographers, it was an indication of Mary's indifference to her daughter, and hatred of Wilkes, that she totally ignored the appeal. But it must, I think, be pointed out that there could well have been a reason for this, by no means so discreditable to the child's mother. It has never been clear if Wilkes, in fact, exercised his legal prerogative in taking charge of his daughter, and how much his wife acquiesced. In eighteenth-century law, the father had sole rights to the child of any marriage in the case of separation or divorce. Thirty years later, in 1784, when Mary Wollstonecraft rescued her sister Eliza from a grievously unhappy marriage, the two sisters had to escape to secret lodgings and leave behind Eliza's very young baby, knowing there was no legal possibility of its ever being permanently kept from the husband. In such cases the mother, if wise enough, did not allow herself to become too attached to a child, or to continue to see it, if that meant reawakening feelings better suppressed. For Wilkes, the devoted and distracted father, his wife's failure to visit her sick daughter was unforgivable, and he never did forgive. But he may well have blinded himself to her reasons, more especially if her parting with Polly had been reluctant.

He and his mother nursed Polly through the crisis, and it was soon after this, when faced with the £7,000 cost of his Aylesbury election, that he made the move to get rescinded the £200 annuity he had settled on his wife. Polly, at least, was to reward him with an affection and a loyalty as deep and, almost, extravagant, as his own for her, although later she was often to visit her mother, apparently on sunnily unclouded terms with both parents. By then, however, she was almost grown-up. To her father, she was to become the anchor to his life in place of a wife, the one reason he can never have regretted the brief, wholly unsuitable marriage of his youth.

Wilkes had not been idle creatively in spite of his loss of a wife. When a new Foundling Hospital was built at Aylesbury, and Wilkes became a Governor, gossip was not slow to remark that this was only appropriate, as he was responsible for so many of the inmates. In fact, as usual, wit exceeded truth. He seems to have had only two natural children, a boy and a girl, and he took full responsibility for both. The boy, Jackie Smith, was only a few years younger than Polly, the son of Wilkes' young housekeeper of the period. This episode had not been without momentarily distressing repercussions: the father of the 'housekeeper', by no means as acquiescent as his daughter, threatened Wilkes with an action for seduction, and Counsel advised Wilkes to double the girl's wages to £20 a year. It would seem this financial arrangement fully satisfied this Mr Doolittle of the eighteenth century. Wilkes had his son well educated and Polly was later to grow fond and solicitous of her little 'cousin', whose identity cannot for long – knowing her father – have been unsuspected by her. Late in Wilkes' life another daughter, Harriet, was to become, almost as much as Polly, the apple of her father's eye, and Harriet's mother the first woman to become a steady and homely influence in Lothario's domestic scene: something akin to a wife, although (and perhaps this was in part the secret) living in a separate establishment.

At Aylesbury Wilkes was active in other ways than as sympathetic Governor of the Foundling Hospital. He was also a Turnpike Trustee, a Justice of the Peace, and a Governor of the Grammar School. He supported a scheme for a workhouse: 'I am persuaded it would be by far the cheapest manner, and the poor would not be supported in idleness as they are now.' How much his interest in poverty was based on a sense of the financial burden on those in better circumstances is equivocal, but he was not an inhumane man. Elsewhere he referred to the 'growing evil of the poor themselves. Unless something effectual is done, it bids fair to ruin you and most of the parishes of England.' At least it was a problem of which, unlike many of his class, he was aware.

In Parliament, however, although silent he was not unobservant. Pitt may have officially given way to Newcastle as first minister, but the War was the national issue and his prestige rocketed. Successes in India and America, defeat of France and the growing invincibility of the Navy – these in the next six years were to put him in an impregnable position. 'You would not know your country again,' wrote Horace Walpole in a letter to Sir Horace Mann; 'you left it a private little island, living upon its means. You would find it the capital of the world; St James's Street crowded with Nabobs and American chiefs, Mr Pitt attended in his Sabine farm by Eastern monarchs, waiting till the gout had gone out of his foot for an audience.'

Pitt's fondness for port in a heavy-drinking age was indulgently overlooked in the light of dazzling success, though in the end it killed him. Probably his drinking was a natural counterbalance to his particular brand of melancholia, which only his deeply understanding wife helped to keep from more frequently overwhelming him. He had married Lady Hester Grenville in 1754, thus welding a family political power-block of tempered steel, very much in the eighteenth-century parliamentary tradition. It was, nevertheless, a love match and it strengthened Pitt's innate distaste for Wilkes' flamboyant and unorthodox style of living.

Wilkes in Parliament remained unassertive to the point of invisibility, but in Buckinghamshire he was still active, being now not only High Sheriff for the county but also a Colonel of the Bucks Militia. The militia had become suddenly an important bulwark of defence, acting as a protection of the country against French invasion while freeing the army for continental service. England was to know a similar rallying of home guard defence, in both the Napoleonic and Second World wars.

As invasion, in Wilkes' time as later, failed to materialize, Wilkes seems hugely to have enjoyed his post as second-in-command to Sir Francis Dashwood. It was not, however, a totally popular position, many of the populace resenting recruitment, enthusiasm for the War being offered more willingly from a safe distance. This cautious attitude was probably intensified by the fact that in Huntingdon the Militia Act had been used as a cover for shipping off volunteers for service overseas, 'an act which smacked of sharp practice', as J. H. Plumb less cautiously comments in his biography of Chatham.

The Buckinghamshire regiment was quartered at Winchester, and Wilkes was there a good deal, describing in one letter an escape of some French prisoners from the camp, which resulted in one of them who was shot having to have an arm amputated. Wilkes gave the soldier who shot him three weeks' leave of absence until the Frenchman's death, or recovery, could be known. Never unready to ballast facial defects with splendour of accoutrement, Wilkes also obtained a good deal of personal satisfaction from his uniform.

Among his acquaintances within the Buckinghamshire Militia was Edward Gibbon, then a Captain of the Hampshire Grenadiers, who in the spring of 1762 sat on a General Court Martial with Wilkes. Gibbon, a serious-minded 25-year-old with an unexpected weakness for 'the prowess of the thoroughbreds' (he had entered a horse in the hunters' plate at one of the race meetings), unpromisingly declared that 'Wit have I none . . .' but this did not prevent him writing, after dining with Wilkes at the officers' mess at Southampton, that he had 'scarcely ever met with a better companion; he has inexhaustible spirits, infinite wit and humour, and a great deal of knowledge'. This did not prevent the future author of the most famous book on decadent Rome from adding that Wilkes 'was a thorough profligate in principle as in practice . . . his life stained with every vice, and his conversation full of blasphemy and bawdy . . . He told us himself, that in the time of public dissension he was resolved to make his fortune.'

The fact that this was obviously true at the time (Wilkes had applied for the premier diplomatic position at Quebec as well as Constantinople) has misled some writers on Wilkes to seeing hypocrisy in his later attitudes. Wilkes was always ready to toss off a witticism at his own expense (like his damaging one to the King later that he was 'never a Wilkeite') but Wilkes was a man whose character developed and whose views widened with adversity: the fight for his own liberty led him into more expansive struggles and vistas.

In October 1760 the old King, George II, died, and he was succeeded by his grandson, the 22-year-old George III. This was a new factor in politics, because the young King had studied to the limit the extent of the King's prerogative since the Revolution of 1688, and dismissal of the Stuarts, had restricted the monarchy. He was the first of the Hanover line to be English born and bred, and to speak English as his native tongue, and had admirable private virtues; but obstinacy, and the desire to rule to the utmost extent constitutionally possible, were to create tensions in government for the next thirty years. He was to build up a 'King's party' using to the full every device the corruption of the times encouraged: the Tories became his mainstay, the Whigs, with a few exceptions, his constant opposition. The conflict was to reach its peak in the long-drawn-out War of American Independence, which need never have taken place with a monarch less bitterly intent on colonial suppression and incapable of compromise.

Wilkes was permanently affected by his first move, the insistence that his former tutor, Lord Bute, should become Secretary of State in the Pitt-Newcastle cabinet. Bute was a Scottish peer of reasonably good character but without experience in practical politics, although it was through his tutelage that the young King had become irrevocably attached to the ideas expressed in Bolingbroke's *Patriot King*. These emphasized the need for a strong and independent monarch, unfettered by any party but that created by himself. In theory, it was to bridge the gap created between the King and his people; in practice, it was to lead to a political despotism in which the King's party, largely Tory, and the Whig opposition were to be locked in an iron vice of mortal combat.

Bute's attachment to the King's mother, the Princess-Dowager, was to create scandal without in the slightest shaking the young King's loyalty and belief in his moral rectitude. His own moral stance was soon evident, in spite of his one certain earlier peccadillo which was hardly even a peccadillo, for rumour had it that he was morganatically married to his Quaker mistress, Hannah Lightfoot, and a descendant of their son in Africa today still claims (or, rather, graciously waives) a right to the British throne.

With the acceptance of a rather plain and homely bride, however, Charlotte of Mecklenburg, George III settled down into an almost Victorian-style matrimony, and sealed his virtue with a proclamation 'for the encouragement of piety and for preventing immorality'. Wilkes' eyebrow must have risen very high above his squint on hearing this noble sentiment, which on Friday, 12 March 1762, was supplemented by deed. This was declared a national day of fasting and humiliation, and all theatres were closed. The Coronation, notwithstanding, was not without what today we would call union trouble: sedan-chairmen, coachmen and the workmen putting up the scaffolding for spectators in Westminster Hall all went on strike.

Wilkes had been re-elected to Aylesbury in the General Election that followed the death of George II. At thirty-five years of age, it secured him his seat for seven years, the span of each elected Parliament at that time. The experience had again been costly; it was a mistake, remarked Wilkes wryly, 'for a gentleman to represent the borough where he lives'. Fortnightly dinners to the independents were among his expenses, and the acquisition of 300 trees (at five guineas a tree) for his grounds for the moment shook the democratic principles of the future apostle of Liberty. 'I love to do acts of humanity', wrote Wilkes, 'and feel a real sense of gratitude towards the few independents who have obliged me. But I will not be the dupe of the mob, nor of a few wretched impertinents.' And he adds:

'I have given Thorpe orders to keep away from the house and gardens all the rabble at Aylesbury. If any of the better sort choose to walk in the garden, the gardener shall attend them, and then I shall get rid of the number of women, children, dogs, etc. You would stare at the number of little thefts they make, I mean the lower sort.'

The best flowers, he added, were picked and carried away. Doubtless the 'rabble at Aylesbury' had the passion of the English race for gardens, but none of their own, and rightly considered their MP had plenty to spare. Wilkes was not to revert openly to this attitude to 'the mob' until the Gordon Riots of 1780; in the interim his political dependence on it was to be too complete for the utterance of such sentiments. Although genuinely liberal in much of his later actions, especially as a magistrate, Wilkes' place in the world of the people was always to be slightly equivocal: poised between upbringing and an often genuine concern for the individual.

Before Pitt's resignation in 1761, Wilkes had applied for a post in the Board of Trade, and also for the Ambassadorship at Constantinople. It was not his last unsuccessful bid for office: his debts were already mounting, and although parliamentary privilege made him, as an elected MP, safe from arrest, this did not free him from the pressures of his creditors. In the autumn of 1761 he at last made his first speech in the House, a competent attack on the dealings of the Ministry with Spain, and in March 1762, primed by Pitt, he published his first pamphlet: *Observations on the Papers Relating to the Rupture with Spain.* Pitt was to inspire some of Wilkes' most picturesque journalism. 'He carried with him the strength of thunder and the splendour of lightning', was his metaphor, and he was to compare his sharply-carved, classical countenance with 'the eagle face of the famous Condé'. But by then it was no longer an admiring description: Wilkes had himself felt the razor edge of Pitt's moral censure. 'His tongue dripped venom.'

It was true in one sense: Pitt had early established his stand against corruption in government, and as he was to write to the most loyal of his younger followers, Lord Shelburne: 'Faction shakes and corruption saps the country to its foundations, while Luxury immasculates and Pleasure dissipates the understandings of men.' While the first sentiments were never alien to Wilkes, who managed for long to maintain a certain independence of attitude in Parliament, the second hit him well below the belt and menaced his most cherished philosophy of life. Pitt himself was not always true to it; although his grandiose rebuilding schemes at his home at Burton Pynsent, and similar outbursts of extravagance, were actually a facet of the mental cloud that so often threatened to engulf him.

Bute and the King favoured peace, although in Pitt's estimate the time was not ripe, as ascendancy over the French was still not completely established. Pitt resigned on 5 October 1761, and in 1762 Bute became chief minister.

The Peace of Paris (February 1763) arranged by Bute and the King was to be the final spark that lit the Wilkes bonfire, which politically was to go on burning merrily for the next twenty years.

Pitt himself flared into a Churchillian display of martial fireworks. For Pitt, with France there could never be any compromise: it was a commercial war to the death, a prolongation of traditional enmity that was to be trounced by Thomas Paine in America just over a decade later, in one of the first and most influential attacks on the lingering mediaevalism of European foreign policy. But Paine's blast of *Common Sense*, that was to blow two continents into the twentieth century with a trumpet call for a world united by commerce and arbitration, not war, went far over Pitt's head and as far over Wilkes'. Liberty of another kind was to stretch, like an umbilical cord, from Wilkes to Paine, heralding a new kind of democracy of which Wilkes himself was only partially aware. But on the Peace of Paris Wilkes stood with Pitt against the King; and the King in this sense had a vision closer to the republican Paine than that prophet of universal brotherhood, seeing monarchy as the fountainhead of human strife, ever quite grasped. This was understandable enough; for whatever the motives behind the young George's tendering of the olive branch to France, they did not extend to his rebellious subjects of America, and the War of Independence was to incarnadine a whole later period of his reign. Civil wars are always the bitterest; and in one sense at least this was to be a civil war, with the nation's own kith and kin.

In 1762 Wilkes with Churchill started *The North Briton*, a political paper in opposition to *The Briton*, a government-financed journal in which Tobias Smollett, its Editor, had already attacked Wilkes as the anonymous writer of *Observation on the Papers relative to the Rupture with Spain*. Smollett, the Scottish novelist, Robertson, the Scottish historian, and Dr Johnson, grandiloquently Tory, were all in the pay of Bute, whose £30,000 of State funds expended on writers was unashamedly bribery to buy their support. Bute's sweeping changes in minor offices of government decimated those with Whig sympathies, and replaced them very largely by Scots and King's party men. It was soon a current joke that 'he turned out everyone who owed office to the Whig party, with the single exception of the King'. The spectre of Jacobitism had been finally laid by the Battle of Culloden in 1746, but the fears and hatreds bred by the Young Pretender's invasion of the North were still unforgotten, and the feeling was rife that the Scots had merely taken over the government of England in a more subtle way. It was on these fears that *The North Briton* played. The unfortunate Bute, who had entered the service of the King's late father, Frederick, Prince of Wales, on the strength of 'a good person, fine legs, and a theatrical air of the greatest importance', as Lord Waldegrave put it in his *Memoirs* (indeed Bute had first attracted attention at Court as an amateur actor of the part of Lothario), became overnight the target of a nation who mercilessly satirized his association with the King's mother, until the supposed secret passage between Bute's mansion and her residence, Leicester House, was as well-known and well-trodden a thoroughfare as Piccadilly.

Although published by Wilkes with strictly anonymous contributors, the main writer of *The North Briton* was soon suspected. In fact, he shared the journalism with Charles Churchill and Robert Lloyd. The first number of *The North Briton* appeared on 5 June 1762, and it was to continue weekly for nine months until No. 45 created a parliamentary explosion that sent Wilkes soaring across the Channel into exile.

Churchill was to be for Wilkes the closest of all his associates, and irreplaceable in his affections on his early death. He was one of those eighteenth-century clergymen who, like Laurence Sterne, John Horne (who later called himself Horne Tooke) and others, did not allow his cloth to interfere with his enjoyment of period pleasures and amenities. Like Horne, he was ordained more from parental suggestion than conviction, as well as from pecuniary need. (He was later to write bitterly of being condemned to 'pray and starve on £40 a year'.) Born in 1731, and therefore a few years younger than Wilkes, he had been a pupil at

Westminster School, where he was a contemporary of
George Colman the dramatist and William Cowper the poet,
as well as of his and Wilkes' friend and fellow-journalist
Robert Lloyd, who was the son of the school's Usher. With the
precocity expected of a later member of the Monks of
Medmenham, he married at the age of seventeen, without
noticeable effect on his sexual adventures, and perhaps for
this reason was forced in 1756 into succeeding his father as
curate at Ramham, when his father was promoted to
assistant Head Master at Westminster.

In 1761 he formally separated from his wife and published
his greatest success as a poet, *The Rosciad*, which had a vogue,
according to Leslie Stephen, 'not equalled by any satire
between Pope's *Dunciad* and Byron's *English Bards and
Scotch Reviewers*'.[1] It was an attack on nearly all
contemporary actors except David Garrick, whose work
Churchill greatly admired for its sensitivity to realistic
impression in a large variety of characters. It was published
anonymously, but after an attack in *The Critical Review*
ascribing the work to others, who disclaimed authorship,
Churchill under his own name published an *Apology
Addressed to the Critical Reviewers*. This included a hearty
lambasting of Smollett, the *Review*'s Editor, and, to a lesser
degree, Garrick. Churchill had no doubt heard that
Garrick, perhaps flattered but not above a witticism at the
expense of one who put him in certain professional
difficulties with his fellow players, had remarked that the
author of *The Rosciad* was probably hoping for a free pass at
Drury Lane.

Churchill, admiring the actor but unawed by the man,
rose nobly to the bait:

> Let the vain tyrant sit amidst his guards,
> His puny green-room wits and venal bards,
> Who meanly tremble at a puppet's frown,
> And for a playhouse freedom, sell their own.
> In spite of new-made laws and new-made kings,
> The free-born muse with lib'ral spirit sings.

[1] *Dictionary of National Biography.*

54

Garrick promptly wrote to Lloyd with a suggestion that he would like to know Churchill.

'At the first reading of his "Apology", I was so charmed and raised with the power of his writing that I really forgot that I was delighted when I ought to have been alarmed . . . In his "rosciad" he raised me too high: in his "Apology" he may have sunk me too low.'

Lloyd showed the letter to Churchill, who was at once invited to 27, Southampton Street, off the Strand, then the actor's home, and a friendship began whose warmth, however, somewhat evaporated with time. Garrick, sedately married to his decorously-retired dancer, Violetti, had long ago found Beaumont and Fletcher's *Philaster* 'very indecent' and, like other plays including some of Shakespeare's, greatly in need of alteration before reaching the Drury Lane stage. In spite of his admiration of Churchill as a poet, he possibly soon found him a sometimes disconcerting teller of tales at the Southampton Street dinner table.

The success of *The Rosciad* enabled Churchill to forget even further his rather nominal profession, although he did not finally resign from it until 1763. A bulky, unprepossessing man physically, although of great charm to many who knew him, Churchill shared with Wilkes a passion for sartorial elegance to offset these disadvantages and he now appeared in considerable glory, in a 'blue coat with metal buttons' and with gold lace on his hat and waistcoat. Perhaps it was this mutual need to conquer nature that helped to draw Wilkes and Churchill together. Churchill also used the *Rosciad* proceeds to pay his debts, an advantage which was not to last, although *The Rosciad* was by no means a flash in the pan. *The Candidate*, an attack on Lord Sandwich, then an unlikely candidate for the high stewardship of Cambridge University, was a later success and although, because of the purely contemporary nature of its satire, Churchill's work is almost unread today, his reputation with scholars has survived for the pungency and brilliancy of his lines. He was the last writer to use lampoons and polemical satires in heroic couplets with poetical distinction. The form lapsed; but the engineer of it remains in literary encyclopaedias.

His association with Wilkes in *The North Briton* was to prove an exhilarating exercise in journalistic notoriety. Fiercely antagonistic to Lord Bute and his paid supporter, Smollett of *The Briton*, *The North Briton* based its policy on the popular anti-Scottish, anti-Jacobite feelings of the time. In a sense, too, it was a vindication of Pitt and Temple, both under fire from Smollett's paper. Its method of presenting anti-Scottish sentiment was ingenious, apart from the more obvious forms of satire:

> 'Some time since died Mr John Bull, a very worthy plain honest old gentleman of Saxon descent. He was choaked by inadvertently swallowing a thistle which he had placed by way of ornament on top of his sallad.'

Frequently, it took the ironic character of a Scot justifying the governmental policy:

> 'My joy and exultation is now complete, for I have seen my countryman, the Earl of Bute, adorned with the most noble Order of the Garter and presiding over the finances of the Kingdom, when nearly the sum of twenty millions sterling will be raised; though, I thank heaven, not a fortieth part of it will be paid by us Scots . . . the Kingdom of Scotland alone pays nearly half as much in taxes as the whole County of York!'

In No. 38, dated 19 February 1763, this sardonic twist took the form of a supposed letter from the Young Pretender, Charles Edward Stuart, to his 'kinsman', Bute.

It is sometimes overlooked that the *North Briton's* forensic ridicule of Bute and scandalous implications about his relationship with the Princess-Dowager were only trimmings on a basically serious attack on Scottish influence and corruption. And there were certainly grounds for the attack: in a promotions list containing sixteen names, eleven of the name of Stuart, and four of the name of Mackenzie, were included (Bute himself was a Stuart). The opening lines of the first number set another key: 'The liberty of the Press is the birthright of every Briton, and is justly esteemed the firmest bulwark of the liberties of the country . . .' It was a maxim that was to be put to the test later and rocket Wilkes into fame in his country's history of civil liberties. 'Under the government of a Stuart', added *The North Briton*, 'the freedom of the press has been openly violated.'

The huge success of *The North Briton*, which was widely read, rested however on its alert appreciation of the need to entertain as well as instruct the public. Its style was what today we would call 'yellow journalism', spiced with amusing and malicious Court gossip. 'Gay Wilkes' had always a sharp eye for the follies or mishaps of the portentous, and he early got himself into trouble with a lively description of an incident at the Coronation, when Lord Talbot, attempting to back his horse, after careful rehearsal, out of the King's presence, had the mortification of being resisted by his anti-Royalist mount, who swung round and left in the usual way, presenting ostentatiously indifferent quarters to the King.

This incident cost Wilkes his first duel. Although spiritedly demanding 'by what right your lordship catechises me about a paper which does not bear my name', Wilkes accepted the challenge, keeping his 'cool' in the face of Talbot's palpably ungovernable temper. 'I must first settle some business about the education of my only daughter, whom I tenderly love', he declared, and demonstrated both his courage and his indifference by offering to agree to Talbot's choice of weapons. Wilkes had brought both sword and pistols, and Talbot chose the pistols. It was moonlight, and Wilkes had tried and failed to put off the meeting until the following morning, on the grounds that he had 'come from Medmenham Abbey, where the jovial monks of St Francis had kept me up till four in the morning'. Both fired and missed, whether deliberately is not quite clear, although it seems not entirely improbable. Duels were matters of honour, and the duellists not always choleric enough to feel it, when it came to the point, a matter of life and death. The fact that both protagonists then departed to the Red Lion, at Wilkes' suggestion, seems to indicate a certain mutual relief as well as a sense of honour satisfied. Talbot, according to Wilkes' account, appears as his passion deflated to have palpably lost his nerve.

Wilkes also fell foul of Dr Johnson, who in spite of his abuse of pensions in his Dictionary (which defined such a dependant as 'a slave of state'), had accepted one from the Bute government. He was later to be equally active, for the same reason, in the cause of the Government during the American War of Independence. Wilkes had already, more genially, crossed swords with 'Pensioner Johnson' in the *Public Advertiser* in 1755, when he had twitted Johnson on his comment on the letter 'H' in the Grammar prefixing his Dictionary. 'The letter H seldom, perhaps never', wrote Johnson, 'begins any but the first syllable.' 'The author of this remark', parried Wilkes, 'must be a man of quick apprehension and compre-hensive genius; but I can never forgive his un-handsome behaviour to the poor knight-hood, priest-hood, and widow-hood, nor his in-humanity to all man-hood.' Nevertheless, to show there was no personal ill-feeling, in March 1759 Wilkes had tried to make amends by using his influence in the Admiralty to procure the release of Johnson's black servant, who had been the victim of a press-gang abduction.

Wilkes' more scandalous baiting of Bute did not entirely please Lord Temple or Pitt. *The North Briton* was one of the first papers to give the full names, not the initials in the eighteenth-century custom, of those it attacked, and Temple at least became nervous of what he anticipated to be the 'unhappy consequences'. 'The sooner this scene of indiscriminate and excessive personality is closed, the better.' On 10th October he added in a letter to his sister, Pitt's wife: 'Mr Pitt and I disapprove of this paper war.' Wilkes' response in a letter to Temple was sharp: 'Such a warning is in character from Mr Pitt, who ought to fear the shadow of a pen for he is the worst writer, as he is the best speaker of his age.' His support for Pitt's war policy, however, provoked something of a *volte face* in November, when Temple was writing blandly that he could not 'sufficiently admire the North Briton'.

Wilkes' final *coup de grâce* in respect of Bute came with the publication of a play, *The Fall of Mortimer*, in which the alliance of Edward II's queen, Isabella of France, with the traitor Mortimer was taken, as it was meant to be taken, as an historic parallel of Bute's supposed illicit attachment to the King's mother and ruling of the kingdom (it was implied) over his head. Bute, the reins of power never easy in his inexpert hands, could take no more. He had always been conscious of Pitt's vast shadow, and his own comparative inexperience. Early in April he resigned, and George Grenville, Pitt's brother-in-law, succeeded him. The King's distracted professions of loyalty to his 'dear Friend', and warning that he would 'ever remember', and 'never forgive', the insults done to his mother, passed unheeded.

No. 44 of *The North Briton* had appeared on 2 April 1763, immediately before Bute's resignation. If Wilkes and Churchill had left it at that, all would have been well. But Parliament reopened later in the month, and No. 45, published in direct response to that event and the King's speech, was to provide the explosive which was to burn the fingers of the Government, and rocket Wilkes to immortality.

IV

No. 45: 'WILKES AND LIBERTY'

The North Briton, No. 45, was published on 23rd April, Shakespeare's birthday, and although there was no comparison in literary content or genius England had probably known no sensation in the world of letters of such magnitude since that time. The year was 1763, one year under two centuries from Shakespeare's birth; and England in both cases never quite recovered from the shock.

No. 45 attacked the speech from the throne on the opening of Parliament: a speech praising the peace of Hubersberg, a consequence of the Peace of Paris, and according to *The North Briton* 'the most abandoned instance of ministerial effrontery ever attempted to be imposed on mankind'. This kind of hyperbole was, in itself, nothing: it was to become journalistic currency (Wilkes privately in more quipping mood had compared the Peace of Paris with the peace of God, 'which passeth all understanding').The article did not attack the King personally, implying, as was usually the case, that the speech he read was compiled by his ministers. ('The King's speech has always been considered by the legislature and by the public at large as the speech of the minister.') It was, however, taken to insinuate that the King was agent of a deliberate political lie. Wilkes wrote the article anonymously, and it would seem indeed that Pitt himself had a hand in its final form, but it was considered 'seditious libel', the stock phrase for supposed censorship evasions of the time. As Peter Quennell wittily and perspicaciously put it, in his essay on Wilkes in *Four Portraits*: 'The administration now took a decision that, in the history of weak governments, has seldom failed to prove disastrous – they resolved that the time had come to act with firmness.' It was, in fact, not their first thoughts on the subject. In November, a warrant for the arrest of the author and publishers of Nos 1 to 26 had been issued but withdrawn, although the writers of a less fortunate paper known as the *Monitor* had been taken into custody. 'Those few, those very few', wrote *The North Briton* triumphantly, 'who are not afraid to take a lover of liberty by the hand, congratulate me on being alive and at liberty.' It was not to be for long. Although only the names of the printers appeared, two warrants were now issued by the Secretaries of State, Lord Egremont and Lord Halifax, for the apprehension of the authors, printers and publishers of the libel. This was done after consultation with the Attorney-General, Charles Yorke, and through him his father, the celebrated lawyer Lord Hardwicke. Not unaffected by wishful thinking, both came to the erroneous conclusion that such warrants were legal and no less than forty-eight people were, in some cases literally, turned out of their beds overnight by constables in an enthusiastic outburst of mass arrests. They included not only Balfe and Kearsley, Wilkes' present printers, but another named Leach who had long ago ceased his connection with *The North Briton*.

It was through the information given by one of the printers that the king's messengers now felt themselves free to arrest Wilkes. Nevertheless, on 29th April they failed to do so, on the rather extraordinary excuse that the intended prisoner was 'in liquor'. He was finally taken at his house at No. 13, Great George Street, Westminster, on 30th April; but the messengers were tardy even here, for earlier in the morning Wilkes had slipped out of the house with the casual comment that he would return for breakfast, and made his way to Balfe's printing shop in the Strand. Here he forced an entry through a first storey window and enterprisingly broke up the type of No. 46 of *The North Briton*, also destroying the original MS of No. 45.

On his return to Great George Street, Charles Churchill, for whom the officers were also searching, walked innocently into the house. Wilkes with his instant flash of wit remarked loudly to his friend: 'How does Mrs Thomson do today? Does she dine *in the country*?' Churchill, as quick-witted as Wilkes in a crisis, immediately took the hint. Mrs Thomson's need to dine in the country was such, he answered suavely, that he could do no more than pay his respects to Wilkes and leave. This he instantly did, rushing home to collect his papers and flee from London. The messengers failed to find him.

Wilkes on his return had indignantly (and with every show of surprise) resisted arrest on the grounds of lack of a warrant, and threatened to run the messenger through when a show of force was indicated. The messenger, considering as intended that discretion was the better part of valour, agreed to discuss the matter inside the house, where Churchill found them before beating his diplomatic retreat. Wilkes, by now enjoying himself, refused point-blank the request of Lord Halifax to present himself for interrogation at his house further down Great George Street, and when coerced by constable reinforcements only agreed to make the journey (a few steps away) in a sedan chair which had to be sent for. Having by now attracted all the attention he desired, from a gathering crowd only too willing to play along with the histrionic entertainment, he graciously allowed the sedan chairmen to carry him to Halifax's house.

He was received in a room overlooking the park, and impressively inhabited by Halifax, Egremont, Philip Carteret Webb, the Solicitor of the Treasury, and a law clerk. Their efforts to incriminate him failed, for Wilkes refused to answer their attempted examination. In fact, he was probably hedging for time; Lord Temple (according to Wilkes' contemporary biographer John Almon) having already been on the scene at the time of the arrest and sent for a writ of *habeas corpus*.[1] There was, if so, a delay in the issue of the writ and Wilkes was committed to the Tower, under a warrant to be kept a 'close prisoner'. Halifax is said to have offered him a choice of prisons, but Wilkes retorted instantly that, except from his friends, he was not in the habit of receiving favours.

In the meantime, Wilkes' house was ransacked and his papers, private and political, seized. The drawers of his writing table were broken open, and all the papers found in

[1] Another version of this story states that Wilkes himself applied for the *habeas corpus* writ, while the Duke of Grafton in his Memoirs says it was 'obtained as soon as could be by two of Mr Wilkes' friends'.

them and other places put into a sack and taken to Halifax's house. The indignation of Wilkes and his friends was rightly vociferous. Public clamour was on Wilkes' side, for *The North Briton* had gained him much popularity and his duel with Talbot even more. The cries of the crowd, formerly 'Whigs for ever' and 'Wilkes and no Excise', now changed to 'Wilkes and Liberty'. (The Excise reference was to Dashwood's Cyder Tax as Chancellor of the Exchequer, which Wilkes had resisted and which had aroused astonishing execration in a country in which cider could not, by the widest stretch of imagination, be claimed as the most popular beverage. But all excise taxes in the eighteenth century were unpopular and evaded almost automatically by large sections of the community, tea being the most widespread commodity of the thriving smugglers.)

The Duke of Grafton in his Memoirs recalls with indignation (he was a liberal-minded Whig at heart if not always in practice) the refusal of the authorities to allow him to visit Wilkes in the Tower:

'Mr Wilkes was apprehended under this *general* warrant; and his papers seized and tumbled about in a manner not warrantable, even had the seizure been less questionably legal. He was committed *close* prisoner to the Tower, under a fresh warrant. Of the close imprisonment, I, with many of his acquaintance, was witness; for we were denied admittance to him; Major Rainsford shewing us the warrant under which he acted. In signing this, as well as the other subsequent warrants, Lord Egremont was equally implicated with his colleague.'

Not only Grafton, in fact, but Wilkes' legal advisers and Lord Temple, were refused admission or contact with the prisoner. Temple, as Lord-Lieutenant of Buckinghamshire, received orders from the King to cancel Wilkes' commission in the militia, and although he obeyed on 5th May he himself was dismissed from the lieutenancy on 7th May. His replacement was Sir Francis Dashwood, a fact which may partly explain Wilkes' later antagonism and the breaking up, about this time, of the more regular meetings at Medmenham Abbey.

Wilkes was particularly nettled by this deprivation of his militia commission, which he seems to have valued, and on 1st May he took pains, in a letter to Polly in France, to maintain his unclouded reputation in a possibly equivocal situation. 'Be assured', he wrote, 'I have done nothing unworthy of a man of honour who has the happiness of being your father. As an Englishman I must lament that my Liberty is so wickedly taken from me; yet I am not unhappy for my honour is clear, my health good, my spirits unshaken, I believe indeed invincible.' The letter never reached his daughter; with an industry and enterprise, like the rifling of Wilkes' desk, not unique in political history, it was intercepted by government agents and found many years later among the papers of the Solicitor to the Treasury.

On 6th May Wilkes was brought into the Court of Common Pleas before Lord Chief Justice Pratt, who was to become famous not only as a result of the Wilkes case but for carrying through both Houses of Parliament, with Charles James Fox, a bill which restored to juries the constitutional right to determine law, as well as facts, in cases of seditious libel. Charles Pratt, Lord Camden, a Whig in politics, was also, while Attorney-General, successfully to sponsor a bill for extending the Habeas Corpus Act to civil cases. Beneath his portrait by Sir Joshua Reynolds in Guildhall is inscribed: 'In honour of the zealous asserter of English liberty by law.' Young Fox, scarcely fifteen years of age at the time of the *North Briton* excitement, was taken by his father, Henry Fox, Pitt's political opponent, to listen to the debates on the issue in Parliament, and Charles Fox was in the gallery of the House of Commons when a resolution was moved and carried to the effect that No. 45 was 'a false, scandalous, and seditious libel'.

Pratt had already, on 3rd May, seen Wilkes in Court and according to Grafton considered the case so important that he had 'desired two days for the consideration of it; and remanded Mr Wilkes back to the Tower, but expressly directing that he was not to be a *close* prisoner'. On 6th May he directed that Wilkes be liberated, declaring, in Grafton's words, 'the unanimous opinion and decision of the Court,

. John Wilkes. Silver medallion.

2. Charles Churchill, by J. S. C. Schaak.

3. David Garrick, by Joshua Reynolds.

4. Mary Mead (Mrs John Wilkes)
by Joshua Reynolds.

5. John Wilkes and his daughter Polly. Portrait by Zoffany.

that publishing a libel did not come within the offences of treason, felony or breach of the peace, which cases alone deprived a member from privilege of Parliament'.

Parliament's (or rather the current Government's) response was almost immediate. When it reassembled, the two Houses resolved by a majority that 'privilege of Parliament does not extend to the case of writing or publishing seditious libels'. Pratt's subsequent ruling that, except in cases of treason, general warrants were illegal, however, established permanently in England the rights of the individual against general warrants. These were warrants for arrest or search in which the intended victims were not named: which could be, and in fact were, used indiscriminately against any members of the public, singly or in bulk. It is true the outcry against the actions in Wilkes' case was based on the fact that they had already been deemed to have lapsed as an instrument for general state purposes, although in fact they had still been operated in time of war, on the excuse of State security: an excuse which can be used to cover a multitude of political and unconstitutional sins, even today. Pitt himself had issued three during the Seven Years' War, in order to incarcerate suspected spies.

Pratt's decision nevertheless ended for ever the English equivalent of the French *lettres du cachet*, although it naturally did not go unchallenged. 'Temple and Pratt are (I fancy) a little mistaken when they call this warrant illegal and unprecedented', wrote Lord Newcastle on 2nd May to the Duke of Devonshire, and the illegality of general warrants for seizure of a person was questioned again in a bill of exceptions, when the case went to the King's Bench as a court of error. Lord Mansfield, although a bitter opponent of Pratt, Wilkes and the Opposition (Pitt had long been at loggerheads with him), left no doubt, supported by three judges, that the warrants were in his opinion illegal. That he did this reluctantly and under public pressure can be gauged from Grenville's statement that 'he had told his Majesty that he should not declare it in public, but that he should tell his Majesty that, according to his opinion, no man had ever behaved so shamefully as Lord Chief Justice Pratt had done;

that Lord Chief Justice Jeffries had not acted with greater violence than he . . .'[1]

Wilkes' Counsel in the case before Pratt was Mr Serjeant Glynn, an association which was to continue into his City days as an Alderman, and Lord Mayor, of London. Pitt was particularly impressed by him when they met: 'Mr Serjeant Glynn has just left me. I find him a most ingenious, solid, pleasing man, and the spirit of the constitution itself. I never was more taken by a first conversation in my life.'[2]

As soon as Pratt's decision was known, Temple, in Wilkes' name, at once took actions against Lord Halifax and the Under-Secretary, Wood, the chief agent in the seizure of Wilkes' papers. The action against Halifax, however, was delayed six years, until November 1769, and in December 1769, the verdict was given for Wilkes, awarding him damages of £1,000.

A young man soon to become an acquaintance of Wilkes in exile was in London at the time of Wilkes' imprisonment. On 3rd May James Boswell walked up to the Tower to see Wilkes brought out, but he arrived too late. Taking a detour to Newgate on the way back, he noticed 'strange blackguard beings with sad countenances', the friends of two prisoners due to be executed the following morning. One was a young highwayman, Paul Lewis, who caught the eye and imagination of the diarist when he came out and passed by, apparently unconcerned and with courage. He was, wrote Boswell, haunted by the image, 'a genteel, spirited young fellow. He was just a Macheath.'

On 6th May, after Wilkes had been discharged from the Court of Common Pleas, a huge crowd followed him to his house in Great George Street, and Boswell watched him bowing from a window. George Onslow, in a letter to Newcastle, his uncle, the same day, described the 'many thousands that escorted Wilkes to his house' as being 'of a far higher rank than common Mob'. The King and Bute had misplayed their hand: their victim was not only popular, but a popular martyr. 'Wilkes and Liberty!' was the established

[1] *Grenville Papers*, vol. ii.
[2] *Ibid.*

cry of the populace, and it was not to be the last time it was heard.

Wilkes can be pardoned for being elated, and elation only added to his natural impudence. The next day he met an acquaintance from the Beefsteak Club and went with him to Bow Street, intending to see Sir John Fielding, the blind magistrate and half-brother of the novelist, Henry Fielding. Fielding was not there, but undeterred Wilkes demanded a warrant from the magistrate present 'to search the houses of the Secretaries of State, by whose order my bureau, desk and escritoire have been broken open and all my papers seized'.

'God bless me!', the magistrate exclaimed: 'Friend Wilkes, you are another John.'

'Whom do you mean? John Hampden?' asked Friend Wilkes hopefully (he had long admired Hampden).

'No, John Lilburne.'

It was not an idle comparison, in the light of Wilkes' new status as a rebel against State inroads on personal liberty. Lilburne, a young man of good family, had been a disciple of the mutilated puritans of the previous century, Bastwick, Burton and Prynne, and in December 1637 had himself been tried and condemned to a barbarous flogging from Fleet Bridge to Westminster, for the distribution of forbidden literature. It was a world in which the 'demonstration', as opposed to open rebellion, was becoming possible, and although rebellion once again erupted into civil war (in which Lilburne served in the army on Cromwell's side), the Commonwealth itself was never able to suppress the individual's newly-found need for political expression. Even beforehand, Lilburne and his Independent colleagues had defied the Presbyterians of the House of Commons. 'I am a free man, yea, a free-born citizen of England', declared this political ancestor of John Wilkes when brought before a Committee of Examination, and the literature of his followers, who became known as the Levellers, poured out between the years 1645 and 1653.

Wilkes might indeed have noted the significant date of '45, for the Levellers in a pamphlet by Richard Overton attacked not only the lack of a free press but suggested, over a century before the eighteenth-century reformers, a Parliament elected freely by all men, without fear and favour. Like Wilkes, Lilburne had the populace solidly behind him, presenting petition after petition for his release from prison, with that of his followers. In the end Cromwell himself, architect, perhaps not entirely by original design, of a military state, quashed a Leveller mutiny in the army and Lilburne was put on trial for high treason. Lilburne's own eloquence, against all the odds, won the day: the 'free men of England', as he called them, returned a verdict of 'Not Guilty'. London celebrated in a characteristically Wilkesian way by lighting bonfires in the streets, and a medal was struck to commemorate the occasion.

How close this was to a feature of his own future history Wilkes could not as yet have known. But the magistrate had made his comparison with an almost prophetic insight. Radicalism, later in Wilkes' century, in many ways had its roots, even if half-forgotten, in the Leveller outlook. Few political movements spring up of themselves: democracy is a continuous process, sometimes in decline or abeyance but with linking threads that are never broken.

On his return home Wilkes found a reply from the Secretaries of State, Halifax and Egremont, to his letter of the previous day. They had been duly provoked. 'In answer to your letter in which you take it upon you to make use of indecent and scurrilous expressions, we acquaint you that your papers were seized in consequence of the heavy charge brought against you, of being the author of an infamous and seditious libel.' They added they were at a loss to understand what he meant by the term 'stolen goods'.

Wilkes was seen next day in the Park 'in high spirits as ever man was', accompanied by Churchill, who had boldly returned to London in the light of his friend's success. Possibly they drafted a reply to the Secretaries of State together.

'Little did I expect, when I was requiring from your lordships what an Englishman has a right to', wrote Wilkes with injured innocence, 'that I should have the expressions "indecent" and "scurrilous" applied to my legal demands.

The respect I bear to His Majesty, whose servants it seems you still are (though you stand convicted of having in me violated in the most offensive manner the liberties of all the commons of England) prevents my returning you an answer in the same Billingsgate language. I will assert the security of my own house, the liberty of my person and every right of the people, not so much for my own sake, as for the sake of every one of my English fellow-subjects.'

It marked the beginning of a new attitude in Wilkes. He may have been, in a well-known phrase, 'a patriot by accident'; but the attack on himself had caused him for the first time seriously to look at general principles, to see himself as an upholder of the liberties not only of himself but of others. 'Wilkes and Liberty' was not to become a meaningless slogan. 'Wilkes' conversion to democracy', wrote his biographer, Charles Chenevix Trench, 'was as sudden as St Paul's to Christianity, and no less sincere.'[1] The sincerity is something that has never been questioned by those who have seriously investigated his life, even by those who on their own admission began the investigation with a prejudice against this assumption.

From Paris on 22 October 1764, Wilkes was to write a long letter to his electors at Aylesbury, which set forth his creed and vindication in a form from which he was not to deviate:

'... The consciousness of having faithfully discharged my trust, of having acted an upright and steady part in Parliament, as well as in other most arduous circumstances, makes me dare to hope that you will continue to me, what I most value – the good opinion and friendship of my worthy constituents. Having the happiness of being born in a country where the name of vassal is unknown, where Magna Charta is the inheritance of the subject, I have endeavoured to support and merit those privileges to which my birth gave me the clearest right ...

'The general charge that "the North Briton," No. 45, is a *libel* scarcely deserves an answer; because the term is vague,

---

[1] *Portrait of a Patriot* (Blackwell, 1962).

and still remains undefined by our law. Every man applies it
to what he dislikes . . .

'The North Briton did not suffer the public to be misled.
He acknowledged no privileged vehicle of fallacy. He
considered the liberty of the press as the bulwark of all our
liberties, as instituted to open the eyes of the people; and he
seems to have thought it the duty of a political writer to
follow truth wherever it leads . . .

'It is, however, most certain that not a single word
personally disrespectful to his majesty is to be found in any
part of it . . .'

And in support of this last claim Wilkes devastatingly quotes
The North Briton's description of George III as 'a prince of so
many great and amiable qualities, whom England truly
reveres. The personal character of our present amiable
sovereign makes us easy and happy that so great a power is
lodged in such hands.'

'Are these the "expressions of the most unexampled
insolence and contumely towards his majesty" which the
majority in his house of commons have declared that the
paper contains? Are these expressions "most manifestly
tending to alienate the affections of the people from his
majesty"?'

If the words describing George III had been used with an
ironic edge, Wilkes was certainly not going to admit it. On
their face value, as he well knew, they not only invalidated
the 'seditious libel' charge but made it look ridiculous.

The correspondence with the Secretaries of State and other
papers were circulated by Wilkes throughout London as
hand-bills, and there were reprints in the Opposition press. A
wit proclaimed that he had no idea how his friend Wilkes
stood in the matter of cash, 'but certainly there is not a man
in the country with so many bills in circulation'.

Wilkes later regretted the tone, although not the matter, of
some of this. He was, he said, 'elated by victory, scarce cool
enough to pay great attention to delicacy of expression . . . It
may be doubted if Mr Wilkes, or the Secretaries themselves,

most forgot on this occasion the dignity of their office and character.'[1]

His popularity was not universal. In the summer of 1762 Wilkes had heard that William Hogarth was about to publish a hostile caricature of Pitt and Temple. According to J. T. Smith, author of *Nollekens and His Times*, Churchill and Wilkes were among Hogarth's 'constant companions', and although the moral judgment of his paintings, such as *The Rake's Progress* and *The Harlot's Progress* series, certainly suggests otherwise, Smith also claimed that Hogarth 'revelled in the company of the drunken and profligate'. How much this was 'revelry' and how much an artist's dedication to the expression of real life is, of course, questionable, and it is difficult to accept some statements that Hogarth was an active member of the Monks of Medmenham, although it is quite true he painted some of the brotherhood. In any case, Wilkes' influence was not enough to deter him from publishing his caricature entitled *The Times*, and as a result No. 17 of *The North Briton* had been devoted to ridicule of Hogarth, who had recently been appointed 'serjeant painter' to the King. 'I think the term means what is vulgarly called housepainter.'

In fact Churchill, rather than Wilkes, was believed to be the main writer of No. 17, and Garrick certainly thought so. It was one of the things that alienated him from the poet: indeed he believed Hogarth's death to have been hastened by Churchill's attack, although considering Hogarth's own tough satiric temperament as an artist he almost certainly endowed his friend here with his own actor's sensitivity to criticism. Hogarth, in any case, had his revenge on Wilkes. He had been present in Westminster Hall, and sketched Wilkes in what was to become his most famous 'likeness', 'a cock-eyed, curious looking sprite' but with more than Byron's merriment. With wig subtly tufted into horns and the leer of a satyr, the portrait was to justify King George's later description, 'That Devil Wilkes'. The artist himself was sardonic. 'A Brutus! A saviour of his country, with such an

[1] Wilkes' own marginal notes to Almon's *History of the Late Minority*.

aspect, was so arrant a farce, that it galled both him and his adherents to the bone.' Later Hogarth did a similar cartoon of Churchill (who also was admittedly no picture), as a bear clutching a pint of porter, while Hogarth's dog, Trump, performed a christening ceremony on a copy of *The North Briton*.

It is doubtful if the two friends, thus coupled in caricature, were 'galled'; but it set Wilkes' image perpetually in history, and there is no doubt it was a deliberate exaggeration. What the avenging artist did not falsify was Wilkes' trim build, which he preserved with care and exercise throughout his life. It gave him an elegance and elasticity of movement that helped to counterbalance other defects. He was never a great eater or drinker: his sensual appetites flowed all in one direction.

At any rate he felt he could afford to acknowledge Hogarthian publicity unruffled: 'It must be allowed to be an excellent caricature of what nature has already caricatured.' In old age he sometimes proclaimed that he grew more like Hogarth's cartoon every day.

Wilkes, though, had damaged one connection, and an important one. Pitt wholeheartedly supported Wilkes' acquittal: he strongly believed a Member of Parliament should be protected by privilege, and that the ascription of libel to *The North Briton* was an attack on the freedom of the press. 'I know what liberty is', he wrote to the Duke of Newcastle (whose correspondence indeed was so voluminous that it must at times have overwhelmed him), 'and that the liberty of the press is essentially concerned in this question. I disapprove of all these sort of papers, the *North Briton*, etc.; but that is not the question. When the privileges of the Houses of Parliament are denied in order to deter people from giving their opinions, the liberty of the press is taken away.'

The disapproval was not sheer expediency. Pitt was aiming to weld England and Scotland more firmly together, and *The North Briton* had been a wedge trying to drive the two races apart. *The North Briton* was, he maintained, 'illiberal, unmanly, and detestable. The King's subjects were one people. Whoever divided them was guilty of sedition.' Pitt was within a few years to become Earl of Chatham, and illness and his transfer to the House of Lords were to weaken his influence. At the moment, however, he was still a formidable friend or opponent, and whatever his original response to Wilkes' ribaldries, his personal contact with him had been limited; although it is true he had received Wilkes at his bedside at Hayes and apparently suggested ways in which *The North Briton* should denounce the peace. When Grenville succeeded Bute, and made it clear he intended to follow his policy, at least to the extent of freeing the King from dependence on the Whig family groups, Pitt and Temple, his brother-in-law and brother, had been understandably alarmed at his apostasy. In fact the attack on the peace in Wilkes' journal had been based on an advance copy of the peace terms sent by Grenville to Temple. Wilkes' usefulness in this family and political quarrel could not, however, be taken as complete acceptance of his views by Pitt, as he was soon to learn, and from now on his support could never be wholly counted on. Grafton, too, was unwilling to stand bail, in spite of his indignation at being excluded from visiting Wilkes in the Tower. He was anxious not to appear openly to affront the King, and probably his gambling and horseracing expenses were worrying him.

Wilkes' siding with Pitt on war and the peace terms was wholehearted: in such matters of foreign policy he was essentially a man of his time, and Bute and the King, in this instance, in some ways ahead of it. So to a degree was Newcastle, whose main misgiving about the peace was its dishonouring of an agreement to aid Frederick, King of Prussia. There were, however, as so often, commercial reasons for the opposition to the Peace of Paris. It sacrificed certain important acquisitions by the English, including the sugar, rum and spices of Guadaloupe and Martinique and, less creditable, the Goree slave trade. Wilkes' later ally in the City of London, William Beckford, who was a close friend of Pitt, vehemently denounced the treaty in the House of Commons, and indeed it was from this moment that Wilkes made himself popular with the city merchants for supporting their commercial interests. It was to be of inestimable help to him in his later career.

'The ministers', declared Pitt, 'seem to have lost sight of the great fundamental principle that France is chiefly, if not solely, to be dreaded by us in the light of a maritime and commercial power – and therefore by restoring to her all the valuable West India islands, and by our concessions in the Newfoundland fishery, we have given her the means of recovering her prodigious losses and becoming once more formidable to us at sea.'

The North Briton had already made the point about the value of the Newfoundland fisheries, and Thomas Paine, who almost certainly had been a reader of *The North Briton*, made it again – on behalf of *American* interests – during the American Revolution. It was widely believed, by Pitt and Temple as well as Wilkes, that the treaty which made these concessions showed the 'iron hand' of Bute still active behind the Government.

Wilkes' fight for individual liberty had an unexpected further supporter in Charles Townshend: unexpected in the sense that Lord Townshend had written his son on 2 March 1763, repeating a paragraph 'out of the North Briton of Saturday last, which is as follows, viz:

"That great reformer of abuses, the new Whig head of the Board of Trade, has just condescended to stipulate for an additional salary, without power, as the price of his support of this Tory government." '

For once the 'shuttlecock', 'the new Whig head of the Board of Trade', had not veered with the wind (in spite of a momentary tremor about offending Grenville). One advantage had been derived from Wilkes, he declared: 'he had stopped a growing evil. Nobody could think what thirty years more might have done'. On 19 January 1764, when Sir William Meredith moved for an enquiry into Wilkes' complaint of breach of privilege, Townshend made a vehement speech in praise of the motion, and on 6th February he voted against the Government on Wilkes and General Warrants, making, according to George Onslow, one of 'the finest speeches that ever were heard'. On 1st August, Townshend even anonymously published a pamphlet: *A Defence of the Minority with regard to General Warrants*.

The anonymity was judicious. Voting in favour of the Opposition on the Wilkes issue was not, certainly, without its dangers. General Conway, who did so, was promptly dismissed by the King from his post attached to the bedchamber, and also from the command of his regiment. It spread a certain alarm and despondency, as doubtless intended. 'I think the calm and submissive reception of such an outrage, done to our constitution in the person of such an officer,' wrote Townshend in a letter to Newcastle on 28th April, 'the deepest and most fatal symptom we have yet seen of general insensibility and incurable indifference . . . Lord Temple returned here yesterday; and Lord Lyttelton thinks him desponding. I am told his relation [Pitt] speaks the language of despair . . . Mr Pitt has relinquished his house in town, and the furniture is removing.'

The 'shuttlecock' Townshend himself was preparing to veer with the wind again, 'and, if possible, obtain reinstatement in office'.[1] Wilkes only gaily faced the breeze, although by now from the safer shores of France. In temperament, he was the opposite of Pitt, the manic depressive: which was as well, considering the further trials to come.

[1] Sir Lewis Namier and John Brooke: *Charles Townshend* (Macmillan, 1964).

V

PARIS AND AN ESSAY ON WOMAN

Wilkes' dismissal by Camden was not, of course, acceptable to the Government, nor did it end their case against No. 45. The Ministry served on him a subpoena to attend the Court of the King's Bench, where Lord Chief Justice Mansfield presided. Mansfield could be relied on to reserve for himself, irrespective of jury, the final judgment as to whether or not a paper in a case of 'seditious libel' really was seditious; and his sympathies would be with the Government.

Wilkes ignored the subpoena. His support was steadily growing, and he had begun to feel himself in a position of strength. 'When I was brought before the court of common pleas', he was soon to write in his Letter from Paris to his constituents at Aylesbury, 'I pleaded the cause of universal liberty. It was not the cause of peers and gentlemen only, but of all the middling and inferior class of people, who stand most in need of protection.' 'Middling' was not a Wilkesian invention, nor did 'inferior' have a personal ring of what today might be called class-consciousness. They were regular terms for the layers of society of the period, and as George Rudé has pointed out, 'middling' derived from Daniel Defoe's grouping of the population (including 'the *middle sort*, who live well') as early as 1709.[1] In any case, the 'middling and inferior class of people' could be relied on to support their champion to the last cheer and, even more dangerously if provoked, the last pike.

Churchill in *The Duellist* underlined the situation:

> Hath he not won the vulgar tribes
> By scorning menaces and bribes?

[1] *Paris and London in the Eighteenth Century: Studies in Popular Protest* (Collins and Fontana Library, 1952–70). *See also* Lucy S. Sutherland: *The City of London and the Opposition to Government, 1768–1774* (University of London, Athlone Press, 1959).

And proving that his darling cause
Is of their liberties and laws
To stand the champion?

The Duellist, published late in 1763, could not be relied on to predispose Lord Mansfield in Wilkes' favour. It satirized the Chief Justice of the King's Bench alongside two others who were also soon to be specially alienated by Wilkes himself, Bishop Warburton and Lord Sandwich. Mansfield was not a popular judge, nor a man whom many found personally attractive. David Garrick, wracked with anxiety for a foreign friend who in 1769 accidentally killed one of a gang which attacked him in the street, and who now stood trial for murder, came to Mansfield with Sir Joshua Reynolds to discuss their friend's trial, and was chilled when the great lawyer, who fancied himself as an amateur critic of the drama, diverted the conversation to an ominous passage from *Othello*, 'Put out the light'. Wilkes was to call Mansfield 'my personal enemy'; and although the rift with Lord Sandwich may have started in the reputed Hell-Fire Club fracas, the satire of Wilkes' known closest friend and journalistic associate, Churchill, in a popular poem, could not have helped.

In the meantime, Wilkes visited his constituents. He and Churchill were met a mile outside Aylesbury by all from the town who possessed, or could borrow or steal, a horse, and that night, amid illuminations for the King's birthday, Wilkes and his admirers managed 'a fine list of patriotic toasts in the nasty wine of the borough'. Nasty wine or not, Wilkes next day had only a small headache although 'poor Churchill was half dead'. Wilkes was assured by his constituents that should Parliament expel him, they would unanimously re-elect him. In this they kept their word.

Wilkes himself recklessly opened the way for this event. He had been calling on the long-suffering Temple for loans in his emergency, but allowing his advice to go unheeded. It was not in Wilkes' nature to go in any direction but his own. Defying reason, he began to set up the press again for the reprinting of No. 45 of *The North Briton*; and promptly and insouciantly, on 20th July, left on a visit to Paris, where his adored Polly was being educated with total disregard of expense. (Wilkes, though his selection of playmates did not automatically suggest it, believed in the education of women, at least from the point of view of everything that was needed for an intelligent woman in intelligent society, and his daughter was getting the best that Paris could provide.)

Unfortunately, Paris also had its pitfalls, and Wilkes ran into unexpected trouble in the form of a challenge by an irate Scottish officer named Forbes, who had resented the slighting treatment of his race in *The North Briton*. Wilkes, perhaps more wary than in the Talbot case on account of his yearning for some Parisian fun, managed to put off this contest – which in principle he accepted – by the ingenious excuse that he had a prior engagement of the kind with Lord Egremont, which must be met first. Unfortunately Charles Egremont took the cue and died; but by this time Forbes had left France. Wilkes could turn to his Parisian consolations with a light mind, fortified too by the welcome he had received at Canterbury and Dover, and the memory of the English sailors who on the Channel crossing he had found 'no enemies to *Wilkes and Liberty*'.

He was soon in full spate to Churchill: 'I long to introduce you to the prettiest bubies I have ever kissed or made oblation to.' And Madame Carpentier, Polly's governess, proved to be an attractive lady by no means entrenched in purely educational battlements. Wilkes laid happy plans to breach the fortress walls, oblivious of the trap which he had laid, back in England, for himself before leaving. 'I am now planning a deep scheme for Madame Carpentier to fall into my mouth within a week.' Though gambling was not one of his vices, he wagered 'a cool hundred' that he would succeed by 1st August. It was late in September before he could bring himself to return to England, after a stay brightened too by reading Voltaire, meeting the *philosophes*, including Diderot and his old friend d'Holbach, and replanning his daughter's education ('I find the house, in which Miss Wilkes is, does not quite answer my plan for her education').

For d'Holbach, it appears, the Wilkesian 'enchantment' of

Leyden days had never ceased, nor 'the friendship which is of all my possessions the firmest and truest'. Wilkes found himself rocketed into the most coveted intellectual circle in Paris: a circle which had already fêted the celebrated author of *Tristram Shandy*, Laurence Sterne, and which was going through 'a great period of Anglomania', as Peter Quennell comments, following the Peace of Paris. At the *salon* of Madame Geoffrin, Gibbon too had found 'a place without invitation', seeing 'more men of letters among the people of fashion' than he had done 'in two or three winters in London'. Both Madame Geoffrin and the d'Holbachs held *salons* twice a week, diplomatically arranged at least in Madame Geoffrin's case to separate the *philosophes* from the *érudits*, a group more devoted to antiquarianism and what we might term 'art for art's sake' than their rivals. The *philosophes* were basically more attached to the Academy of Sciences, and therefore modern and political in their outlook. The Baron d'Holbach was a geologist of distinction, as well as a writer and wealthy man.

The liberal attitude of the *philosophes* fitted into Wilkes' newly-awakening political awareness, bred of his recent experiences. D'Holbach's *Système de la nature* Goethe found merely dull: 'We did not understand how such a book could be dangerous. It appeared to us so dark, so Cimerian, so deathlike . . . we shuddered at it as a spectre.' This hardly seems congenial in temperament to John Wilkes, and perhaps it is true d'Holbach had changed somewhat with the years. But like so many of the *philosophes* he was revolutionary and critical in principle, although the expression was too metaphysical, as so much of pre-Revolution French writing, to lead to any direct action.

By 1789 the major *philosophes* were dead, and in 1763 when Wilkes was with them, this first time, in Paris, Diderot and d'Alembert were still working on their great *Encyclopédie*, which, published in seventeen volumes between 1751 and 1765, launched the group into historic significance. La Mettrie, author of *L'Homme Machine* with its remarkable biological equations of man and animal, and anticipation of Thomas Paine in its humane attitudes to the alleviating

79

causes of crime unobserved by society in its punishments, had died prematurely in 1758, but his work had first been published at Leyden in 1748, only two years after Wilkes left the university, then 'the most modern and highly respected in Europe',[1] and although Wilkes wore his university-lore lightly (like the epicurean La Mettrie) some of its philosophical distinction had doubtless brushed off on him. His new liberalism can only have been stimulated by the surviving *philosophes*, although in Diderot he must have early found, too, a spirit equally responsive to pornographic jovialities. Diderot, like La Mettrie, was either to influence or curiously anticipate Paine, seeing in insect life and the wing of a butterfly signs indicating the existence of God.[2] Wilkes, no countryman, was blind to such intimations of human immortality; but Diderot as author of *Les Bijoux indiscrets* and *La Rêve d'Alembert* would be a congenially salacious companion.

Wilkes, therefore, in Paris had the best of both worlds: the ribald and the politically liberal. It was presumably through conversations with the *philosophes* that he became aware of the more sombre conditions in France, and the revolution which his companions, like Voltaire, were already anticipating. 'The distress in the provinces', wrote Wilkes, 'is risen to a great height, though Paris is as gay as usual. The most sensible men here think that this country is on the eve of a great revolution.' He was twenty-six years out in his prophecy, but not the only Englishmen to make it: the fate of the Bourbons was foreseen across the years by almost everyone except themselves. Arthur Young, the agriculturist, travelling across France on horseback in 1787 and 1788, noted everywhere a poverty and *laissez faire* of a standard unknown in his native England: splendid bridgebuilding and roadbuilding projects on the one hand, cottages and houses

[1] R. J. White: *The Anti-Philosophers* (Macmillan, London; St Martin's Press, New York, 1970). White also points out La Mettrie's curious affinity to Bernard Shaw's 'creative evolution' in *Back to Methuselah*: 'The original shape of a creature degenerates or perfects itself through necessity. . . . I wouldn't rule out that man might end by being nothing but a head.'
[2] *Les Pensées sur l'interprétation de la nature* (1753). *See also* Paine: *The Age of Reason* (1794).

West Wycombe House and Park, showing St Lawrence Church (with golden ball) and Mausoleum.

7. The Earl of Bute.

8. King George III, *c.* 1767.

without glass windows, and peasantry in rags without shoes, on the other. The landed gentry made no attempt to farm their vast estates, which they visited, in the main part, only to hunt. The result was hunger in the land, and even Paris was 'vastly inferior to London':

'The streets are very narrow, and many of them crowded, nine-tenths dirty, and all without foot pavements. Walking, which in London is so pleasant and so clean, that ladies do it every day, is here a toil and a fatigue to a man, and an impossibility to a well-dressed woman. The coaches are numerous, and, what are much worse, there are an infinity of one horse cabriolets, which are driven by young men of fashion and their imitators, alike fools, with such rapidity as to be real nuisances, and render the streets exceedingly dangerous, without an incessant caution. I saw a poor child run over and probably killed, and have been myself many times blackened with the mud of the kennels . . . To this circumstance also it is owing, that all persons of small or moderate fortune are forced to dress in black, with black stockings; the dusky hue of this in company is not so disagreeable a circumstance as being too great a distinction; too clear a line drawn in company between a man that has a good fortune, and another that has not. With the pride, arrogance, and ill temper of English wealth this could not be borne; but the prevailing good humour of the French eases all such untoward circumstances.'[1]

Young added that lodgings were not half as good as in London, yet considerably dearer, a circumstance that probably did not diminish Wilkes' expenses twenty years or so before. But if there was a lack of pavements and colour in the clothes, these things did not disturb Wilkes' own butterfly temperament. Paris was still gay Paris, with its 'prevailing good humour' which Mary Wollstonecraft was to notice, with slightly scandalized amazement, only a month after the execution of Louis XVI. And Wilkes, unlike David Garrick on his first visit to Paris in 1751, was hardly likely to be

[1] *Travels in France during the years 1787, 1788 and 1789* (Ed. Constantia Maxwell: Cambridge University Press, 1950).

disturbed by the French women 'all heavily painted', nor to be cheered, as Garrick was, by observing later two very pretty clean faces unpainted 'which was a greater curiosity than any I had yet seen in Paris'. Even Garrick was susceptible enough to be impressed by their attractive, gay and easy manners and their well-shaped figures, adding: 'They tread much better than our ladies.' No doubt Wilkes made his own measurements of the shapely figures, and the easy resilience of Paris and the Parisians was, in fact, very much in the spirit of John Wilkes' own.

Perhaps this was as well, for he was to revisit the French city more quickly than he had anticipated. He returned to London on 28th September, and set to work, with characteristic untroubled defiance, on printing a collected edition of *The North Briton*. But Lord Egremont's sudden death had opened the way for a former rakish colleague, now to become Wilkes' implacable political enemy. His successor as Secretary of State was Lord Sandwich: that Lord Sandwich, member of the Monks of Medmenham, whom Wilkes is supposed to have frightened by setting a baboon in the guise of the Devil on his back. The new Secretary of State had attached himself to the 'Bloomsbury Gang' and in spite of his private life had won the regard of George III, who had a puppy-like eagerness to lick the hands of those willing to devote themselves to his interests. Later, the King was to declare that of all the First Lords of the Admiralty, 'he valued Lord Sandwich above them all'.

Where the Wilkes issue was concerned, Sandwich had decided, at least on the surface, to play it respectable; and fate played into his newly respectable hands. Wilkes had a private printing press on which, before he left England, he had printed a pornographic *Essay on Woman*, intended purely for the delight of his more rakish friends. How much he wrote of it himself is highly disputable, as are the various extant copies reputed to comprise the text. On the chronological evidence it was obviously originally by Thomas Potter, who had died in June 1759. Many of the references were topical long before Wilkes' maturity. The version dedicated to Fanny Murray, for instance, celebrates a courtesan most active in Bath between 1735 and 1745, although as the wife of David Ross, an ex-actor of David Garrick's company currently attempting a disastrous new career as a theatre manager in Edinburgh, she was to meet the pruriently interested James Boswell at dinner as late as 1772: 'as decent a lady at her own table as anybody', wrote Boswell. There is a reference to 'Hussey's Duchess', readily understandable only near the year 1746 when the Dowager Duchess of Manchester caused a stir by marrying Edward Hussey, and although the scurrilous footnotes attributed to Bishop Warburton were almost certainly mainly Wilkes' work, Potter's own disreputable connection with the Bishop dated back to 1756, when Mrs Warburton, childless in eleven years of matrimony, happily bore a son just nine months after becoming friendly with Potter.[1] Dr William Warburton was then aged sixty, and neither a likeable character nor a sensitive and understanding Editor of the works of Shakespeare. 'Besides your giving an elegant form to a monstrous composition', he wrote to Garrick, whose alterations and omissions in his stage versions were notorious, 'you have, in your own additions written up the best scenes in the play, so that you will imagine I read the reformed Winter's Tale with great pleasure.' (Garrick's 're-formed Winter's Tale' had become the story of Florizel and Per-dita, with all the opening scenes of Leontes' jealousy left out.)

Warburton had also edited Pope's *Essay on Man* (1751) and *The Dunciad*: and both were the cue for the form taken by the *Essay on Woman*, which was a parody of the former with footnotes attributed to Warburton; just as Warburton, with equal malice if not scurrility and wit, had attributed his *Dunciad* introduction and notes to the scholar Bentley, purely in order to bring Bentley into disrepute. Warburton, in fact, was hoist with his own petard, a fact some of his sympathizers have overlooked.

---

[1] Garrick's excellent biographer, Carola Oman, was apparently unaware of this by no means uncelebrated connection, as indeed was Garrick, who wrote his congratulations to the Bishop who was 'curt in his acceptance' of them. This Miss Oman attributes to the fact that Warburton may have felt 'his own success tactless in view of Mrs Garrick's disappointment'!

Wilkes' later declaration, however, that 'I am not the author of the "Essay on Woman". It was written by Potter', must be taken as a gloss on the full truth, produced for self-protection purposes. It is true Potter had written him on 31 July 1755 that he was about to 'attempt an "Essay on Woman" '; but the ironic reference in the work to 'the most intrepid hero George Sackville' can only be to the Battle of Minden in August 1759 (three months after Potter's death). Sackville, later prominent as a Minister in connection with the British defeat at Saratoga, under the title Lord George Germain, had been cashiered for cowardice at Minden and accused of homosexual tendencies by Wilkes. Pitt was also his bitter opponent. Internal evidence of the poem's style is less convincing. Pornographically, of course, Wilkes was perfectly capable of it, and also the use of Latin and Greek and the quotations from Homer. But the prolific (and authentically eighteenth-century) use of four-letter words and deification, as it were, of the penis rise little above what today we call schoolboy lavatory humour, although the Pope-like verse construction gives it all a kind of literary *double entendre*.

The 'Pego' or 'Prick', in the period terminology (the probably most authentic copy of *An Essay on Woman* is given as 'By Pego Borewell Esq.'), is much, if sometimes weakly, in evidence:

> Presumptious Prick! the reason wouldst thou find
> Why form'd so weak, so little and so blind?
> Observe how Nature works, and if it rise
> Too quick and rapid, check it ere it flies;
> Spend where we must, but keep it while we can:
> Thus Godlike will be deem'd the ways of man . . .

There is a good deal of salacious brooding on the Virgin doomed 'to bleed today' (with a footnote by 'Warburton' on the Englishwoman's failure, unlike the European, to wash the vagina, which sounds curiously modern in the light of certain advertisements of chemical products today; as indeed does Arthur Young's complaint, in his *Travels in France*, that the English, unlike the French, have no idea of the uses of the

84

bidet). And Pope is neatly if scurrilously parodied on occasion, his

> Who sees with equal eye, as God of all,
> A hero perish, or a sparrow fall,
> Atoms or systems into ruin hurl'd.
> And now a bubble burst, and now a world.

becoming:

> Who sees with equal Eye, as God of all,
> The Man just mounting, and the Virgin's fall;
> Prick, cunt, and bollocks in convulsions hurl'd,
> And now a Hymen burst, and now a world.

Wilkes may well have 'touched up' Potter as well as providing the 'Warburton' notes; yet after the wittier and less obviously vulgarized quotations given by Wilkes of Dashwood's fancies at Medmenham, it is difficult not to feel that the *Essay on Woman*, taken as a whole, is not only below the Dashwood style but below that of Wilkes who so admired it. Certainly he claimed that 'the most wretched and impious lines' in the version produced by the Government were forged, and on all the evidence it seems unquestionable.

Nevertheless, this was the weapon which had now fallen, by a series of betrayals, into the Government's hands, and it would be asking rather more than eighteenth-century political honour could bear for the King's party to make no use of it to support their case against *The North Briton*. The Earl of Bute, conscious of his unpopularity and perhaps too thin-skinned for a politician of that day, had finally resigned in 1763, to the distress, as we have seen, of his 'dear friend' the King. 'I hardly meet with anything but cruel abuse and base ingratitude', wrote the aggrieved favourite. 'The Gaveston of the eighteenth century' as he had been called, not quite accurately, had been succeeded on the King's choice by George Grenville, and it was in a weak attempt to preserve some of his independence from throne influence that Grenville had made an unlikely alliance with the Whig faction headed by the Duke of Bedford – a faction called the

'Bloomsbury Gang' because it was centred at the duke's residence, Bedford House, Bloomsbury. Grenville was therefore now a governing force behind Wilkes' prosecution, and only Temple of the family associated with Pitt remained Wilkes' friend.

In a sense, Wilkes had impudently contributed to his own downfall. On 10th May in the *Public Advertiser* he had inserted an advertisement: 'Speedily will be published, an "Essay on Woman" by P. C. Webb'. This can only have been a revengeful gesture to put the fear of God into Philip Carteret Webb, the Solicitor to the Treasury, whom Wilkes considered responsible for the searching of his house and removal of his papers; for Wilkes obviously had no intention of publishing the poem, which would have laid him open to prosecution, and in fact on 20th June he broke up the type in order to use it to set a new expensive reprinting of *The North Briton*. (He had been warned against this financially, as it would mean charging half a guinea instead of the original 2½d a week, and in fact only 120 subscribers out of the required 2,000 had been obtained. Although Temple had contributed £500 towards the cost, 'I am not a little out of pocket by it', wrote Wilkes, 'but *The North Briton* and Wilkes will be talked of together by posterity.' He felt, he added hopefully, 'the spirit of Hampden in it'.)

At the time the type of the *Essay on Woman* was broken up only nine pages had been printed (it seems obvious the extant versions are of an incomplete poem). The fact that twelve copies had been made suggests an assumption that these were printed privately for the perusal of the twelve 'inner brotherhood' of the Monks of Medmenham. Whether a thirteenth was deliberately taken off by the printer Michael Curry, from whom the Government obtained it, or was simply stolen by him, is unclear. The frontispiece, inevitably phallic, had been sent to Wilkes in November, 1762, by his main printer Kearsley, with a bill for £2 15s. The Government's story of their windfall, which few believed, was that one of the compositors had picked up a proof page from the workshop floor and shown it to a workmate, who had been so shocked that he had delivered it into the hands of his foreman, who in his turn had passed it on to his employer. Michael Curry was certainly implicated in obtaining the rest, and so much a marked man in the printing world (which even in those days was linked by a sense of what we would call 'union' honour) that he could not obtain employment and eventually committed suicide.

The implication of the Rev. John Kidgell was more equivocal. Kidgell was a reprobate chaplain of the Earl of March, now Under-Secretary of State and notorious in unvenerable old age as 'Old Q', still ogling the passing girls from his eyrie in Piccadilly. Correspondence between the two a few years later, when Kidgell had been forced into exile in Holland through his unpopularity over the affair, makes it clear Kidgell was in possession of a secret involving forgery in the Wilkes business. On 18 September 1767 he wrote to March:

'It was in obedience to your command that I undertook to join in the persecution against Mr Wilkes . . . I informed you I had seen a forgery in Mr Wilkes' papers, a proceeding I could see so plainly Your Lordship detested from his observations upon it, and thought he who could have been concerned in it deserved to be hanged.'

Kidgell most significantly adds that he later saw 'the same forgery, two months after its discovery, made instrumental to Mr Wilkes's condemnation. Now I humbly submit to Your Lordship to consider whose reputation I consulted by that precipitate retreat out of the kingdom, which ruined my reputation and saved your Lordship's.'

He received an evasive reply and on 6th October Kidgell tried again:

'I am surprised that the action which fills me with remorse can be looked upon by Your Lordship with indifference . . . I am determined to lay the whole affair before my Lord Chief Justice, who, I take it, will either rehear the case or take such methods to satisfy the injured party as shall be consistent with strict justice and public tranquillity.'

He informed March he had not *yet* communicated with Wilkes, 'though the intelligence I could have given him was beyond all price'.

It seems some counter-threat was made, for on 6 May 1768 Kidgell apologized 'for the liberty I have taken in making intercession for the most contemptible of men', although by 29th November, perhaps driven by necessity, he was claiming he had refrained from seeing Wilkes when he was in Holland and the hint of blackmail recurs. 'Forgive me, my lord, when I assure Your Lordship that unless some consideration is taken of me that I may be indemnified in part for my losses... I shall be under a necessity of publishing my apology.'

A letter from a master printer, William Faden, to Philip Carteret Webb on 24 September 1763 had also referred to 'tendering down the money to Michael Curry, who I believe will not resist the temptation', showing that Wilkes' rash outburst of advertising humour had in fact alerted Webb and its perpetrator had been easily guessed.[1] Faden was the employer of the foreman printer, Lionel Hassall, who was alleged by the Government to have brought Faden the copy of the proof which so shocked the staid compositor in Wilkes' unlikely employment. Faden was, by a curious chance, staying at the time in the house of the Rev. John Kidgell, Rector of Godstone and Horne in Surrey and chaplain of the Earl of March.

What is in any case clear is that the methods taken to secure the document were of the dirtiest for political ends: if Wilkes could not be got rid of on a genuinely political charge, then he must be got rid of on another. It should be added that Wilkes was not present at his trial, his attorney, Phillips, was believed to have been bought by the other side, and no record was kept of the trial because Lord Mansfield ordered those taking notes to cease doing so. As a result Wilkes himself complained he never knew exactly what had taken place or 'what he had been convicted of'.

Wilkes when Parliament reopened on 15 November 1763 was aware that he was to be charged for reprinting and

---

[1] *Guildhall MSS* 24/3.

publishing No. 45: he had informed the Speaker that he intended to complain of the breach of privilege he had endured, but was ready to waive this privilege (as a Member of Parliament) in the case of the new trial. He rose to speak on 15th November but was stopped by Grenville, who indicated there was a message from the King to be read first. In spite of a wrangle with Pitt over privilege, this in fact was done: and the House learned that 'His Majesty having received information that John Wilkes Esquire, a Member of this House, was the author of a most seditious and dangerous libel', this John Wilkes Esquire had been apprehended but discharged by the Court of Common Pleas on grounds of privilege. He had ignored a summons issued to him for the same offence, and His Majesty, thinking it 'of the utmost importance not to suffer the public justice of this kingdom to be eluded', laid the libel before the House for its consideration.

Most of this was known already, and also most of what followed regarding the seizure of Wilkes' private papers and person. A new element was introduced by Samuel Martin, Secretary to the Treasury, who had been savagely attacked in *The North Briton* for his involvement in Bute's governmental briberies and what was known as the 'Massacre of the Pelhamite Innocents', in other words the toppling of the Duke of Newcastle, head of the Pelham family and receiver of so much interesting correspondence, from power. Martin, who had been practising with his pistols ever since the attack was published in No. 40, now reminded the House of this and, looking Wilkes in the face, deliberately repeated twice the words: 'A man capable of writing in that manner without putting his name to it, and thereby stabbing another man in the dark, is a cowardly, malignant and scandalous scoundrel.' Wilkes, whose case was based on the anonymity of the writings, failed to rise to the bait; although it was to involve him in a duel later. The House eventually divided on Lord North's resolution that Number 45 was a 'false, scandalous and seditious libel, containing expressions of the most unexampled insolence and contumely towards his Majesty, the grossest aspersions on both Houses of Parliament and the most audacious defience of the authority of the whole Legislature' etc. In North's defence it must be said that when offered the leadership of the attack in the House of Commons he had at first refused, since he had 'received civilities from Mr Wilkes'. But this honourable stand had eventually been undermined by Grenville. The resolution was passed by 273 votes to 111. It was by now early morning, and the half-somnolent MPs went home.

All this, apart from Samuel Martin's intervention, Wilkes must to some extent have expected. What he could not have anticipated was an attack in the rear simultaneously taking place in the House of Lords. Dr William Warburton, Bishop of Gloucester, was a member of the House of Lords, which gave an opening for the matter of the poem to be brought up in the House as concerning a member's privilege. The unfortunate Warburton probably did not relish this airing of unsalubrious linen in public, and was perhaps caught unawares. It was Lord Sandwich, new Secretary of State, who brought up the motion; and indeed he had written to Webb on 22nd October, 'I wish to play a forward part in this business'. [1] He had in his hand, he said, a paper abusing the Bishop of Gloucester in the grossest manner; it was infamous, filthy and blasphemous, and he shuddered to read it; but read it he must, and did. Dashwood, who after his brief failure as Chancellor of the Exchequer had now been despatched to the Lords as Lord le Despencer, was heard to remark audibly that it was the first time he had heard Satan preaching against sin. Sandwich's relish in his recital outraged the good Lord Lyttelton, who cried out that he should stop (he was known to have a reprobate son, reputedly belonging to the Monks of Medmenham, who gave him great anxiety); but the House, which well knew Sandwich's own reputation, was riven with shouts of 'Go on' and the members it would seem had an uproarious good time, not in the least abated when Warburton exclaimed that 'the hardiest inhabitants of hell' could not listen to such blasphemies.

[1] Sandwich-Webb correspondence (thirteen letters), 22 October to 14 November, 1763. *Guildhall MSS* 214/1.

He had, of course, been libelled, as he certainly did not write the scurrilous notes attributed to him, but the Ministry was not concerned with him. The target was Wilkes, and Sandwich moved that Wilkes be named as the author. But at this even Lord Mansfield had the honesty to comment that before condemning a man, one should at least give him the right to be heard in his defence. Temple also complained of the methods used by the Government, but could not prevent the passing of a resolution to the effect that the essay was 'a most scandalous, obscene, and impious libel'.

Wilkes himself, in the Paris letter to his Aylesbury constituents, put his finger firmly on the real criminal in this issue of 'impious libel':

'I will always maintain the right of private opinion in its fullest extent, when it is not followed by giving any open, public offence to any establishment, or indeed to any individual. The crime commences from this point; and the magistrate has then a right to interpose, and even to punish outrageous and indecent attacks on what any community has decreed to be sacred. Not only the rules of good-breeding, but the laws of society, are then infringed. In my own closet I had a right to examine, and even to try by the keen edge of ridicule, any opinions I pleased . . . it was in private I laughed. I gave no offence to any one individual of the community. The fact is, that, after the affair of the North Briton, the Government bribed one of my servants to steal a part of the Essay on Woman, and the other pieces, out of my house. Not quite a fourth-part of the volume had been printed at my own private press. The work had been discontinued for several months, before I had the least knowledge of the theft. Of that fourth-part only twelve copies were worked off, and I never gave one of those copies to any friend . . . After the servant had been bribed to commit the theft in his master's house, the most abandoned man of the age (who in this virtuous reign had risen to be secretary of state) was bribed to make a complaint to the house of lords, that I had published an infamous poem, which no man there had ever seen. It was read before that great assembly of grave lords and pious prelates (excellent judges of wit and poetry!), and was ordered to lie on the table, for the clerks of the house to copy, and to publish through the nation. The whole of this proceeding was, I own, a public insult on order and decency; but the insult was committed by the house of lords, not by the accused member of the house of commons.'

He added a sardonic rider on Kidgell and his employer: 'The neat, prim, smirking chaplain of that babe of grace, that *gude cheeld* of the prudish kirk of Scotland, the earl of March', and maintained (which the later discovery of the March-Kidgell correspondence confirms), 'The most vile blasphemies were forged, and published as part of a work containing in reality nothing but fair ridicule on some doctrines which I could not believe.' Perhaps realizing that the rather glowing innocence of this description might, to put it mildly, prove not entirely credible, he admitted to 'two or three descriptions, perhaps too luscious' and smartly returns to the attack: 'Besides, it is not given to every man to be as pious as Lord Sandwich; or as chaste, *in* and *out* of the marriage bed, in all thought, word, and deed, as the bishop of Gloucester.'

Wilkes was now caught, nevertheless, on a double hook: he would now go on trial as printer and publisher, if not as proved author, not only of No. 45 of *The North Briton* but also of the scandalous *Essay*, and both were condemned in advance by a vote in both Houses. Already exhausted by the overnight sitting in the House of Commons, where he had been under fire almost the whole time, he was perhaps over-ready to let Martin's insult rankle, and the irritation betrayed him into not only taking up the challenge (which the gentleman's code of honour of the day forced him to do) but into an indiscreet admission of his authorship of at least the passages about Martin in *The North Briton*, in a letter to Martin the next morning:

'SIR,
You complained yesterday, before five hundred gentle-men, that you had been *stabbed in the dark*; but I have

reason to believe that you was not so *in the dark* as you affected to be. To cut off every pretence of ignorance as to the author, I whisper in your ear, that every passage of "The North Briton" in which you have been named or even alluded to was written by

Your humble servant,

JOHN WILKES.'

Martin, in a letter the same day (16 November 1763), took great care to repeat Wilkes' own admission as well as his own original insult, and challenged Wilkes to show him 'whether this epithet of *cowardly* was rightly applied or not' by meeting him in Hyde Park immediately with a brace of pistols each, 'to determine our difference'. He added he proposed to call at Wilkes' house to deliver the letter, and then to go directly to the ring in Hyde Park, concealing his pistols and intending to wait one hour, 'in order to give you the full time to meet me'.

It has been pointed out, and rightly, that Martin reversed the usual procedure by which the challenged, not the challenger, should have the choice of weapons, and gave Wilkes no time to find a second or a surgeon. The fact that ever since the attack in *The North Briton* appeared Martin had been practising with his pistols is fully attested. He chose the range (twelve yards) and himself gave the signal to fire, both giving an advantage to a practised shot. Moreover, as a Treasurer of the Princess-Dowager's household, and a friend and close neighbour of Hogarth, he could well have been backed, officially and unofficially, in a plan to eliminate Wilkes. Horace Walpole certainly thought so. According to Wilkes himself, in a debate on the Civil List fourteen years later, Martin handled £41,000 of Secret Service money in the year before the duel, implying that some of this could well have been given him as a bribe.

If so, the plot misfired, but only by the narrowest margin. Martin left two sets of unpublished notes describing what took place, the first considerably altered and corrected, and Wilkes' version appeared in the biography written by his friend, the publisher John Almon. There are several differences, but the general account seems clear. Wilkes followed Martin to the park alone, soon after receiving the letter, and together they sought a more private place while Wilkes made the point about seconds and 'previous regulations'. To this Martin replied shortly that he had come to risk his life with no fear of unfairness, that they should walk a dozen paces and turn round and fire, and that (when Wilkes queried this) they should both fire together, 'or in what way each thinks fit'.

While they were talking a man and woman passed, and so they moved on further to a rail near a low, watery place. Wilkes exercised his choice of this spot for the duel, and Martin agreed. He also agreed on Wilkes' insistence that they should each use one of the other's pistols. When this exchange was made they parted as arranged, but when Martin turned round to fire he saw Wilkes bending down, apparently to examine the pistol. Martin paused at Wilkes' request, but when Wilkes had adjusted his position, they both fired. Both missed. When Wilkes presented his second pistol, Martin fired again, Wilkes 'snapping his pistol in his hand at the same moment'.

When Martin asked if his pistol had misfired, Wilkes replied 'No, dammit, I am wounded'. He showed a large patch of blood under his waistcoat, buttoned up his clothes and, ducking under the rail, walked towards Grosvenor Gate. Martin followed with the pistols. As he drew nearer Wilkes he saw someone helping him. He ran up and offered to help, but Wilkes cried 'No, No. Take care of yourself. I will say nothing of you'.

Martin notes that on examining the pistol used by Wilkes on his return home, he found it loaded, but the pan clean and without powder. He surmised that when he saw Wilkes stooping, he was opening the pan to see if it were primed, and by accident spilled the powder. Wilkes' own short account was to the effect that Martin fired first, and missed, and Wilkes' own pistol flashed in the pan. They then each took one of Wilkes' own pistols, and Wilkes missed while Martin's shot wounded him in the stomach.

It was, on the face of it, a complicated business and although Martin obviously took pains with his account of it, and saw he had the best of things in advance (Wilkes himself might well have chosen swords, and he was an expert swordsman), he does not attempt to cover Wilkes' generosity towards himself, and admits, rather as an afterthought, that the pistol that did not fire was the one he had given Wilkes. Wilkes makes no accusations of possible foul play in his account, and as far as one knows never did so. His situation, however, was grim and the wound might well have proved mortal. He was confined to his bed in considerable pain, when it was found that a button had deflected the bullet from the stomach into the groin. It kept him from attending the House, and he was not unnaturally incensed when the Ministry sent doctors to discover if he was malingering. Otherwise, when the danger was past, he had a gay time entertaining a throng of friends and well-wishers in his bedroom, and wrote to Polly: 'My antagonist behaved very well. We are both perfectly satisfied with each other.'

Although Wilkes was careful to conceal the name of his opponent it was, of course, widely known and not all shared Wilkes' view of his assailant's honour in the matter. 'I shall not be thought to have used too hard an expression', wrote Horace Walpole, 'when I called this a plot against the life of Wilkes.' He was not alone, and Wilkes' followers in the London crowd probably agreed. Some of them serenaded the invalid with French horns outside his house (it confirms, as before remarked, that the Wilkeite 'mob' was of various class levels and included not only artisans but musicians).

Walpole, indefatigable gossip, expanded further in a letter to George Montague:

'Your cousin Sandwich has out-Sandwiched himself. He has impeached Wilkes for a blasphemous poem and been expelled for blasphemy himself from the Beefsteak Club. Wilkes has been shot by Martin, and instead of being burnt at an *auto da fé*, as the Bishop of Gloucester intended, is

95

reverenced as a saint by the mob; and if he dies, I suppose
people will squint themselves into convulsions at his tomb in
honour of his memory.'

The *auto da fé* actually attempted was the burning of No. 45
of *The North Briton* by the public hangman, as ordered by the
House of Commons. This fiasco took place on 3rd December,
the reluctant and alarmed City Marshall having requested
military assistance, and the event justifying his dolorous
anticipation. The mob managed to soak the faggots so that
they would not burn, and smashed the coach windows of
Sheriff Harley, who had to walk with his escort of constables
amid a shower of mud. Authority took refuge in Guildhall,
while the mob, cheered on by young gentlemen behind
coffee house windows, ostentatiously burned a jackboot and
petticoat (the cartoonists' symbol of the Earl of Bute and the
Princess-Dowager).

The King was not amused: 'the continuance of Wilkes'
impudence is amazing, when his ruin is so near'. He had
ordered the Prime Minister to send him an account of each
debate on the matter, 'be it ever so late'. It took place on
24th November, when Pitt, to Wilkes' disgust (and also some
hurt: his armour of impudence was not impenetrable), finally
showed which side he was on by coming to the House
ostentatiously wrapped up in flannel against ague and gout,
and declared that the author was 'the blasphemer of his God
and libeller of his king'. Using his arm outstretched, crutch in
hand, as emphasis (Pitt would have made no mean actor), he
added: 'I have no connection with him. I never associated
nor communicated with him. I know nothing of any
connection with the writer of this libel.' From the man who
Wilkes believed had laughed with Potter over his ribaldries,
and who certainly had had a hand in the attack of *The North
Briton* on the Peace of Paris, this was apostasy, and Wilkes
said so. 'This marble-hearted friend' was his expression, in a
letter to the Duke of Grafton.

He had, however, a consolation. On 6th December Sir
Charles Pratt heard the case against Under-Secretary of State
Wood for illegally arresting Wilkes and others, and awarded

£1,000 damages to Wilkes. Pratt's summing up settled the individual's rights for the future:

'This warrant is unconstitutional, illegal, and absolutely void: it is a general warrant, directed to four messengers to take up any persons, without naming or describing them with any certainty, and to bring them, together with their papers. If it be good, a Secretary of State can delegate and depute any one of the messengers, or any, even from the lowest of the people, to take examinations, to commit or release, and, in fine, to do every act which the highest judicial officers the law knows can do or order. There is no authority in our law books that mentions these kinds of warrants but in express terms condemns them . . .'

On the same night Alexander Dun, a Scottish lieutenant of Marines, was overheard in a coffee house threatening to 'cut off Mr Wilkes', and two days later was seized at Wilkes' house. His only weapon was a penknife, but Wilkes' friends saw to it that the matter was debated in the Commons, the suggestion conveyed being that the Ministry had hired Dun to assassinate a sick man. The House found Dun unbalanced, and no one, of course, prosecuted Martin for his duel.

Wilkes decided it was time he sought diversion and convalescence, out of reach, perhaps, of pistols and penknives. It is possible also that Chief Justice Pratt's £1,000 damages was (in expectation) burning a hole in his pocket. He knew he had been watched for months by government spies, and his letters tapped by the Post Office. 'I take it for granted', his friend George Onslow had written, 'that all my letters to you are opened. I must beg one favour from the inquisitive rascal who does it, that he will communicate to all the world my opinion of John Wilkes and also my opinion of the Ministry.'

On Christmas Eve Wilkes was reported by a government agent to have been seen leaving his house 'about 11 o'clock in a post-chaise and four horses and two large trunks well packed'. There were various rumours as to where he had gone for Christmas, Walpole favouring exile in preference to martyrdom and Lord Chesterfield a simple flight from his creditors. In fact, his alliterative targets were Paris and Polly, both equally enticing for one reviving in health and spirits. It was not a totally wise move politically, nor even medically at the time. The journey, in a lurching coach and on an equally lurching sea, seriously inflamed his wound and left him weak from seasickness. More invalid than roué, he arrived on 29th December. It had been probably the most miserable Christmas of his life.

VI
ITALIAN TEMPESTS

Notwithstanding his indignant stance, there were certain indications of the shock to Wilkes of the discovery and use of the *Essay on Woman*. Although within the House (in fact both Houses) it was fairly generally known that there was a high proportion of libertines, and there was little attempt at concealment among members, these were not always publicly known and some attempt at moral conformity was made, outside the certain groups. The wide dissemination of the matter of the *Essay on Woman* therefore could be damaging to Wilkes politically and perhaps even with some of his lower-class followers, who were his greatest political bulwark and strength, and he knew it. As it happened, any rumours that got around, and plenty did, about the nature of the Essay seem to have had no effect whatsoever on his popularity with the mob or most of his political followers; but neither the Government nor Wilkes could be sure of this at the time.

His leaving for Paris was construed as flight, but in fact Wilkes at the time had every intention of returning to appear in the House on 19th January, and ordered a dinner in London on that date. But his journey had genuinely made his wound worse, and on 11th January he wrote to the Speaker sending medical certificates signed by French doctors. The certificates were refused on the ground that they were not witnessed by a Notary Public. Wilkes promptly sent authenticated certificates, but these were ignored and on 20th January he was expelled from the House. This loss of his parliamentary privilege loosed his creditors on him and he stood in danger, should he return, of arrest for debt. Wilkes' affairs were now handled by his friend Humphrey Cotes and his brother Heaton. Cotes was a Whig wine merchant and Wilkes had shared his mistress, giving rise to his pun, '*Fungor vice Cotis*', i.e. 'I play the part of Cotes' or alternatively 'I play the part of a whetstone', a play on the Latin *Cos-Cotis*, a whetstone. Cotes was now to share Wilkes' troubles and joys in quite different, more economic, directions.

Expulsion from the House and its likely effects made Wilkes change his mind about returning, although his lawyer Phillips had requested him to do so.

'If I return soon, I may be found guilty of the publication of No. 45 and of the "Essay on Woman". I must then go off to France, for no man in his senses would stand Mansfield's sentence upon the publisher of a paper declared by both Houses to be scandalous, seditious, etc. . . . I have experienced the fickleness of the people. With all the fine things said of me, have not the public left me in the lurch as to the expense of so great a variety of lawsuits . . .? Can I trust a rascally Court, who bribe my own servants to steal out of my house?

'I will now go to the public cause – Liberty. Is there any point left to be tried? I think not. The two important decisions have secured forever the Englishman's liberty and his property . . .'

This was no more than the truth: on 17th February the Commons debated a motion affecting the illegality of general warrants (which Pitt supported with his full strength) and it was only narrowly defeated. On 12th March Wilkes allegedly expressed his gratitude to his supporters in *A Letter to a Noble Member (Temple) of the Club in Albermarle Street.* Although his actual authorship is disputable (it has been claimed to be a satire of his style from a government source), in a private letter on 25th February he had indeed been uncharacteristically contrite: 'I owe what I suffer to the neglect of your Lordship's advice. I foresee all the consequences of being entirely at the mercy of an abandoned Administration and vindictive judge, and intend never to put myself in their power, though I leave my dear native country, and all the charms that it ever had for me.' On 21 February 1764 he had been convicted in his absence before Lord Mansfield on both charges of libel, not as author, still unproved, but as the person responsible for printing and publishing No. 45 and the Essay. As he failed to appear, he suffered the sentence of outlawry, which took effect on 1st November.

There was now nothing for Wilkes to do but to accept exile and make the most of it, which he was exceptionally qualified in temperament to do. Polly was now fourteen years old, and an age to delight her father with indications of coming womanhood and all the social graces she had been quick to acquire. Her adoration of her indulgent and randy father seems to have been quite unquestioning, and she gave indication of being precociously aware of the situation with her pliant governess, Mademoiselle Carpentier, and not in the least disturbed by it.

Nevertheless, it would be interesting to query why Polly never married, in spite of a lively social life which certainly could not have excluded possibilities. Could no man come up to her dazzled image of her father? Was there a sexual repression, certainly not a reaction in Jackie Smith, Wilkes' natural son? She does not appear even to have taken lovers. Possibly her father's lack of any permanent woman companion in his home left a blank there which she was delighted to fill, and the domestic relationship became for her in the end the equivalent of a marriage, but with a far livelier, adored host than she might have got through marriage, and allowing her to retain her property and freedom in addition. Much later, when her father became Lord Mayor of London, she became his official hostess, a very exacting social role, and carried it off to general praise and with distinction. Wilkes certainly never had cause to regret the money and affection he lavished on his daughter.

In Paris, Wilkes' contacts were of the highest. He was again fêted by the *philosophes*, and formed a friendship with David Hume, the Scottish historian and philosopher, now Private Secretary to the English Ambassador in Paris. Hume's friendship with Rousseau, whom he brought to London in an excess of admiration, broke up as dramatically as Wilkes' was later to do with his own young admirer, Horne Tooke; few political associations escape the human hazards of personal disillusionment, and Hume, like Wilkes, was not by nature a radical of the more advanced school of thought. Far from being an atheist like d'Holbach, he was particularly impressed by Wilkes' demure attendances at the Embassy Chapel, where 'Sir Shandy Sterne', as the d'Holbach group called him, sometimes preached. 'I never see Mr Wilkes here but at Chapel, where he is a most regular and devout and edifying and pious Attendant. I take him to be entirely regenerate', he wrote home on 16 May 1764.

'The sleepy lion of a brilliant bevy of admirers', in Peter Quennell's appropriately descriptive phrase (Hume was a very large man and much shrewder, as was sometimes observed, than he looked, in spite of some psychological naïvety), he was later a favourite author of King Louis XVI and probably useful to Wilkes in Court and social circles. Wilkes was certainly received in both, and Madame Geoffrin is said to have commented to him that pride was an extravagance that the poor should not allow themselves. '*Quand on n'a pas de chemise, il ne faut pas avoir de fierté*' ('when one hasn't got a shirt, one has no need of pride'). Wilkes promptly asserted the contrary: '*Au contraire, il faut en avoir afin d'avoir quelquechose*' ('On the contrary, one needs it more than anything else'). Shakespeare's shirtless Don Armado would have agreed with him. It was a typical philosophy of the eighteenth-century gentleman intent on keeping his end up. 'Poor' in these circles meant not the peasantry, but the 'genteel poor', or gentry momentarily out of funds. D'Holbach's splendid mansion in the Rue St Anne, so international in its visitors that it was known as the 'Café de l'Europe', was again a regular haunt, especially on Thursdays and Sundays when the d'Holbachs officially held their *salon*. Madame Geoffrin's, neatly dovetailed, was devoted on Mondays to artists and on Wednesdays to writers. Among the visiting English writers whom Wilkes met was Lawrence Sterne, who joined him (according to Wilkes in a letter to Churchill) in 'an odd party' in which 'goddesses of the theatre' were prominent. Sterne, whose cloth did not preclude him from any of the more delightful of eighteenth-century pursuits, varied his gambols among the Yorkshire Demoniacs and Parisian actresses with a lively interest in a different kind of gamble; by June he was back in England, travelling north for the races at York.

No one in France seems to have been disturbed by the commotion Wilkes was causing in the English Parliament, which seemed, complained the virtuous if prerogative-minded young King George with reason, to be taken up entirely with the affairs of Wilkes to the exclusion of all other and more important business (the same might be said of the London streets and theatres, where, with Lord Sandwich in mind, audiences were reacting with appreciative roars to the lines of Macheath, the imprisoned highwayman, in Gay's *Beggar's Opera* then being performed at Covent Garden: 'But that Jemmy Twitcher should peach I own surprises me.' Sandwich, for the rest of his life, was ribaldly referred to as 'Jemmy Twitcher', sometimes it is said in his presence. Years later, the young Fanny Burney, who rather liked him, wondered why).

He took it with reasonable jollity: like Wilkes he seems not to have been a man to bear personal malice for long, however oblivious to political loyalties and hypocritical when it served his purposes. It is interesting to conjecture if it was before, or long after, his betrayal of Wilkes over the *Essay on Woman* that Wilkes' most celebrated piece of wit in repartee took place. Sandwich made the laughing assertion that Wilkes would die either of venereal disease or on the gallows. 'That depends, my lord', answered Wilkes instantly, 'whether I embrace your mistress or your principles.'

Wilkes' correspondence back to England concerned other financial matters than debt, in which both Cotes and Heaton were to prove singularly inept (in their favour, it must be confessed that a master economist would probably have been baffled by the intricacies of Wilkes' finances, and Temple's generosity was still continually called on). 'I have a boy, two years old, at nurse near Hounslow, a lively little rogue who goes by the name of John Smith. His mother was my housekeeper. There is about five pounds due to the nurse. May I trouble you to settle it, and to mention what plan I should pursue for him at that age?' He added, 'My library is very good: if it can be saved, I shall be glad; if not, it must go.' Like a later famous radical, the actor-playwright Thomas Holcroft (who at this period had just left a happy youthful apprenticeship as a stable-boy at Newmarket), the sale of his library to meet his debts was one of the blows from which Wilkes, resilient though he was, suffered most.

Financial problems or not, he was happily planning to go 'for a year to Rome, with Miss Wilkes'; and afterwards 'to Constantinople, alone, for six months'. Constantinople, a city which in the end Wilkes never visited, is an extraordinary recurring theme in the Wilkes story. His earliest political manœuvre had been to try and badger an Embassy appointment there, and it was not his only attempt. What, one wonders, was the specific attraction? Could it have been the houris? It was certainly an international diplomatic centre of some standing in the eighteenth century and two prominent figures in the French Revolution, Joseph-Marie Chénier, the dramatist, and his ill-starred brother André, the poet, were born when their parents were in the French consular service there.

'My daughter's education is the greatest expense to me', Wilkes wrote, 'and that is a point I cannot dispense with . . .' Daughter's expensive education or not, he moved from the Hotel de Saxe to a house in the Rue St Nicaise, where he vastly increased his expenses by taking to himself a young Italian mistress, Gertrude Corradini, whose considerable physical attractions were somewhat mitigated by a flaming temper, delicate health and a pack of Italian hangers-on including a formidable mother. Corradini was not in-experienced as a money-gatherer and charm-dispenser: her former protector, John Udny, British Consul in Venice, was said to have been bankrupted mainly as a result of this dubious position.

Wilkes, for so experienced a roué, was besotted, and seems never quite to have got over her. He described her 'perfect Grecian figure cast in the mould of a Florentine Venus. She possessed the divine gift of lewdness, but nature had not given her strength adequate to the force of her desires. In conversation she was childish and weak, but in bed she could not be called *fatui puella cunni*. Her two prevailing passions were jealousy and a fondness for being admired. By these she tormented herself and all about her'. He was not entirely without compassion and social understanding of her position. She was, he thought, doomed to perpetual exploitation, partly through her own lack of intelligence: 'her whole life had been sacrificed to the interests of others'. She came from Bologna, which inspired Wilkes to the witticism that of all the delights in France, he took most pleasure in his frequent excursions to the Bois de Boulogne.

Wilkes did not find the early going easy: with neither looks nor much money to commend him, and brains and wit totally lost on the childish Italian, he finally succeeded by rescuing Corradini's favourite crucifix (or rather, finding its replica in a market, after she had lost it), and so by an astonishing and happy chance attained the Italian through her grateful piety (he was later amused to find that before receiving him in bed she superstitiously, or with a misplaced delicacy, turned the face of the Madonna in the picture over it to the wall).

Wilkes dined with Polly, as a rule, and supped with his mistress, thus having, he wrote, 'the happiness of remarking all day the openings of a sensitive and intelligent mind in his daughter, while in the evenings other passions were gratified'. For his daughter, however, he had momentarily more economical plans: probably because the acquisition of Corradini had made Polly's inclusion in the Italian tour impracticable. He wrote on 1 November 1764, to Temple saying he proposed to leave Paris and travel to Italy (this, he had convinced himself in some unexplained and optimistic process of reasoning, would save money) and to send Polly in the meantime back to England to live with her uncle Heaton. Polly, at the age to have a mind of her own and used to being spoilt, rebelled in vain at this arrangement, writing tearfully to her father that her uncle had dismissed her French maid as unnecessary luxury and threatened her with the slipper when she complained she could not dress herself without one. ('My God!' exploded the enraged and adoring father, forgetting this was a deity he had little right to call upon, 'Heaton is a barbarian! He has done the cruellest thing in the world by

Miss Wilkes, and has held a language to her about me which is false, insolent and infamous. What! Set a daughter against her father?') Whatever cat Heaton had let out of the bag, or Wilkes imagined he had let out of the bag, regarding her father, failed to alter Polly's devotion, and in fairness to Heaton it must be said that he was basically a kindly man and in the end the adolescent handful he had taken into his home settled down amicably enough, as adolescents are wont to do, finding much interest in any scene around them.

In the meantime, Wilkes was having problems with Corradini, whose physique broke down so that her physician forbad her to sleep with her protector for two months. Given Wilkes' nature he apparently sought consolation elsewhere, and Corradini saw him come out of a doorway at night and jumped (probably with reason) to the obvious conclusion. More than usually tempestuous storms were the result, and perhaps helped to distract the harassed lover from the noble task, he had written to Temple, that he had set himself, which was no less than writing a 'History of England' (for which he had already accepted an advance from Almon. It was not to be the only one). Certainly he wrote an Introduction; but Wilkes was not a writer of great fluency, unlike the polemical Junius who was soon to burst on the English scene, and there was little value in this, which in the end was as far as he got with the project.

In October 1764, however, Wilkes had written his *Letter to the Electors of Aylesbury*, re-examining the whole matter of his treatment by the Government, and he even proposed to risk return to England to help forward his case against Halifax for wrongful arrest. Charles Churchill and his new mistress were to come to meet him at Boulogne to discuss this possibility, but in late October it was left dangerously late, for on 1st November the pronouncement of outlawry on Wilkes was finally made and the friends' plans turned towards a joint trip to Italy. La Corradini, in fact, had already been despatched ahead with her mother, a dubious 'uncle', and an expensive coach, her assets including a draft on a Lyons bank for one thousand livres to pay for the journey. She also had Wilkes' permission to draw on his bank account in

Bologna, though it is extremely doubtful how much this was actually worth. Wilkes let his Paris apartments in the Rue St Nicaise to David Garrick, and proceeded to Boulogne.

The whole plan was darkened for Wilkes by the death of Churchill on 4th November. He had caught a fever, possibly intensified by heavy drinking (unlike Wilkes he drank to excess, and like many stout, heavy-framed men was physically less hardy than he looked) and he died within a few days. He was only thirty-three years old, if much older in debauchery, and Wilkes, admitting to thirty-seven himself, was appalled. He was also genuinely grief-stricken. Basically without home roots, and in spite of his purely physical companionships, he was a lonely man: Churchill had remained for many years his only close and unshakeably loyal friend, a companion after his own heart, a sharer of joys and tales of bawdry, and one who could be implicitly trusted to enjoy and cap them. He was also, in the opinion of his time, a considerable satiric poet, one whose work did not outlast that time (it was too orientated to contemporary politics and scandals) but which earned him a lasting place in encyclopaedias. 'Churchill's verse', writes Peter Quennell, 'has a tumultuous energy that sweeps the reader along. The invective strikes home in a succession of hammer-blows; Churchill's use of the English language is always fresh and lively – it produces something of the same effect as Hogarth's use of paint; and from the poems of the one, as from the pictures of the other, emerges a whole vision of eighteenth-century London . . .'

Neither Churchill nor Wilkes would have relished the comparison with their enemy Hogarth, but the loss of Churchill had for Wilkes far more significance even than that of personal friendship. Anonymously, he had shared equally in the labours and excitements of writing and publishing *The North Briton*. A whole era of the past had vanished with him.

'I have never a moment in my life been low-spirited', Wilkes boasted to Boswell a few months later in Italy. It was a deliberate, self-supporting lie, perhaps a final jerk towards revival. For there is no doubt Churchill's death plunged Wilkes into the deepest melancholy, of a kind which in a different kind of man might well have proved suicidal. It is a tribute to Churchill's charm and generosity that the poet Robert Lloyd, who had shared with the two friends the work on *The North Briton*, pined for him to such an extent that he died shortly afterwards. In 1763, when Lloyd was in the Fleet prison, Churchill had allowed one guinea a week for his support and raised a subscription for his release. Churchill's own financial position was far from stable. He left his property to his two sons, and on his deathbed dictated a note leaving £60 to his wife and £50 to his mistress; but the property no longer existed and one of the sons in later years constantly appealed to Wilkes for help.

Wilkes sent his friend's body back to Dover, where Churchill was buried in the old churchyard of St Martin, with a line from *The Candidate* on the stone: 'Life to the last enjoyed, here Churchill lies.' In 1816, Byron visited the grave when leaving England for the last time. To Cowper, in a letter to Unwin written in 1781, he was still 'the great Churchill'. With more optimism than judgment, Wilkes undertook the editing of his papers (Churchill had named him his literary executor). Like the History, this project never made much headway, presumably sinking into the background as Wilkes' never inelastic spirits gradually rose.

Wilkes set out for Italy, only too conscious of the lack of Churchill's friendly weight on the seat of the coach beside him. It was Christmas Day when he left Paris, and he must have reflected that Christmas was not becoming his luckiest or happiest festival. For the moment, at least, shocked by Churchill's death, he was prepared, with more optimism than logic, to face turning over a new leaf. 'I will be in everything prudent', was his New Year's resolution, 'and my eye is ever fixed on my two great works, Churchill's edition and the "History".' This did not preclude his eye taking in his surroundings with appreciation, and Polly was the recipient of long letters describing his travels.

'How do you like England?' he wrote her from Turin, after crossing the Alps perilously and joltingly in mid winter. 'Is it not a little *triste*? The Sundays especially, between you and me, are very dull.' (Seventy-five years later another epicurean, Richard Wagne , was to echo the complaint, after briefly, en route for Paris, experiencing 'the horrors of a ghastly London Sunday'. London has not heard the last of it yet.)

At Turin Wilkes found to his annoyance that Corradini, whom he had expected to meet him, had gone on to Bologna, but met agitated notes from Boswell trying to make his acquaintance. It became a comedy of missed invitations, like a French Feydeau farce, although Boswell saw him at the opera, where he (Boswell) was sitting in a box with his latest conquest, a Contessa twice his own age. Boswell's notes were scrupulous in dissociating himself from Wilkes' politics and anti-Scottish sentiments, but anticipated immense enjoyment from a hoped-for companionship. Wilkes was not unwilling for he was avoided by the English, either from principle or fear of the consequences of associating with a newly-proscribed outlaw.

But the association with Boswell was to bloom later. Wilkes went on to Milan, where he studied the pictures and began, he wrote to Polly, to make himself understood in Italian, and to read 'tolerably well' the best Italian authors. At Bologna he at last caught up with Corradini, whose welcome was all he could wish: the madonna's face was duly turned to the wall, although there were no curtains to the windows and, wrote Wilkes, 'the visual ray had sometimes in contemplation the two noblest objects of the creation, the glory of the rising sun and the perfect form of naked beauty'. Polly's version was somewhat Bowdlerized: 'I went to pay my respects to Mlle Corradini.'

Wilkes moved on to Florence and Rome, where there was a carnival, the Pretender's Court (hardly welcoming to the publisher of the anti-Jacobite *North Briton*) and the Secretary to the Vatican, the Abbe Winckelmann, an antiquarian and an obliging host who tried (a difficult task) to entertain Corradini's mother while the fair Italian made discreet disappearances with Wilkes into another apartment. Wilkes needed the consolations: like many womanizers he had a slightly more than normal antipathy to homosexuality, and heartily disliked Rome. 'Could a Promethean fire animate the Venus of Medicis, she might walk in all security from Turin to Naples. So far from a rudeness being offered her, she would be treated with the most cruel neglect. Should the same thing happen to Antinous, the whole *orbis Romanus* would rise in arms and a million of drawn weapons dispute the glorious prize.' Modern psychology tends to equate the Don Juan pressures with a subconscious tendency in the opposite direction and urge to prove a possibly suspect virility; but it is very difficult to apply this to as hearty and intolerant a heterosexual as Wilkes. It is interesting (and an indication of the sometimes surprisingly wide range of women's sexual knowledge at that time) that Mary Wollstonecraft, in her *Vindication of the Rights of Woman* written thirty years later, also pinpoints Italy as a centre, with Portugal, where 'men attend the levées of equivocal beings, to sigh for more than female languor'. Mary had herself visited Lisbon, to tend a friend who died in childbirth, in 1785, but it would seem that the Roman scene was still a matter of comment.

Wilkes also disapproved of the Romans on other, more compassionate grounds: a man without cruel facets, he was sickened by their habit of shooting hordes of small birds in order to protect their vines. The ancient ruins, which exactly a year before had given the enchanted Gibbon his first inspiration to write 'the decline and fall of the city', left Wilkes unmoved. Apparently, however, he approved of some of the city's products, for he sent Polly a dozen pairs of Roman gloves as well as a French book of maps.

The departure from Rome was rocked by one of Corradini's most extravagant storms of temper, this time directed against Wilkes' young servant Brown who had banged down a picnic basket in front of her. (It was never easy, reflected Wilkes with philosophical resignation, to make 'any kind of servant preserve a due respect to his master's female favourite'. The one form of service was doubtless too obviously underpaid in comparison with the other.) Naples, however, proved the most pleasant place in Europe, or so Wilkes informed Polly, alongside instructions not to forget her French and to read Molière, Racine and Corneille.

At Naples he and Boswell finally merged, two stars in conjunction, and met William Hamilton (it was, by chance, the year and indeed almost the month of the future Lady Hamilton's birth). Wilkes, hearing rumours in later years, may well have considered that he met Hamilton in Naples twenty years too soon. It would have been interesting to know Emma's reactions to this other timeless charmer. Her future husband, saddled with a plain wife patently devoted to him, had arrived at the British Embassy in mid-November 1763, a handsome, ambitious man of very good connections, who at that time looked on Naples as a stepping-stone to greater things. He was an antiquarian and archaeologist of distinction and a keen collector, pursuits which in the end acted as consolation for any disappointments in office and in love.

The two new friends talked eagerly in Boswell's lodgings at Bertollo's 'Strada Andalusia al Mare'. Wilkes even grew confidential on the subject of Corradini: 'I love this girl, I'm not hurt by her follies – her stupid mother and her foolish cousin. In these connections, there's no good mother in any case. I keep my eyes open and my pockets shut.' Dining at Stefano's after ascending Vesuvius, Boswell grew melancholy in his cups: 'What shall I do to get life over?' Wilkes told him firmly that 'While there's all ancient and modern learning and all the arts and sciences, there's enough for life even if it lasts three thousand years.' After this surprising intellectual echo of Thomas Paine (who was referring to the consolations of old age as experienced by the great Benjamin Franklin) and Bernard Shaw, Wilkes went on to advise Boswell to forget what he called 'the problem of Fate and Free Will' and told him (or at least so Boswell maintained in his notes) he was an original genius. 'I talked much to Baxter of the immateriality of the soul', proclaimed Wilkes, 'and read his two quarto volumes, and have never thought of the matter since. But I always take the sacrament. Dissipation and profligacy . . . renew the mind. I wrote my best *North Briton* in bed with Betsy Green.' Andrew Baxter was a Scots philosopher, author of *An Inquiry into the Nature of the Human Soul*, whom Wilkes, a much younger man, met and charmed at Spa in 1744.

The next day, Friday, 15 March 1765, Wilkes and Boswell, mounted on asses, ascended the height of Vomero to inspect a villa Wilkes had thought of renting. 'I am always happy', declared Wilkes, putting Churchill out of his mind. 'I thank God for good health, good spirits, and the love of books . . . A man who has not money to gratify his passions does right to govern them. He who can indulge them does better. Thank Heaven for having given me the love of women. To many she gives not the noble passion of lust.'[1] It was indeed a comfortable philosophy for one who (debts or not) always considered he had the means to indulge it, and it shows how far Wilkes was, by nature and outlook, from the true radical theory – so soon to be proclaimed in America and France – of the equality of man. It was not so unlike, strangely enough, the Wesleyan evangelical doctrine which, later in the century, was to begin to undermine the radical political aspirations and send the bulk of the working class, laundered, puritanical and unprotesting, into the factories of the newly rich. It was the doctrine, the bulwark of Victorian society and the cult of Empire, that the good citizen should remain in the place in society to which providence had called him. By an anomaly, Wilkes himself was to provoke one of the last large-scale rebellions of the poorer class before it settled down into the rut provided for it: the Wilkesian riots in three years' time seemed at least to the frightened Government a herald of revolution, and with a different man from Wilkes as leader this might indeed have been the case. As it was, by the time of the French Revolution, in spite of frantic measures by the Government and some active radical societies, the danger for England was past. It had blown itself out in the wake of Wilkes and the Gordon Riots in which he had played so unexpected a part.

But this was a type of volcano which, dining under the shadow of Vesuvius, neither Wilkes nor Boswell could anticipate in 1765. Nevertheless, it was aptly to Rousseau, whose *Social Contract* had been published three years before, that Boswell wrote at this time about his new friend. 'All

[1] F. A. Pottle: *James Boswell: The Earlier Years, 1756-62* (Heinemann, London; McGraw Hill, New York, 1966).

theories of human nature are confounded by the resilient
spirit of that singular functionary. He is a man who has
thought much without being gloomy, a man who has done
much evil without being a scoundrel. His lively and energetic
sallies on moral questions gave to my spirit a not unpleasant
agitation, and enlarged the scope of my views by convincing
me that God could create a soul completely serene and gay
notwithstanding the alarming reflection that we all must
die.'

Boswell does not reveal if it was Wilkes' 'lively and
energetic sallies on moral questions' which enabled him
(Boswell) eventually to decamp with Rousseau's mistress
Theresa, with an untroubled conscience: at the moment his
love life was complicated by a lady named Belle de Zuylen,
on whom he tried to make Wilkes a sympathetic listener.
Wilkes, whose moral conscience was a singularly unclouded
entity, permitted himself a little impatience at young
Boswell's scruples. 'You too like the thing almost as well as I
do, but you dislike the talk and laugh about it, of which I am
perhaps too fond.' Nevertheless, he was perhaps the first to
encourage Boswell in his particular, as yet unacknowledged
talent, the ability to record with vividness the life of his time
and the more famous characters within it. 'You're the most
liberal man I ever met with, a citizen of the world . . .' It was
a curious anticipation of the radical ideal, very much used in
that sense later in the century: Wilkes must have used the
phrase with a rather different and more worldly intent.

Corradini marked the month of May with another storm.
She had read in an English paper that a Devon farmer had
died, leaving Wilkes £5,000. How true this was seems
uncertain – he never received the money – but Corradini
made it an excuse to demand a lavish settlement and
permission for her father, uncle and brother to join them.
Wilkes refusing, Corradini (with what truth again seems
uncertain) claimed she was pregnant and must go to Bologna
for treatment. Wilkes, not surprisingly, replied to this that
there were perfectly good doctors in Naples for such a
common eventuality. As a result, she decamped during his
brief absence, reputedly with everything belonging to him

that she could lay her hands on and could reasonably transport.

Wilkes, after the first shock, pulled himself together and wisely sent a letter after her dismissing her. It looks very much as if the pregnancy claim was merely a device, or she would not have risked losing his protection. He never quite got over her, and occasionally in the future asked for, or received, news of her. Apparently there was no son or daughter, or he would have been willing enough to support the child, as he did in two other cases. 'Though I have a tolerable share of gullibility', he wrote to Boswell, 'it is only a sinking fund which you may draw upon till exhausted.' But he was not used to being made a laughing stock and far too many in Naples knew the story. His mind, receptive to certain news from home, began to turn to England again and he started to make his way back through France.

He chose to go by boat, in a 'wretched French Tartan' sailing direct to the South of France. It was a deliberate detour to avoid Bologna, 'lest the dear enchantress shou'd again draw him within her powerful circle, and melt down all his manhood to the god of love'. In Marseilles, where the women were 'more beautiful than in any other part of France and not to be reproached with cruelty', he bought Polly a print by the painter Angelica Kauffmann, whose work he particularly admired, seeing in it the grace of Raphael, the warmth of Corregio's colouring and the delicacy of Guido. Posterity in the art world has not supported this estimate, although Angelica Kauffmann was to be nominated a founder-member of the Royal Academy and Sir Joshua Reynolds was a close friend of both her and Wilkes. Wilkes may well have known of her personal beauty (Goldsmith and other poets acclaimed it) and admired it as much as that of her paintings.

At La Grande Chartreuse, the Carthusian priory near Grenoble, founded in 1084, he paused to admire the scenery and take advantage of the monks' hospitality, which included the best Burgundy he had ever tasted. The monks lived in isolated cells, yet clustered in little groups of houses among the lofty rocks and trees. For a roué, he sometimes found himself in strange company, yet carried the situation off with invariable charm and aplomb. He made a graceful entry in the visitors' book, and moved on to Geneva, where he found the atmosphere depressing (Calvin's tomb gloomily over-grown with nettles) except for the presence of Rousseau, that 'divine old man, born for the advancement of true philosophy and the public arts'.

From Rousseau it was a natural step to visit Voltaire at Ferney. This was a literary pilgrimage regularly undertaken by the Englishman on the 'Grand Tour', and the entertainment was by no means purely philosophical. Voltaire's reputation was founded also on his plays, which were to be constantly revived in Paris during the French Revolution, and his talents were also displayed as an actor in his private theatre. In August 1763, Gibbon had found him, at seventy years old, acting a Tartar Conqueror with a broken voice, and making love to an ugly niece of about fifty. This dubious piece of theatrical excitement was, however, followed by an elegant and substantial supper provided for the audience, with dancing afterwards until four o'clock in the morning. Voltaire told Wilkes he must live either 'in London, or Paris, or Heaven, or Hell' and Wilkes characteristically chose the last, where he announced he would find 'most of the popes, many cardinals and almost all kings', again anticipating Bernard Shaw. [1]

He reached Paris on 29 September 1765 and began to consider plans to get back to London.

---

[1] Epilogue, *Saint Joan;* Act III ('Don Juan in Hell'), *Man and Superman.*

VII
THE MASSACRE OF ST GEORGE'S FIELDS

What had drawn Wilkes' attention to England again was a change in the political atmosphere. In July 1766 the Grenville-Bedford ministry had been overthrown, one of the instruments in its collapse being an attempt to impose a Stamp Act on the American colonies, a form of taxation which the colonists (who had no representation in Parliament) bitterly resented. The tone of Charles Townshend's speech in support of this American Stamp Bill introduced by Grenville on 6 February 1765, could hardly have conciliated any colonist who heard of it.

'And now will these Americans, children planted by our care, nourished up by our indulgence until they are grown to a degree of strength and opulence, and protected by our arms, will they grudge to contribute their mite to relieve us from the heavy weight of that burden which we lie under?'

Its patronizing timbre brought a quick response from Colonel Isaac Barré:

'They planted by your care? No! Your oppressions planted them in America . . . They nourished by your indulgence? They grew by your neglect of them . . .'

Riots and disturbances in America followed throughout the autumn of 1765, in the wake of attempts to enforce Grenville's Act, and on 17th December Grenville moved an amendment to an Address declaring the colonies in a state of rebellion. The Assembly of Massachusetts Bay had passed an Act pardoning the rioters in the Stamp Act disturbances, and New York had refused to comply with the Mutiny Act and make provision for British troops stationed in the colony.[1]

[1] Sir Lewis Namier and John Brooke: *Charles Townshend* (Macmillan, 1964).

116

A new Government and Whig alliance was formed headed by the Marquis of Rockingham as First Lord of the Treasury (the office which in the eighteenth century put its holder in the position of a modern Prime Minister) and the Duke of Grafton as a Secretary of State; but Grafton's real support was still given to Pitt who like himself strongly opposed the Stamp Bill. 'It is my opinion', declared Pitt, 'that this Kingdom has no right to lay a tax upon the colonies . . . The Americans are the sons, not the bastards of England. As subjects they are entitled to the common right of representation and cannot be bound to pay taxes without their consent.'[1] Grafton, steadfastly loyal to Pitt, was also sharply aware of the resistance of Boston in particular to this 'absurd tax', as he described it. The Stamp Act was repealed, partly owing to the good offices of Benjamin Franklin as well as Grafton's own efforts in alliance with Conway. Unfortunately, Grafton had not the strength of will, later, to resist Townshend's renewed attack on the colonists in the form of suspension of the legislative powers of the New York Assembly, and the attempt to raise a revenue from America by import duties. An American Customs Board was established at Boston in an attempt to end smuggling, 'in which all New England merchants were happily engaged', as Professor Plumb puts it. The weakness of Grafton's will in office is shown by his genuine opposition to the American War later, although its causes lay deep in the mistakes of the English Government in these earlier years. In his Memoirs he admits to lack of foresight, and blames it partly on the difficulties of making decisions while Chatham, on whom he greatly relied, was inaccessible owing to illness.

Grafton was a contemporary of Thomas Paine, who like Grafton was born in Thetford, which the Dukes of Grafton successively controlled as a 'rotten borough' (its thirty-two voters, out of a population of 2,000, were all in Whig control and General Conway in fact had been Grafton's unopposed nominee for Member of Parliament for Thetford). Augustus Henry Fitzroy, the third Duke, had succeeded his

[1] J. H. Plumb: *Chatham* (Collins, 1953; 'Makers of History' series, 1965).

grandfather in 1757 at the age of twenty-two, and he was a great-grandson of Charles II by Barbara Villiers, Duchess of Cleveland. With such a genealogy it is not surprising that he early entangled himself with a beauty named Nancy Parsons, whose delicate charms were immortalized by Gainsborough, and in 1769 divorced his first wife, a circumstance which laid him wide open to attacks by Junius. He inherited also from King Charles a passion for horseracing: Holcroft in his Memoirs recalls a brief period as stable-boy at the stables in Newmarket where thirteen of the Duke's horses were in training.

It was an expensive hobby, which led him to the gaming tables, but the Duke at worst as a politician was indecisive, and basically an amiable character with strong liberal tendencies. His autobiography, in later life, proved notably without personal rancour, and although it was with relief that in 1783 he finally retired from politics and devoted himself to the country activities he preferred, he was never less than conscientious as a politician and in fact resigned as a minister on the issue of the War against the American colonists. He was a reader of Locke and the classics (as correspondence with his close friend Charles James Fox shows) and has been maligned and underrated by Wilkes' biographers and some other historians, who have been far too influenced by Junius' heavily prejudiced estimates of his character. By most of his contemporaries in Parliament he was obviously liked, and treated with respect and consideration. They included Wilkes' legal champion in the General Warrants case, Charles Pratt, Lord Camden, one of Grafton's lifelong friends.

He had earlier tried to visit Wilkes in the Tower, as we have seen, although he hesitated to stand bail when Wilkes wrote and asked him to do so. To Temple, who had paid the bail, Grafton had pleaded loyalty to the King, supposedly maligned by No. 45, and he is fair enough to include Temple's implied rebuke to himself in a letter in his Memoirs. It is possible that the beautiful Miss Parsons, as well as a run of losing horses, may have contributed to his reluctance to meet Wilkes' request, put forward persuasively

in a particularly flattering letter. In May 1766 he resigned as
Secretary of State, in order to support Pitt, but in July 1766
reluctantly allowed himself to be appointed First Lord of the
Treasury, Pitt with failing health resisting all attempts to
persuade him to undertake the post. Pitt chose instead the
office of Privy Seal and elevation to the House of Lords as
Earl of Chatham. His subsequent illness left Grafton, fully
aware of his own shortcomings ('how little suited the post
was to my inexperience and my feelings'), in charge of the
Government.

Rockingham was the casualty in these 1766 changes,
having been brought down by the 'King's Friends'; but in
the meantime Wilkes had been receiving in Paris much
correspondence and implied promises from Rockingham
supporters such as George Onslow and Laughlin Macleane, a
Member of Parliament attached to Lord Shelburne, and
Wilkes was being encouraged to hope for government
positions in Jamaica, the Leeward Isles or Constantinople
(Constantinople once again eluded him, the post going to
John Murray, a Scot, which could not have in any way
consoled the late Editor of *The North Briton*). Instead he
received an offer of £1,000 which he was told was placed to
his credit in Paris and would be renewed annually. It was
undoubtedly a bribe to keep him away from England and
Wilkes described it as 'equally precarious, eleemosynary, and
clandestine. I claim from the present ministers a full pardon
under the Great Seal for having successfully served my
country . . .' But in spite of rumours that the French
Government (for reasons which seem obscure) also contributed to his support, Wilkes in Paris was running out of
funds and the 'pension' (as he referred to it) was tempting.

Letters to Humphrey Cotes had failed to obtain for him the
£1,000 damages awarded him against Under-Secretary
Wood, and in the end he drew £500 on the other £1,000
against the advice of his new young friend, the Rev. John
Horne of Brentford, a freedom-loving clergyman (in both the
political and sexual meaning of the term) who had scraped
an acquaintance with him in Paris and who was to prove an
ally of vacillating strength. Horne, who was later to take the

name of a benefactor and become famous in radical circles as Horne Tooke, had already been nettled by Wilkes' failure to answer long letters he had addressed to him when accompanying a pupil on a European tour, and his sensitivity to slights and public attacks on Wilkes (in which Wilkes' supposed acceptance of the Government's pension in Paris was a prominent charge) were to aggravate an always rather uneasy alliance. Wilkes, in Paris, maintained he had not received Horne's letters and tried to pass the matter off genially as a joke, but Horne obviously brooded. Ploughing through the stormy waves of his friendship with Wilkes, it is, in fact, hard to account for Tooke's reputation, later in the century, as an irrepressible wit and also as a greatly admired candidate for legal honours, in which detached judgment and a balanced presentation of a case are surely necessary. [1]

In the meantime, his support of the Wilkes cause was enthusiastic and helpful and had included, in 1765, an anonymous lampoon, *The Petition of an Englishman; with which are given a Copper-plate of the Croix de St Pillory, and a true and accurate Plan of some Part of Kew Gardens.* The Kew Gardens reference was that now elderly joke on the supposed connecting passage between the mansions of the Earl of Bute and the Princess-Dowager, and Lord Mansfield as well as other Scots were also victims of the pamphlet. Its more general tenor was libertarian. 'Spirit of Hampden, Russel, Sidney! animate my countrymen. I invoke not your assistance for myself: for I was born INDEED A FREEMAN.' For all his prickly antagonisms, a freeman Horne Tooke was to remain, a scholar whose *Diversions of Purley* was to immortalize his interest in philology and whom bribery could never corrupt. He was to be a founder of the Society for Constitutional Information, a friend of Thomas Paine, and one of the radicals victimized but released in the Government treason trials of 1794, in the wake of Paine's *Rights of Man* and the panic aroused by the French Revolution.

[1] He studied the law but was never allowed to practise, probably because of his known political radicalism, although his having taken Holy Orders was the official excuse given for his rejection by the Bar.

Another friend of Wilkes in Paris was also now unexpectedly addicted to freedom. Boswell had returned to the French city after travels in Corsica and enthusiastic conversion to the cause of Paoli (in Garrick's 1769 Shakespeare Jubilee, in a rain-drenched Stratford-on-Avon, he was to turn up in full Corsican dress, with dagger and pistols and wearing a cap embroidered in gold, *Viva la Libertà!*). The friends exchanged gossip about their travels and Boswell was particularly grateful to Wilkes for the older man's kindness to him when he had the shock of reading of the unexpected death of his mother, to whom he was devoted, in an English newspaper. Nevertheless, Wilkes was finding French society uncongenial, and his income (little helped by his writing) was conspicuously failing to support him in the style to which he had grown accustomed. He had settled his entire property on Polly, partly to evade his creditors or other confiscation.

In May 1766, he risked slipping over to London, hoping to interest Grafton in his plight. There was no response and he returned disillusioned to Paris: Burke had also failed to respond to letters. Recently returned as Member of Parliament for Wendover, much be-bannered with re-minders of 'Wilkes and Liberty', Burke had written that the Rockinghams 'had not the least intention of taking up that gentleman's cause: he is not ours, and if he were, is little to be trusted: he is a lively, agreeable man, but of no prudence and no principles'.[1] Burke's own principles were to be, on occasion, considerably more corruptible, and flexible for reasons of prudence, than Wilkes'.

Again advised by Grafton's brother, Colonel Fitzroy, that Grafton could use his influence on his behalf, in October Wilkes again visited London, sending a letter dated 1st November to Grafton which 'surprized me much', commented the Duke, 'as he was under a verdict of outlawry'. It was flattering to the point of obsequiousness, and very difficult to assess as regards its sincerity, as it is true Grafton's reputation abroad as well as in England was good

[1] *Correspondence of Edmund Burke.*

at this time: he had travelled in Europe with his sick wife, was believed to be honest as well as amiable, and there were some hopes for the success of his ministry. Wilkes wrote:

'It is a very peculiar satisfaction I feel on my return to my native country, that a nobleman, of your Grace's superior talents and inflexible integrity is at the head of the most important department of the State. I have been witness of the general applause which has been given abroad to the choice His Majesty has made, and I am happy to find my own countrymen zealous and unanimous in every testimony of their approbation.

'I hope, my lord, that I may congratulate myself as well as my country on your Grace's being placed in a station of so great power and importance. Though I have been cut off from the body of His Majesty's subjects by a cruel and unjust proscription, I have never entertained an idea inconsistent with the duty of a good subject. My heart still retains all its former warmth for the dignity of England, and the glory of its Sovereign. I have not associated with the traitors to our liberties, nor made a single connection with any man who was dangerous, or even suspected by the friends of the Protestant family on the throne. I now hope that the rigour of an unmerited exile is past, and that I may be allowed to continue in the land and among the friends of liberty.'

He implores the Duke to lay his request for clemency before the King, and is sure 'a heart glowing with the sacred zeal of liberty must have a favourable reception from the Duke of Grafton'.

The Duke, by no means so sure himself of his 'superior talents', was more harassed than flattered by this missive from a returning Hamlet set naked upon the kingdom. He showed the letter to the King, who 'read it with attention; but made no observation upon it' (it sounds very unlike George III, not normally unloquacious on the subject of Wilkes) and then to Chatham, who remarked on 'the awkwardness of the business'. [1] Grafton was indeed not in a happy position to help, with the King literally at his elbow

[1] Grafton: *Memoirs with Political Correspondence* (Ed. Sir William Anson: John Murray, 1898).

and depending on the King's favour to hold his place. The situation was not of his making, and he felt forced to bow to it. He told Wilkes to write to Chatham, which in view of what he thought of as Pitt's betrayal Wilkes had too much pride to do. He returned to Paris on 12th December, publishing a *Letter to the Duke of Grafton* which appeared in London, Paris and Berlin. It also attacked Chatham ('private ambition was all the while skulking behind the shield of a Patriot . . . Friendship is too pure an emotion for a mind cankered with the lust of power'). It did not help his cause: and Grafton fled to Newmarket, his inevitable reaction in a crisis. (Although apparently unruffled on leaving, he came back furious, reported Wilkes' brother Heaton: perhaps his horses lost.) Temple also did not take kindly to this *Letter*, but Heaton wrote on 11 May 1767 that nevertheless this baiting of Grafton 'has done you infinite service in the City and on the Exchange'.[1]

In London on his first visit Wilkes had stayed with Laughlin Macleane in Holles Street. It is an interesting connection (which had commenced in Paris) as Macleane was one of the men to be identified with the mysterious pamphleteer 'Junius', soon to erupt into polemical journalism in vigorous support of Wilkes' cause. In 1949 an investigator, Cordasco, in fact publicized the discovery of a note by Lord Shelburne definitely naming Macleane, his Under-Secretary as 'Junius'. On his next visit Macleane was in office and Wilkes stayed at Wildman's tavern in Albemarle Street. It was the meeting place of the Opposition Club and John Horne was Wildman's brother-in-law.

Wilkes spent 1767 working at his *Introduction to the History of England, from the Revolution to the Accession of the Brunswick Line*, which was published in London the next year. In February he had faced his biggest disaster: Cotes had gone bankrupt, taking some £1,300 of Wilkes' money (including the Wood damages) with his own into limbo. He refused to give up Polly to her rich mother, one possible economy, although Mary Wilkes had now legally tried to get custody of her

[1] ADD. MSS. 30866, f.121.

daughter, and somehow scraped together enough money to sustain them both, partly through advances from Almon in respect of the work on the *History*.

In England there was a wet harvest and a food crisis, and Wilkes decided to try and stand in the coming General Election. In December 1767 he began his journey back to England via Holland and Leyden. Kidgell heard of his presence in Holland, with what pangs of conscience (except as a blackmailing device) we can only guess. Wilkes enjoyed the skating and reported to Polly that the Dutch thronged to see if he was like the Hogarth print. He had slipped over to England for a few days on 3rd December, but fearing arrest for debt had immediately returned to Holland, from where he also wrote to Polly rapturously about 'the wondrous productions of Rubens and Vandyke *(sic)*'. He had heralded his return to England, in October, with a statement, published in a London newspaper, that he would shortly return to England and stand as a parliamentary candidate in the General Election of 1768.

In spite of the outlawry, the Government was at a loss what to do, especially with an election looming and no foreknowledge of what the public might do. Grafton hopefully hinted at a pardon to the King, who proved implacable and complained privately to the Lord Chief Justice 'of the conduct of the present Ministers, particularly of the Duke of Grafton, that a man in his situation should propose a pardon'. (Wilkes' private reputation did not help him here: good King George was distressed enough already by the known moral laxity of some of his ministers, and the attacks on Bute and his mother had left their mark.) Grafton, throwing up his hands, went off to Newmarket, and the more congenial company of his racehorses.

On 6 February 1768 Wilkes reached London, taking a house at the corner of Princes Court, close to his old residence at Great George Street, Westminster. Here Polly might have 'every convenience, every elegance, every pleasure', as her doting father put it. On 4th March Wilkes made a formal application for the King's pardon by letter, handed in to Buckingham House by a servant (Buckingham

House, forerunner of the Palace, had been acquired by George III in 1762, although the dilapidated and inadequate St James's Palace continued to be the official royal residence). Wilkes' letter was ignored, and it is interesting to speculate into whose hands it was finally delivered. Biographers of Wilkes seem to have overlooked the Duke of Grafton's Memoirs, which show he obviously had no knowledge of it, for he states clearly that had Wilkes applied for a pardon it would probably have been granted, and all the later parliamentary disputation over his ineligibility for re-election been avoided. The failure of his own hint to the King of a pardon he had either forgotten by 1804, or preferred to forget, and he was not the only minister to suggest that Wilkes' own application for a pardon would have succeeded. Lord Barrington certainly stated, 'from the lenient character of those who serve the Crown I believe a pardon would have been granted if properly applied for: and I for one would have been glad to have it brought about'.[1] This may well, however, have been a vindicating cover for Barrington's own motion, on 3 February 1769, for Wilkes' expulsion. The ministerial ignorance of Wilkes' application to Buckingham House seems, nevertheless, clear, unless someone had suppressed the letter and was covering up. More likely the letter never got beyond Buckingham House.

Friends having purchased for him the freedom of the City, Wilkes appeared on the hustings as a candidate for the City of London. It was, wrote the harassed Grafton, 'as sudden as it was unexpected by us all'. Indeed, Wilkes had allowed himself too little time, for the Government had two strong candidates, and his election to the Joiners' Company as a liveryman appeared in the minute-books of the guild only on 10th March, six days before the start of the poll. The 1768 *Battle of the Quills*, however, racily poetized this honour:

The Joiners Joined: or, Jack Gimlet the Joiner Triumphant.

Ye joiners of England and joiners of France,
Come join all your hands and then join in a dance.

---

[1] *Cavendish Debates:* quoted in footnotes by the Editor, Sir William Anson, of Grafton's Memoirs (1898).

> For since Joiners made joints such a joint ne'er was hit
> Nor did Fate join to Joiners a Joint of such wit.
> Each join in his praise who has joined such a joint,
> And join in a chorus, then take off your pint.
> Let Liberty join tho' disjointed and torn,
> For a Joiner like Gimlet sure never was born . . .

And, more literally racy, it provided an advance commentary on the City Races, in the form of 'A List of the Horses that are to start on Wednesday, March 16, placed in the order in which it is expected they will come in':

> '1. The famous horse Liberty, formerly belonging to Mr Pitt, and since sold by Lord Chatham; he was got by Magna Charta, his dam by Freedom. This horse is too well known on the turf to need much description; there has been a great deal of Jockeyship made use of to prevent his starting, as the knowing ones are too well acquainted with his mettle to wish to have him brought again on the course; however, he is now entered, and very large betts are depending; the odds on him are four to one against the field.'

The famous horse Liberty, in fact, came in last, after a good start from the stalls. His supporters on 16th March heavily shortened the odds, but this was a seven-day race and by 23rd March fear of damaging the City's commercial interests, and a sense that Wilkes' entry was splitting the more radical vote, took hold. William Beckford, Pitt's friend and a vociferous Member of Parliament, and Barlow Trecothick had been more or less promised the support of what in a normal situation would have been the Wilkeite followers, and the poverty of those who deserted them for Wilkes was a subject of jest. (When one of them was said to have turned his coat, Wilkes rapidly replied that it was impossible, 'none of them has a coat to turn'.) In the end, the Government candidates, Sir Thomas Harley, the Lord Mayor, and Sir Robert Ladbroke, topped the poll, with Beckford and Trecothick third and fourth and Wilkes (with 1,247 votes as against Harley's 3,729 and Ladbroke's 3,678) seventh. Today,

Wilkes would probably have quipped that the bookmaker always wins. [1]

The horse Liberty, however, was a horse of phenomenal stamina. On 28th March he ran again, in Middlesex, and won. The feat staggered his one-time supporter, Charles Pratt, now Lord Chancellor and Lord Camden, who wrote to his friend Grafton:

'The event is disagreeable, and unforeseen, for I am persuaded that no person living, after Wilkes had been defeated in London would have thought it possible for him to have carry'd his election for the County of Middlesex. Sure I am, that if the Government had arrested him while he was a candidate, that step would have secured his election, and would have been considered as the cause of his success, if it had been taken. I cannot pretend at this distance without further information to advise what proceedings are now necessary to be taken, but the only subject for consideration seems to be what measures are to be taken by the House of Commons at the meeting of the Parliament. If the precedents and the Constitution will warrant an expulsion that perhaps may be right. A criminal flying his country to escape justice – a convict and an outlaw – That such a person should in open daylight thrust himself upon the country as a candidate, his crime unexpiated, is audacious beyond description . . .

'Whatever may be the heat of the present moment, I am persuaded it will soon subside, and this gentleman will lose his popularity in a very short time after men have recover'd their senses.'

'Lord Camden soon after altered his opinion', as Grafton comments, adding: 'It was much to be lamented, that Administration were at so early a period of this business, deprived of the advice of this great lawyer whom posterity will justly rank among the most able, learned and distinguished of our Chancellors, both in Parliament and in the Courts of Westminster Hall' (Camden in fact wrote from

[1] Ladbrokes is England's oldest-established bookmakers for the aristocracy.

Bath, where the triumphant Wilkes, he adds, was expected that night).

Wilkes' election for Middlesex with a large majority was not as surprising as would at first sight appear. Middlesex, like Southwark and Westminster, was open in the eighteenth century to a free democratic vote and the franchise was enjoyed by those who paid certain small municipal dues. Even some unskilled workers could vote, and half a century later Francis Place, the radical tailor, by organizing skill made it a certain radical seat. It was one of the arguments against the Reform Bill of 1832 that in fact its more limited terms of franchise, applied to the whole country, actually disenfranchised voters in a few towns which had earlier allowed a full vote. Preston (in this 1768 election successfully contested by Colonel John Burgoyne, later the unlucky General, 'Gentlemanly Johnny', defeated by the Americans at Saratoga) was one of these. As the seventeenth-century edict in the House of Commons had maintained, 'the right of electing members of parliament was not limited to the mayor and burgesses but extended to "all the inhabitants"'.[1] This privilege of universal suffrage Preston actually lost with the passing of the Reform Bill of 1832.

Wilkes at Middlesex had the help and support of Serjeant Glynn, the brilliant lawyer who had defended him in 1763 on the matter of General Warrants, and of John Horne, who electioneered throughout the parish, emphasizing Wilkes' services to liberty. Temple had also helped by presenting Wilkes with a small strip of land which made him eligible as a Middlesex freeholder.

On polling day, and before, the Government had reason to know Wilkes was back in harness. 'Wilkes and Liberty' was once again a rallying cry, the crowd broke the Mansion House windows, and Boswell, travelling by fly to Oxford on Saturday, 26th March, found the road to Brentford in possession of a mob roaring 'Wilkes and Liberty' and chalking the now sainted slogan of 'No. 45' on every coach or chaise that passed. 'Wilkes and Liberty' was the cry of

[1] Edward Barrington de Fonblanque: *Life and Correspondence of the Rt Hon John Burgoyne* (Macmillan, 1876).

Serjeant Glynn, Wilkes and Horne Tooke. Contemporary painting by R. Houston.

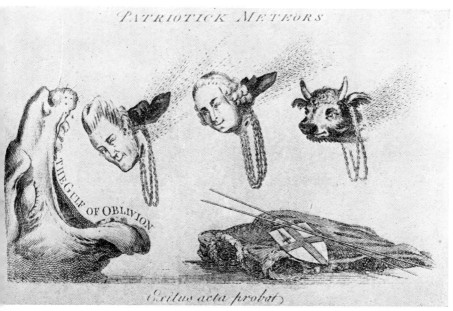

'Patriotick Meteors': Wilkes, Brass Crosby and Bull. Contemporary cartoon.

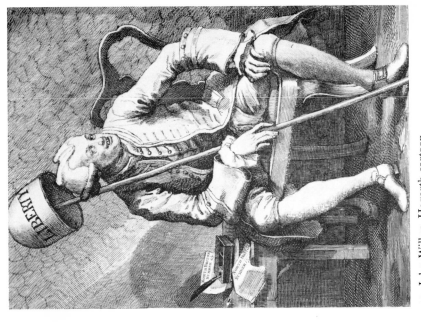

11. John Wilkes. Contemporary drawing by R. Earlom.

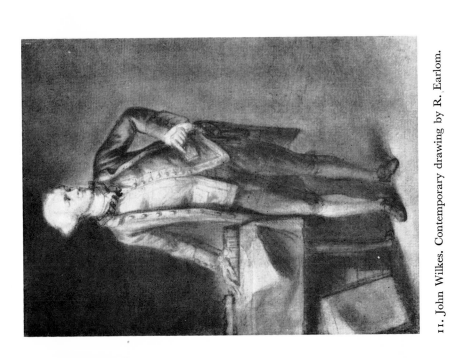

12. John Wilkes. Hogarth cartoon.

election rioters as far away as Lancaster and Newcastle. The coal-heavers at Wapping had gone on strike for higher wages and had been repressed only by force, and strikes by sailors, sawyers, tailors and weavers were soon to follow. Spitalfields weavers had mustered in Piccadilly, giving out blue cockades (signs of a Wilkeite) and papers marked 'No. 45, Wilkes and Liberty'. It was the silk weavers of Spitalfields who had begun the wave of London labour unrest with riots in 1765. It was not surprising the Government was alarmed. The Lord Chancellor was in Bath, and Grafton (needless to say) fled to Newmarket. Only the King stood his ground. 'I shall not stir from home', he told Barrington, the Secretary at War, 'so you may send to me if anything arises that requires my immediate attention.'

Wilkes' chances were the subject of lively betting. 'Today they give sixty to return one hundred if he was elected', wrote a correspondent of George Selwyn. The low odds were justified. Wilkes headed the poll, it was announced, with 1,292 votes, his two opponents having only just over 800 each. London was illuminated, and the mob threatened any who put out their lights. Benjamin Franklin estimated that two nights had cost London £50,000 in candles alone (he was the son of a tallow chandler, and doubtless interested in compiling the statistics), not to count broken windows. Glaziers, said to be Wilkeites, did a brisk trade, perhaps on the same basis of custom achieved by glazier Charlie Chaplin in *The Kid* 150 years later, when Chaplin's adopted child, Jackie Coogan, dodged round the streets throwing stones through windows, which Chaplin nonchalantly passed with a sheet of glass some minutes afterwards. 'At night', reported the *Annual Register*, 'the rabble was very tumultuous.'

After his victory, Wilkes characteristically snatched a few days' relaxation in Bath, where it is to be hoped he did not bump into the Lord Chancellor. But on 20th April he duly presented himself, as Camden had anticipated, to surrender his outlawry. In the Court he raised every technical objection possible and impossible, and to general surprise Lord Mansfield, hearing the case, refused to take cognizance of his presence in Court as it had not been procured by a writ of *capias utlegatum*, necessary in an outlaw. As an outlaw, moreover, 'Mr Wilkes is not regularly entitled to bail, and on the other hand it appears that this Court cannot commit him'.

Willes, the Judge, concurred: 'The officer of the Crown cannot put his office upon us.' In other words, the Court was passing the buck: let the Ministry shoulder its own responsibilities.

Wilkes waited a week at his house, and then sent a note inviting the sheriffs to serve the writ on him. The fact is they and the Government were in a ferment of indecision, though the King thought it 'proper to apprize Lord North that the expulsion of Mr Wilkes appears to be very necessary and must be effected. He declared No. 45 a paper the author ought to *glory in*, and the blasphemous poem a mere ludicrous production.' The King remained morally outraged, and the Bloomsbury Gang naturally supported him.

The Lord Chancellor's sense of justice had reasserted itself, and he urged caution. 'Your Grace will be pleased to understand', he wrote to Grafton on 20th April, 'that Mr W. stands at present *convicted* only by *verdict:* and if there shall appear to be any material defect in the record, that the judgement must be stayed: in which case, he must be discharged, and he becomes a free man upon this prosecution, as much as if he had never been convicted ... till judgement is finally pronounced against Mr W., by the Court, no man has a right to pronounce him guilty, more especially, as he *appears*, and intends to object in arrest of judgement . . . For, how can the House expel a member, either as an outlaw, or a convict, while the suit is pending, wherein he may turn out at last, to be neither the one, nor the other.' On 9 January 1769, he added: 'As the times are, I had rather pardon W. than punish him. This is a political opinion independant of the merits of the cause.'

In spite of the King's anger, there was some need for caution: Franklin was not the only one to suggest that perhaps 'the English soldiers cannot be confided in to act against the mob, being suspected as rather inclined to favour and join them'. And the mob, varied in composition though it was, was always a potent factor in Wilkes' affairs.

The Scots in the army were another matter, in view of their resentment at the anti-Jacobite *North Briton*; but the food crisis and price of bread, the highest ever known, made riot possible on other counts. The harvests between 1764 and 1768 had all been bad, and a severe winter, in which the Thames had been frozen over, had further drained the resources, and exacerbated the tempers, of the poor. Already there were Luddite-style breakages of labour-saving machinery in the sawmills, and the destruction of silk-looms by Spitalfields weavers. When some tailors were hanged, their colleagues stoned to death two of the prosecution witnesses. With the troubles among the sailors and coal-heavers, some of whom as Grafton reports clashed and murdered each other, the Government had every reason to fear a further explosion. It was a violent age and the law itself set the example with its own savage penalties, which grew in number and ferocity as the century progressed, until even a minor theft by a starving mother or child could be expiated on the gallows. The people learn violence, as Thomas Paine wrote, 'from the Governments they live under, and retaliate the punishments they have been accustomed to behold'.[1] It was 1772 before the last head of an executed traitor fell from its spike on Temple Bar.

On 27 April 1768 Wilkes was at last brought into Court again, but Mansfield adjourned the affair to the next term, remanding Wilkes in custody. This prevented Wilkes taking his seat in the Commons, which the Government required, but without committing Mansfield to a legal decision. Most people, including Franklin, thought Mansfield was frightened.

Wilkes set off to the King's Bench Prison with the Marshal and John Horne, but the mob intercepted them and harnessed themselves to his cab. Instead of the King's Bench, as he requested, they took him to the Three Tuns in Spitalfields. Wilkes, enjoying his popularity but with no mind to put the Government in the right by disobeying the law, made his escape through a back door and delivered himself

[1] *Rights of Man* (1791).

up to prison by hackney coach (the Marshal had been dropped at Temple Bar).

On 5th May, from prison, he issued a spirited address to his constituents, and in the next few days crowds began to gather in St George's Fields, near the prison, probably because there was a rumour he would be released, to take his place in the new Parliament. There were one or two cases already of hooliganism, and Wilkes on 8th May made a short speech from his prison window, aimed at mollifying and dispersing his followers. Some sailors, the following day, and probably alerted as to his exact whereabouts by the speech, clambered to his windows and offered to rescue him, but he politely told them that he had no doubt the laws of his country would do him justice. The next day, 10th May, was the date for the opening of Parliament, and the Lord Mayor had urged master tradesmen to keep their journeymen and apprentices off the streets: these were always a source of agitation and revolt and they were rumoured to be gathering in several parts of the City. The prison Marshal, fearing an attempt to rescue Wilkes, sent for troops, which by ill-luck or judgment proved to be a detachment of the Third Regiment of Guards, all Scots. One of the crowd stuck up some verses on the prison wall, and the magistrate, Gillam, ordered their removal. This started the mob throwing stones. The Riot Act was read twice, the second time stating that if any stones were thrown, the soldiers would be ordered to fire. This was a red flag to the crowd, some of whom defiantly threw some stones, one of which hit Gillam on the head. He panicked or lost his temper, and ordered 'Fire'. The Guards fired several volleys, killing half a dozen people and wounding a dozen or so more. Some were bayoneted. The soldiers went berserk, killing several innocent passers-by, including a pregnant woman and a girl with a basket of oranges.

An Ensign Murray and three grenadiers then gave chase to a man with a red waistcoat who they thought might have thrown the stone at the serjeant. They gave chase across a road, over a rail, round a windmill and through a cowshed, a distance of 400 or 500 yards. There they came across the farmer's son, William Allen, who had not even been in St

George's Fields but was wearing a red waistcoat. Private Donald Maclane is said to have shot him, although another version of the events maintains he was shot by the third grenadier, Maclaughlin, whose officers allowed him to desert to escape trial. On 7th July the Middlesex Grand Jury did, however, give a verdict of wilful murder against Justice Gillam, who had given the order to fire in the case of a weaver named William Redburn, who was killed. A few days later the Old Bailey reversed the verdict.

On 8th August Wilkes was taken to Guildford to give evidence at the Surrey Assizes against Maclane (and the High Sheriff had to send out an order to silence the church bells being rung in Wilkes' honour). He was presented with a basket of fruit by admirers, and characteristically kept a pineapple to give to Polly. Wilkes in the end was not called and Maclane's trial was adjourned until the next day, when the jury, faced with conflicting evidence, gave a verdict of Not Guilty.

It was said, bitterly, in London that not since Prestonpans had there been such a massacre of Englishmen by Scots. But the next day Lord Barrington, Secretary of State at War, congratulated the Guards on behalf of the King: 'His Majesty highly approves of the conduct of both the officers and the men.' In this, among much else, the 'Massacre of St George's Fields' resembled the 'Massacre of Peterloo' in 1819.

VIII

THE KING'S BENCH

Massacre, accidental or fore-designed, is nearly always a political mistake. All the Government gained by the massacre of St George's Fields was a further burst of popularity for Wilkes, and the King had the galling experience of seeing Lord Bute, still blamed for everything as presumed power behind the throne, caricatured mercilessly by the cartoonists (in Almon's *Political Register* he was shown sneaking into a bedroom openly identified by the Royal Arms). The device of No. 45 was now seen everywhere, not only in London but up and down the land (Franklin said that for fifteen miles out of London there was hardly a door or window which had not had 45 chalked on it: and an anti-Wilkeite named Alexander Cruden boasted he had gone all over London with a sponge, wiping out the offending symbol as soon as it was made).

Lord Mansfield continued his decided role of sitting on the fence and on 8th June achieved a remarkable feat of equilibrium: he reversed Wilkes' outlawry on a technical point, although he confirmed his prior convictions. He had been jostled by the crowd on the way to Westminster Hall, and his verdict was widely attributed to fear. Yet Mansfield, according to his lights, could be open-minded on a point of law, although his reaction to the St George's Fields massacre was not endearing: Boswell in 1772 was to note:

'. . . A report of several people having been killed in a sort of mob in the north of Ireland was mentioned. Lord Mansfield, smiling and addressing himself to Lord Barrington, said, "This beats St George's Fields all to nothing." What would Junius, what would the Patriots, as they call themselves, have said had they been present! The massacre of St George's Fields has been a bloody and terrible charge against Lord Barrington in particular, and much, too, against Lord Mansfield. Many of the English would suppose that the great culprits would grow pale at hearing the very name of St George's Fields; and yet here were they making it a point, a jest, in conversation.'[1]

On 18 June 1768, therefore, Wilkes was sentenced to one year and ten months' imprisonment (exclusive of the time he had already spent in gaol) for the printing of No. 45 and the *Essay on Woman*. He was also fined £1,000, and required on his discharge to enter into recognizances in £1,000 with two sureties in £500 each for good behaviour for seven years. Supporters paid the fines, but he was confined to King's Bench until 17 April 1770.

On the whole, he was to prove more inflammatory in prison than out of it, with admirers loudly singing his praises on both sides of the Atlantic. On 1st November he issued a *Letter on the Public Conduct of Mr Wilkes*, putting his case in full and the best possible light, and on 3rd November followed it with an *Address* to his constituents. His most triumphant and politically destructive gesture was the production of a copy of Lord Weymouth's instructions to the Chairman of Lambeth Quarter Sessions, in which he and his brother magistrates were ordered to make prompt use of the military in event of riot. This most damaging document for the Government was dated 17th April, three weeks before the massacre in St George's Fields. Wilkes entered a writ of error making appeal against his sentence, presented both in the House of Commons and the Lords (Grafton, as nervous as one of his own thoroughbreds, strongly advised him to abandon it but without avail, and Wilkes continued to press parliamentary proceedings). Grafton undoubtedly at the time had some liberal pangs of conscience about the Wilkes expulsion, desiring at first that no obstacle should be interposed to the member for Middlesex taking his seat. Wilkes' writ was dismissed finally on 19 January 1769.

Nevertheless, Wilkes was incorrigible and unsilenceable.

[1] *Boswell for the Defence, 1769–1774* (Yale Editions of the Private Papers of James Boswell, Ed. William K. Wimsatt Jr and Frederick A. Pottle (Yale University, 1959; Heinemann, London, 1959)).

He produced an article in the *St James's Chronicle* which was voted libellous by both Houses, and on 4th February he was expelled the House (to give a colour of legality, account was taken of his previous offences and he was stated to be a condemned criminal). Wilkes had been brought to the House and spoke there for the last time for five years. He acknowledged that he transmitted to the press the letter of the Secretary of State, 'and, Sir, whenever a Secretary of State shall dare to write so bloody a scroll I will through life dare to write such prefatory remarks, as well as to make my appeal to the nation on the occasion. I ask pardon, Sir, that I made use of too mild and gentle expressions when I mentioned so wicked, so inhuman, so cowardly a massacre as that in St George's Fields on the tenth of May.' Having shot his bolt of irony, he demanded that Ponton (the magistrate who received Lord Weymouth's letter) be sent for and examined that in fact he did receive the letter (it was afterwards ascertained that he did receive it).

Wilkes was indicted on a triple charge, not only the publishing of a state secret in the *St James's Chronicle* (a matter which he rightly considered once again raising the liberty of the press) but on the publication of No. 45 and the *Essay*. As he had already suffered a fine and imprisonment for the last two publications, certain of the Opposition, including Edmund Burke and Wilkes' one-time turncoat friend, George Grenville, strongly opposed this; but the deliberate implication was that Wilkes had libelled the King and he was expelled by a majority of eighty-two. Grenville, out of office, perhaps felt now freer to revive some loyalty to Wilkes: he warned the House that Wilkes' 'popular favour is not confined to this capital or to its neighbourhood alone, but is extended to the most distant parts of the kingdom' and added the prophecy: 'Mr Wilkes will certainly be re-elected: you will expel again and he will return again. What is to be done then, and how is so disgraceful a conflict to terminate?'

Walpole saw the dangers: 'Instead of dipping into Roman or Greek histories for flowers to decorate the speeches of false patriotism, principles are revived that have taken deeper root; and I wish we do not see quarrels of a graver

complexion than the dirty squabbles for places and profit.'
Prophecy was in the air, and Philip Francis (whom men were
soon to be identifying as chief suspect in the role of the
anonymous pamphleteer Junius) saw no reason 'why he may
not be Sheriff and Lord Mayor in regular succession, and
why not Prime Minister before he dies'. Only in the last was
Francis wrong.

In the meantime Parliament was as good as its word, but
so were the good electors of Middlesex. Wilkes, in an
address to them as freeholders, ventured on a prophecy of
his own: 'If the Ministers can usurp the power of declaring
who *shall not* be your representative, the next step is very easy
and will follow speedily. It is that of telling you whom you
shall send to Parliament.' Indeed, the Duke of Grafton,
attempting to justify the events thirty-five years later, and
forgetting his original doubts, maintained just this:

> 'If I was asked, as to my opinion on this perplexing
> subject, I should readily answer, that on the first step of
> expulsion, all dignity was gone from the house, if they could
> admit a person under a verdict of outlawry, to sit one hour,
> as a member of it. When he was returned member again and
> again, I cannot see why the repetition of an insult to the
> House of Commons should have altered the right, provided
> it be granted, that it had existed. The two Houses must
> separately be sole judges of the seats of their members.
> Destroy that right, and their independence is gone: for
> where else can it be placed? The most just rights and
> powers may be abused, but it does not follow, that they are
> to be abolished, unless it can be shewn that they may be
> placed elsewhere, without injury to the Constitution.'

There are times when the consideration that the House of
Commons was an *elected* body hardly seems to occur to the
eighteenth-century ministerial mind. Many of the seats were
simply bought, and franchise could be largely disregarded.

On 16 February 1769, proposed and seconded by two
City magnates, Townsend and Sawbridge, Wilkes was again
elected for Middlesex, no one daring to oppose him. On the
17th he was again expelled, and on the 18th he again put up

Wilkes

as candidate. This time, with a month to elapse before election day, a royalist stigmatized by Junius as 'the miserable Dingley' decided to oppose Wilkes. He had made a large fortune for a timber-sawing invention, was William Pitt's landlord at North End, and at one time had been Charles Churchill's landlord also. (It is uncertain if this financially unfortunate experience at all activated his antagonism to Wilkes.) He started the campaign pugnaciously enough by knocking out the teeth of a Wilkeite named Reynolds, who being a lawyer promptly had him arrested. However he was released in time to appear on the hustings on 16th March, but as no one could be found bold enough to propose him, Wilkes was again elected unanimously. Monotonously, the House next day declared the election void.

Before the next farce of election and expulsion could take place there were riots of a serious nature, as indeed Grafton later realized was inevitable in the circumstances. On 22nd March an anti-Wilkes petition was due to be presented by the smarting Dingley at St James's Palace. The worst was expected (Horace Walpole hurriedly inscribed the magic talisman '45' on his valued painted windows) and indeed the mob was prepared for the procession of petitioning merchants from the City. They shut the Temple Bar gate, built barricades, flung the only too plentiful London dirt at the coaches, pulled some gentlemen out of these coaches and sang 'God Save Great Wilkes our King' (some years later it was to be adapted to 'God Save Great Thomas Paine'). The Riot Act was read twice without effect and the crowd had to be dispersed by a charge of Horse Guards. Only twelve merchants reached the King, it is said bedraggled and in sorry plight. The address was lost, although the King behaved with his usual courage (it was one of the qualities he did share with his antagonist Wilkes).

Grafton (as can be taken for granted) had fled to Newmarket. He had other worries on his mind. In January that year (1769) there had appeared in the *Public Advertiser* the first letter signed 'Junius', a castigator of the corrupt Government whose identity (to escape certain prosecution)

138

was so successfully concealed that it remains conjecturable to the present day. Written in a style which had a permanent influence on later journalism, full of polemical wrath but with a literary grace that drew the admiration of Coleridge and others, the letters continued for more than three years and their special target from the start was the unhappy 'Sporting Duke' (who naturally thought the letters anything but sporting). Grafton was 'the pillow upon which I am determined to rest all my resentments', wrote Junius in 1771, and already he had established this in March 1769, when he sent a broadside flying after the Duke to Newmarket where in 'rural retirement and in the arms of faded beauty' (suggested Junius) 'he lost all memory of his sovereign, his country and himself'.

What special grudge, if any, he nursed against the unfortunate Grafton cannot be known: his victim was by no means the least amiable or politically honest of the King's ministers, nor even was he Wilkes' most virulent enemy, and Wilkes was certainly an object of Junius' support. In an Epistle to the Duke of Grafton Junius had particularly lambasted him for a matter on which it is difficult to see that the Duke was personally to blame, although there is no doubt the Government had some blame in it. This was concerning a young Wilkeite lawyer named George Clarke, who had been murdered, or at least had died from head wounds received, during the election. Two Irishmen, McQuirk and Balfe, had been arrested in a Covent Garden alehouse, partly through the efforts of John Horne, whose courage seems to have been fortified by an unparsonly amount of alcohol at the time. At the subsequent trial both McQuirk and Balfe were acquitted, it was considered on deliberately concealed medical evidence regarding Clarke's death. Junius chose to put the whole blame on Grafton, though the Duke's knowledge was in fact likely to be far more on the veterinary side of medicine than the physician's. The whole dubious episode helped to stoke the Wilkesian fires, and fix the blundering ineptitude of the Government.

Meanwhile, the Government had to think out its next move in the Aylesbury saga. Grafton decided 'it required a man of the firmest virtue, or a ruffian of dauntless prostitution, to undertake the office of opposing Wilkes', and the governmental choice, decidedly nearer the latter, was of a young Colonel Henry Lawes Luttrell, profligate son of Lord Irnham.

If he was named after Henry Lawes, the charming lutanist and composer who had the previous century created the incidental music for Milton's *Comus*, Luttrell can hardly be said to have lived up to any parental ideal. He was claimed to be a seducer of a worse kind than Wilkes, the kind who left his women in the lurch, and had kidnapped an eleven-year-old girl and bribed witnesses to swear that the child was already a prostitute. He had resigned a Bute pocket borough in order to stand, and Wilkes pretended he had been bribed by the offer of Bute's daughter as his wife. In Lloyd's, gamblers took out insurance policies on his life. Wilkes, it had been noted, was to be supported by one of his most notorious Irish admirers, a Captain 'Tiger' Roche, who proclaimed he would stand alongside Wilkes.

The Government nevertheless were not unhopeful; in fact it was already arranged that Luttrell should win the seat even if without (as misplaced optimism still anticipated) a 'fair majority of legal votes'. How wrong they were and how much they misjudged the public, including many freeholders, clergymen and MPs, was shown by the fact that not only did many express their disapproval of Luttrell personally by abstaining from voting, even although they had voted against Wilkes at previous elections, but a great number actually transferred their vote to Wilkes on this occasion, while MPs refrained in the House of Commons from voting for the admission of Luttrell in Wilkes' place.[1]

Junius, poised for the kill, started the campaign with another letter to the wincing Grafton. 'Your Grace can best inform us for which of Mr Wilkes's good qualities you first honoured him with your friendship . . . For my own part, my Lord, if I had been weak enough to form such a friendship, I would never have been base enough to betray it . . . But, let

[1] George Rudé: *Wilkes and Liberty: A Social Study of 1763 to 1774* (Clarendon Press, 1962).

Mr Wilkes's character be what it may, circumstanced as he is, even his vices plead for him. The people of England have too much discernment to suffer Your Grace to take advantage of failings of a private character, to establish a precedent by which the public liberty is affected, and which you may hereafter, with equal ease and satisfaction, employ to the ruin of the best of men in the kingdom.'

Junius, of course, like many after him to the present day, was concerned not just with the moment of time, but the dangers of establishing an iniquitous precedent for the future. In times of danger, or conceived danger, governments have a habit of passing laws, or taking actions, which can lead to powers of repression in totally different and less questionable cases. But with a mob barking '45' at its heels, both the normally easy-going Grafton and the Government probably had some reason to fear anarchy. Their mistake was not in realizing that they were going about the best way to provoke it.

There were two candidates besides Luttrell: Roche and Serjeant Whitaker (who failed to turn up). Luttrell arrived with a mounted escort, somewhat depleted en route through being recognized by the mob at Hyde Park Corner and pelted with dirt, after which some of the victims apparently decided that soap and water would be a pleasanter experience than a journey into Buckinghamshire. The Wilkes supporters arrived on horseback and in coaches, all lavishly decorated with his election colour, which was blue. They had behaved peacefully enough, en route, in the streets of London; and Sir John Fielding's precautions against disorder proved largely unnecessary. One group had almost anticipated later Trade Union processions with their craft banners, setting out 'from the Prince of Orange in Jermyn Street, before whom were carried six or seven flags (Bill of Rights, Magna Carta, etc.) all badges of the different societies of which Mr Wilkes had been made a member'. Another 'preceded by a band of music, with colours flying, marched along Pall Mall and stopped fronting the Palace, where they gave three loud huzzas, and the music began to play. This alarmed the Guards, who marched out of the gate with their bayonets fixed; but the company marched on peaceably for Brentford, and the soldiers returned into barracks.' The candidate Roche, pondering on Whitaker, beat a last-minute retreat and Wilkes won the election with 1,143 votes as against the 296 polled by Luttrell and the almost indecent five achieved by the absent Whitaker.

The City, once again, burst into illumination and the King's Bench resounded to the cheers of Wilkes' supporters who arrived to congratulate the prisoner. The following day, true to form, the Government declared the election null: the Commons, by a majority of 54, voted that Colonel Luttrell 'ought to have been returned'. Burke remarked that thus ended the fifth act of 'a tragi-comedy acted by His Majesty's servants, for the benefit of Mr Wilkes and at the expense of the Constitution', and Grafton again had indecisive doubts. 'Whether the decision that Colonel Luttrell was duly elected . . . was in strict justice determined, I will not take upon myself to decide.' It would appear Grafton, liberal-minded by nature when expediency did not take control, was wavering again: on 22nd April, 1768, a year before, he had written to the King on 'the desire of His Majesty's principal servants jointly expressed that Mr Wilkes should not be allowed to sit in Parliament if it could be avoided by any means justifiable by law and the Constitution and conformable to the proceedings of Parliament'. The tentative search for legal justification suggests an uneasy conscience.

Nevertheless, the vote that Luttrell was elected and should enter the House was finalized on 9th May (it was the first case in Parliament of 'whipping in' members of the Government party to ensure a majority: Treasury officials rounded up members as far afield as Paris, and Burke coined the phrase). Temple, who had become reconciled and joined forces with Grenville (whose support of Wilkes' rights had been accompanied by a malicious attack on his personal character), maintained it was 'a glorious day', without a 'shadow of argument in favour of disqualification'. The young Charles James Fox, later a Whig liberal of some courage but now deeply in the shadow of his Tory father,

Henry Fox, Lord Holland, blotted his political copybook with a reference to Luttrell's 'noble action', and Fox's brother Stephen referred to those who elected Wilkes as 'the scum of the earth', a remark which may have been echoed in Burke's notorious 'swinish multitude' in his *Reflections on the Revolution in France* twenty years later.

It is worth noting that although the Wilkes situation was unique, not dissimilar examples of chicanery in electing members, contrary to the actual vote, were not uncommon in the corrupt eighteenth-century system of electioneering, so devastatingly lambasted by Hogarth a decade before. Colonel Burgoyne's passage into Parliament with Sir Henry Hoghton at Preston was also a tempestuous one. Although supported by the Earl of Derby, his father-in-law, and although Burgoyne and Hoghton received a very large majority of the votes, the Corporation of Preston, itself solidly Tory and suspected of Jacobite sympathies, saw to it that the returning officers declared the Corporation candidates to be duly elected. The grounds given for this were that the votes of all other than 'freemen' were null and void, despite the City's century-old tradition of virtually universal suffrage. In this case a Committee of the House of Commons, on petition, confirmed the franchise originally granted and Burgoyne and his colleague were enabled to take their seats.

In 1770, at a by-election at New Shoreham, there was a similar incident, when Thomas Rumbold, a Whig candidate in opposition to the Government, gained 87 votes as compared with the 37 and 4 polled respectively by his two opponents, a Mr Purling and a Mr James.

'Notwithstanding the great majority of votes in behalf of Mr Rumbole [*sic*], (who opposed the ministry)', reported *The Sussex Weekly Advertiser or Lewes Journal* of 26th November, 'the returning officer deemed Mr Purling duly elected, and returned him as such; and we are informed, he has taken the oaths and his seat in Parliament accordingly.' In this case, too, there was an immediate explosion of public wrath, and on 17th December the Lewes column in the paper gave the glad news:

'The contested election for Shoreham, which has been under the consideration of the committee of elections ever since last Tuesday, Thomas Rumbold, Esq., petitioner, against Purling the sitting member, was on Saturday morning decided by the latter giving up; and we hear that the conduct of the Returning Officer on this occasion will be taken into consideration. It is said, that upon the arrival of the express, which was dispatched immediately, the bells were rung, and a universal joy filled the place and its environs, some few excepted.'

Rumbold was supported throughout by Wilkes' lawyer and friend, Serjeant Glynn, who must by now have become an expert in such election reversals. Another supporter, who probably gained much knowledge of political graft from the experience, was Thomas Paine, an exciseman based at nearby Lewes, who wrote an election song for the Whig candidate and was paid three guineas for it. Wilkes, on a holiday tour of Kent, Sussex and Hampshire with his daughter, had visited Lewes in the middle of August. He had stayed at the Star Inn, not at Paine's Whig haunt, the White Hart, but Paine could hardly have been unaware of the presence of the celebrated fighter for liberty, very recently released from the King's Bench. *The Sussex Weekly Advertiser or Lewes Journal*, a very good paper for political news, had reported at length on the Wilkes case and included letters both from him and from Junius. On 27 August, 1770, it recorded his visit in detail:

'On Wednesday last, about 6 in the evening, arrived at the Star Inn, in this town, in their way from Tunbridge Wells to Brighthelmstone, Mr Alderman Wilkes, and Miss Wilkes, his daughter; on their arrival being known, the bells in our several churches were immediately rung, and vast crowds of people assembled to see the great patriot, at whom they expressed their pleasure by joyful acclamations: they lay at the above inn, Wednesday night, and on Thursday morning, after going to take a view from our castle (at which he expressed a satisfaction, and at which time the inhabitants again thronged in prodigious numbers

13. William Beckford, Lord Mayor, 1769–70.

Silver cup presented to Wilkes by City of
Lon, 1772.

Prince's Court.
Oct. 5. 1784.

My Lord,

                        yesterday I received the hon
of your Lordship's letter of the thirtieth of September, with one
enclosed for Mr Donaldson in St Paul's Church Yard. My servant h
carried it to him, with the assurances of my readiness to address any co
to your Lordship, which might be sent here for that purpose.
                              The grea

business of a Parliamentary reform will, I suppose, be agitated early
the ensuing Session, and I observe the same anxiety, as well as zeal
for this important object in the more northern parts of the island
as among the patriots of the South. The political horizon is inde
at present very generally clouded over, but fair weather will, I trust,
soon return, and we remark, that it often comes from the North.

               I am, with great regard,
               my Lord,

                      your Lordship's obedient,
                      humble Servant,

                        John Wilkes

Addressed to the Earl of Buchan.

(Original in possession of W. Upcott Esq)

15. Letter written by Wilkes to the Earl of Buchan, Oct. 5, 1784, on parliamentary refor

once more to behold the object of their adoration) they proceeded (Mr Wilkes on horseback, and Miss Wilkes in a post-chaise) on their journey to Brighthelmstone, where, we hear, the bells were likewise rung, and other marks of pleasure shewn on the joyous occasion. He seemed to avoid popularity, and affect a degree of privacy; notwithstanding which, every mark of real esteem was shewn him by the inhabitants of this town, that could, in such circumstances, be expressed to a gentleman so highly deserving the public Regard. We are informed, they will remain at Brighthelmstone a week.'

It is interesting to speculate if Paine, as well as Rumbold, met Wilkes at this time, and Rumbold then obtained the services of Wilkes' able lawyer, as well as a propaganda song writer, for the coming election. Paine's customs duties may well have prevented his mixing with the 'vast crowds assembled to see the great patriot', but of the ringing bells and 'joyful acclamations' he was bound to hear much, quite apart from reading about it in the excellent local journal. His mind was in any case being stocked and formed, ready for a career as political writer which was to surpass in fame even Wilkes' own.

In the meantime, Luttrell retained his ill-gotten seat, and Wilkes, his ears as yet unassailed by Lewes church bells, remained in the King's Bench Prison. His lot was not in the least what the reference to 'prison' suggests to a modern ear. Like others of his class, he was lodged in a 'most spacious and pleasing apartment' on the first floor, overlooking the green pastoral setting of St George's Fields, and although he could not go beyond the gates the prison was built like a small town, including even a little street containing shops, a tennis court, a coffee-house and a tavern. Visitors could be received (Polly and his mother came to see him) and political deputations also, at any time; and Wilkes was even able to arrange a diversion which several years later was to prove costly and cause him some regret. Mrs John Barnard, attractive wife of a City Alderman, had been Wilkes' mistress before her marriage and she now visited him both with the unsuspecting Alderman (a Wilkeite) and without him. In between some delightful 'happenings', charming and coquettish letters passed between them. The renegade parson John Horne seems to have been involved in some way with this happy arrangement: he was to be referred to later bitterly by the betrayed Mr Barnard as Wilkes' 'pimp general'.

Nor was the 'inner man' forgotten. For the rest of his incarceration Wilkes was snowed under with gifts, including food and drink on a colossal scale, from admirers and organizations of reform, both in his own country and far-off America (even live turtles travelled across the Atlantic, with 'Wilkes' printed on their shells). On 20 February 1769, at the London Tavern in Bishopsgate Street, Horne helped to form a Committee of Supporters of the Bill of Rights, which made a remarkable and successful effort to appeal for generous gifts towards the covering of Wilkes' by no means inconsiderable debts. A number of wealthy City figures and Members of Parliament were among its founders, and the Committee discharged liabilities of £17,000. (Debts remaining of £6,821 were covered during the summer of 1770.) As a result, Wilkes, who had entered the King's Bench a ruined man, left it completely free from debt, and the 'idol of the populace'. Public houses were named after him and still exist in a few cases. A public house in Carteret Street, Westminster, was called the 'Three Johns' (its sign showed the head of Wilkes between those of John Horne Tooke and John Thelwall), and a landlord who had adopted the 'Wilkes Head' as a sign, was refused a licence by the Surrey magistrate unless he altered it. In the celebrated British satirical tradition of the freedom-loving spirit, the landlord retorted that he had hung up Wilkes as criminals were usually hanged, but that if their worships pleased he would have no objection whatever to taking him down, and hanging one of their worships in his place. Busts of Wilkes in marble, bronze, or china were said to decorate half the mantelpieces in the metropolis, his portrait took a star position in shop windows, and trinkets and souvenirs decorated with his face were sold to hordes of admirers and tourists.

On the occasion of his birthday, 28th October, there were widespread demonstrations during which windows not illuminated in his honour were broken in the now customary fashion: it was, commented a newspaper, 'everywhere celebrated as a day of festivity. The Committee of the Bill of Rights presented to John Wilkes Esq., a silver cup of £100 value; which contains a gallon and half a pint, and is of curious workmanship. On the outside is the figure of John Wilkes Esq., with a cap of Liberty over his head, held by Britannia; before him lies Magna Charta and the Bill of Rights.' On Friday, 3rd March the same year, 1769, the officers and members of the Freemasons' Lodge, at a meeting held at the Jerusalem Tavern in Clerkenwell (his birthplace), quite irregularly elected him a freemason, and sent a deputation to the King's Bench to inform him of the fact. It was said in the papers that a dispensation was obtained from the Grand Master, but this was later denied.

The demonstrations did not calm the Government's nerves. Industrial unrest had been rife throughout 1768: not only the weavers and coal-heavers, but sailors, dockers, coopers, hatters, glass-grinders, sawyers and tailors demonstrated in varying degrees of anger and violence as the price of wheat, in mid-May, rose at the London Corn Exchange to 56s a quarter. On 20th August, the Spitalfields weavers destroyed the silk on two looms, and it was not the only action that seemed to anticipate the Luddites' destruction of machinery over fifty years later. Even incipient trade unionism, not officially recognized until the ending of the Combination Laws in 1824, had begun to emerge among the journeyman tailors as early as 1720, when their masters had complained to Parliament about their 'combinations' to raise wages and reduce working hours. Grafton was not the only person in authority to ascribe some of this dangerous unrest and alliance for better conditions among the workers to the Wilkes movement: 'Artisans of almost every denomination also combined for an advance of wages, and their discontents and disobedience to the laws, led them to join often, in numbers, those mobs which the consequence of the election for Middlesex frequently produced.'[1]

---

[1] *Memoirs with Political Correspondence* (Ed. Sir William Anson: Murray, 1898).

Meantime, the agitation for Wilkes' release increased. A Bill of Grievances and Apprehensions had been drawn up on Horne's proposal, and petitions were presented by the City. Wilkes himself sent one to the House of Commons complaining of his treatment since his arrest. David Garrick was persuaded by Grafton to visit him with Fitzherbert, to try to dissuade him from this (Garrick was supposed by the Duke to know that 'Mr Wilkes was not always correct in his reports of conversations'). Wilkes did not abandon the petition, but submitted another for clemency, presented by Sir Joseph Mawbey, MP for Southwark. This peace feeler in the King's direction was totally ignored. Nor was George III amused when on 6th May, at Epsom Races, he and the Queen were exposed to the audacious cry of 'Wilkes and Liberty for ever!', from 'a fellow who stood near His Majesty'.

'With firmness', the King had insisted in April, 'this affair will vanish into smoke'. The smoke was proving surprisingly persistent, and petitions from all over the country continued to pour in. The freedom of Norwich was presented to Wilkes in a gold box. Norfolk, a county as yet unaware of the apostle of liberty it had spawned in Tom Paine, had a long tradition of radicalism and dissent which was to increase as the century progressed. As Burke wrote to Garrick the following year: 'Yorkshire has begun to move and its progress will be, I trust, great and powerful like a giant refresh'd with wine.' The hope was realized and no Wilkeite could be disappointed.

The repeal of his outlawry had left the way open for Wilkes' case against Lord Halifax for wrongful arrest. It came to trial at the Court of Common Pleas in Westminster Hall on Friday, 10 November 1769. The trial lasted until eight o'clock, when the jury brought in a verdict for Mr Wilkes, awarding him £4,000 damages. 'Several gentlemen gave two guineas to obtain admittance into the court early, at about ten the price fell to a guinea, and at three in the afternoon people got in for five-and-threepence.'[1]

---

[1] William Purdie Treloar: *Wilkes and the City* (Murray, 1917).

148

Even Chatham, pulling himself out of the slough of melancholic despair into which port and natural temperament had plunged him, appeared like a ghost in the House of Commons to propose a bill of Wilkes' reinstatement. Lord Mansfield made reflections on Wilkes' character in opposing the motion, and Chatham's response was worthy of his political judgment at its best:

'The character and circumstances of Mr Wilkes have been very improperly introduced into this question, not only here, but in that court of judicature where his cause was tried, I mean the House of Commons. With one party he was a patriot of the first magnitude; with the other the vilest incendiary. For my own part I consider him merely and indifferently as an English subject, possessed of certain rights which the laws have given him, and which the laws alone can take from him. I am neither moved by his private vices nor by his public merits. In his person, though he were the worst of men, I contend for the safety and security of the best; and God forbid, my lords, that there should be a power in this country of measuring the civil rights of the subject by his moral character, or by any other rule but the fixed laws of the land.'[1]

Thirty-six voted for Chatham, 203 against. He was not silenced. 'I do avow that Colonel Luttrell is no representative of the people', he declared a few months later. 'He is a mere nominee, thrust in by enemies of the laws of the land, and to the principles – the established principles – of the Constitution.' The whole Middlesex business, he later added in a fine phrase, was an 'alarm-bell to liberty'.[2]

When his motion for Wilkes' reinstatement was negatived (he failed to carry the Rockingham Whigs), he suggested an address to the King for immediate dissolution, which was defeated by the same means. By this time (May 1770) Wilkes was out of prison, which he had left on 17th April. His cup of triumph was full.

[1] *Parl. Hist.* vol xvi; W. F. Rae: *Wilkes, Sheridan, Fox: The Opposition under George the Third* (1874).
[2] *ibid.*

IX

'WILKES AT LIBERTY'

Although many of the City merchants were traditionally puritan (at least in comparison with the aristocracy) and politically conservative, there were signs of a serious change of heart. On 2 January 1769, before his discharge, Wilkes had been elected Alderman for the Ward of Farringdon Without, 'the largest and best ward in London' according to the author of *Wilkes and the City*, W. P. Treloar, who had himself been elected to it in 1881. The City was beginning to consider its interests were on Wilkes' side.

Wilkes was not initially unopposed: at noon '. . . the Lord Mayor held a wardmote at St Bride's Church in Fleet Street, for the election of an Alderman of Farringdon–Ward Without in the room of the late Sir Francis Gosling, when John Wilkes Esq. and Mr Bromwich a paper-hanger on Ludgate Hill were severally put up; at which time there appearing an amazing number of hands in favour of Mr Wilkes, and very few for Mr Bromwich, Mr Wilkes was declared elected; but a poll being demanded by the friends of Mr Bromwich, the same began immediately and closed at three.'

In fact, Wilkes had received 255 votes and Bromwich 69, and 'about three o'clock in the day Mr Bromwich declined giving his friends any further trouble, and Mr Wilkes was declared duly elected admidst the shouts of a prodigious number of people'.

Wilkes celebrated in jail, giving a dinner by invitation in the King's Bench Prison to common-councilmen of his new Ward. 'Mr Wilkes received them in the politest manner. The dinner was plain and elegant and composed of presents received from Mr Wilkes' friends in town and country as a testimony of their joy and satisfaction at his election'. . .'the evening concluded with greatest mirth, decency and unanimity'. It would seem from the decency that Wilkes was on his best behaviour and in no mood to damage his new City status with even a *risqué* story. It is doubtful if he needed the presents of food on his election, and earlier gifts though elegant had certainly not been 'plain'. Apart from turtles from Massachusetts, 'during the space of last week', reported the London column of *The Sussex Weekly Advertiser* on 4 December 1769, 'Mr Wilkes has received from his friends in different parts of the kingdom upwards of 100 braces of partridges, pheasants, hares, and other game'.

On 14th March the next year, the Lord Mayor had presented to the King a 'remonstrance of the livery' on Wilkes' behalf. It was naturally dismissed, but motions continued to be made in Parliament, and petitions from various parts of the country supported the demand for Wilkes' release and the removal of Luttrell from his seat in the House of Commons. The campaign was personally stimulated by Wilkes' followers, who travelled to many of the areas, notably John Horne and two new young Members of Parliament, both soon to be deeply involved in City affairs, James Townsend and John Sawbridge. (Sawbridge became Alderman in 1769, Sheriff from 1769–70, and succeeded Wilkes as Lord Mayor, 1775–6.) Eighteen counties in all sent petitions and over a dozen boroughs, including, outside London, Canterbury, Exeter, Bristol, Liverpool, Berwick-on-Tweed (apparently regretting its earlier rejection of Wilkes as parliamentary candidate!), Worcester, Durham and Newcastle. In Yorkshire, the progress of the petition was watched with misgivings by one of the substantial class of freeholder always most likely to be opposed to Wilkes, John Robinson, of neighbouring Westmorland: 'It gives me concern to find the Quakers and Dissenters are so infatuated . . . as to sign and support it.'[1] Ecclesiastical dissent, as the radical movement grew, was often to ally itself to such movements for reform, and the Quakers had issued a resolution against slavery as early as 1724. In Kent, Essex and elsewhere also petitions survived the disapproval of the local

[1] Brit. Mus. Add. MS 38206: letter dated 3 November 1769.

gentry.[1] It was not only in Westminster, Middlesex and the City, but throughout the country, that the Wilkes issue and its parliamentary and libertarian implications had taken hold of the public imagination. The demonstration as a source of protest, begun in the time of John Lilburne, had revived and become an integral part of English political life.

Although in prison Wilkes could take no direct part in City affairs, his civic career was open for him on his emergence from the King's Bench, and he seized on it as his next objective. Already he had his eyes on the Mayoralty. He took a house in Fulham (then in the country) and no doubt enjoyed the repercussions of his release from prison, celebrated throughout England and beyond on a gratifying scale. In Bradford:

'. . . the morning was ushered in with the ringing of bells, which continued till ten at night, and in the evening were illuminations, and the following, we hear, was given at the sole expence of Mr Richard Shackleton, at the Bull's Head, viz. A bonfire of 45 of coals: a curious representation of the figures 45, composed of 45 candles, under which was wrote in large characters, Wilkes at Liberty: also a supper to the sons of Liberty, which consisted of 45 lbs. of roast beef; legs of mutton and tongues 45 lb.; three hams 45 lb.; 45 fowls; a lamb, 45 lb. of bread; 45 lb. of vegetables; 45 gallons of ale and 45 bowls of punch.'

In Boston, far away in America, the health of 'the illustrious martyr to Liberty' was drunk at a public dinner. Illuminations in Bristol, celebrations in Lynn and other Norfolk towns, the hanging of Luttrell in effigy in the West Country, and the decoration of Alderman Beckford's mansion in Soho Square with the word 'Liberty' in bold white letters three feet high, were only a few of the outward marks of public delight.

[1] Lucy S. Sutherland: *The City of London and the Opposition to Government* (University of London, Athlone Press, 1959). Miss Sutherland points out that only eighteen out of forty English counties sent petitions: but her underestimate of Wilkes' character and reform record causes her to tend to overstress the views of the squirearchy inevitably opposed to him and to underestimate the substantial nature of this movement of support, among a people without franchise or any official procedures for protest.

William Beckford, Pitt's friend, born in Jamaica (which made him valuable on West Indies trade and affairs), and successively Member of Parliament for Shaftesbury and London, had been Lord Mayor from 1762-3 and again from 1769-70. He was therefore Lord Mayor at the time of Wilkes' release (17 April 1770) and had already by this year produced (in Lucy Sutherland's words) 'the three-fold programme of reform – shorter parliaments, a place and pension bill and the more equal representation of the people'. Wilkes' own later support of similar measures in the House probably owed something to his association with Beckford.

In Parliament, the King had acquired a new 'Friend'. 'Stormed at by Pitt, scurrilously libelled by the able but malignant political writer who signed himself Junius, hooted down by the mob of London, and abandoned by the "King's Friends" in his moment of distress, Grafton resigned.'[1] The new equivalent of Prime Minister was Lord North, who for the next twelve years (1770–82) was pliant enough to allow himself to be used as the King's instrument. The loss of America was to be the epitaph of the George III/Lord North administration.

Wilkes, before settling down to his duties as an Alderman, celebrated his release with a trip to that eighteenth-century city of eternal pleasure, Bath, and in August made the first of what was to be an annual holiday tour of Kent, Sussex and Hampshire, frequently extended to Cambridgeshire, Norfolk and the West. Not only Lewes rang the church bells in his honour; it was to be a feature of Wilkes' almost royal progress in towns across the whole of southern England from East Anglia to the farthest reaches of the West Country.

One of his first objectives after Bath was the welcoming country house of the new Sheriff Sawbridge in Kent, as indeed had been rumoured in the London column of *The Sussex Weekly Advertiser* as early as 31 March 1770, a fortnight before his release. Nor were his excited prospective hosts always City men. 'Great preparations are already making among the nobility against the enlargement of Mr

[1] Charles Oman: *A History of England* (1895).

Wilkes', reported the same columnist, 'who is said already to have received upwards of fifty invitations from the most respectable personages.'

The progress, however, was not entirely for pleasure. Wilkes began it on 1st August at Guildford, where John Horne, following a trial for defamatory libel (with Lord Mansfield as his formidable judge) at Kingston the previous year, was now further arraigned on the same charge at the Surrey Assizes. [1] At Guildford he lost his case, the plaintiff being awarded damages of £400; but it did not repress the buoyant Horne's spirits, and in fact he successfully challenged the verdict, and got it reversed, in April the following year. Meantime, on the evening of 1st August, he and Wilkes dined at the house of Serjeant Glynn (lawyer to them both) together with Alderman Oliver and other blithe spirits undimmed by the Guildford verdict.

Wilkes then passed through Epsom to Croydon, staying overnight at the George Inn, and proceeded on 2nd and 3rd August through Dartford, Rochester and Sittingbourne to Dover. Here he met Polly, joyously recalled from Paris to join the ex-prisoner. A wit on *The Sussex Weekly Advertiser* celebrated these mixed adventures in metaphorical verse:

SHIP NEWS EXTRORINARY

Arrived at Guildford, the Englishman, Capt Horne
At ditto the Verdict, Capt Onslow.
At Dover, the Liberty, Capt Wilkes,
At ditto, the Supporter, Capt Trevarion.
At the Treasury, the Grafton's Prize, Capt North.

(Lord North, sailing towards American tempests, had just succeeded Grafton at the head of the Government.)

On 3rd August the reunited father and daughter moved on from Dover to Canterbury, according to Wilkes' Engagement Diary, and by 7th August they had reached Margate, where, reported a Canterbury columnist in *The Sussex Weekly Advertiser*, they 'dined with Mr Macnamara; in the evening

---

[1] Mansfield had overplayed his hand by trying to take the matter out of the hands of the jury: comparisons with Star Chamber had resulted in a re-trial on the ground of 'misdirection on the part of the judge'.

he went to the rooms, where was a brilliant assembly. Mrs Brooke (relect of the late Robert Brooke Esq.) very politely made him an offer (which he accepted) of her house, with the bed and apartments reserved for, and used by his late Majesty on his return from his German dominions . . . The bells rung, and there was a general display of colours from the steeple and vessels in the harbour, with the firing of the large cannon on the fort, which have not been discharged sincethe landing of his late Majesty, and an exhibition of fireworks on the parade concluded the joyous day. During his stay here, he was treated, by all degrees of people, with the greatest respect.'

The royal nature of the reception could hardly have been more emphasized. There is, though, a discrepancy between Wilkes' Engagement Diary and the newspaper, for it was not until the Sunday after, the columnist reports, that the travellers arrived at Canterbury, where they stayed one-and-a-half hours, inspected the Fountain, and 'then set off for the seat of John Sawbridge, Esq., at Ollintigh'. Tunbridge Wells, Uckfield, Lewes, Brighthelmstone, Rottingdean and New-haven were visited by the indefatigable travellers from 14th August, and by the end of the month they reached Bramber, Chichester, Goodwood and Petworth, working their way back home through Hampton Court to Fulham.

In February 1771 Wilkes again visited the Rose Inn, Cambridge, and moved through Wisbeach to King's Lynn, where he was sworn in as a Freeman of the town and dined with the Mayor and Corporation, and at the Mayor's house the following day. In July the same year he visited the dockyard at Chatham and (according to his Diary) 'went on board the *Victory*, a man of war of 100 guns, repairing there'. (At the end of his long life, but seven years before the Battle of Trafalgar, Wilkes was to meet the *Victory*'s most famous commander, Admiral Nelson, when Nelson was given the freedom of the City of London.) The following year, 1772, his itinerary embraced Portsmouth, the Isle of Wight, Exeter, Exmouth and Southampton; from July to August 1773 he was 'rambling about Sussex'; and in August 1774 he was once again in Lewes, although it is unlikely this time he met

155

Thomas Paine, who earlier that same year had parted from his wife and his situation in the Excise, and returned to scientific pursuits in London. In September, with the recommendation of Dr Benjamin Franklin, Paine left for America, at a momentous moment in its history. Wilkes had dined with Franklin at Fitzmaurice's in Pall Mall on 14 May 1773, and it is tempting to wonder if Franklin, when he met Paine a year later, mentioned meeting the 'liberty' hero and if Paine compared notes, remembering Wilkes' visit to Lewes with the acclamations and ringing bells of four years before.

In London, Wilkes gathered round him a fairly new set of friends, not from the aristocracy but by no means all deeply involved with him in politics. David Garrick, the actor, was one, in spite of amicably acting as go-between between Grafton and Wilkes in prison; and he proved amenable, when John Horne, unexpectedly remembering his original profession, protested at a dubious reference in a play to meddling priests, to making the required excision. Wilkes had, of course, known Garrick some ten years before, when he let his Paris apartment to him. Garrick had descended on London from Lichfield in 1737, in company with his friend and tutor Dr Johnson, and Johnson, after some earlier passages of arms, was becoming resigned to accepting Wilkes in the community, and was soon to meet him at dinner under Boswell's discreet manipulation. Wilkes' solicitor Reynolds; the fencing and riding master Angelo, who had been one of Garrick's most imaginative theatrical designers;[1] John Horne; Humphrey Cotes the wine merchant (readily forgiven for his bankruptcy *débâcle*): these were among his regular companions.

More exotically, there was the strange transvestite figure, the Chevalier d'Eon, whom many believed to be a Mlle d'Eon more especially when he took, rather late in life, to appearing constantly in woman's dress. Wilkes already knew him from Paris, where in fact, as throughout Europe, d'Eon

---

[1] His real name was Domenico Angelo Melevolti Tremondo and he had adapted for Garrick's Christmas Harlequinade in 1758 the idea of Canaletto's first *tableaux mouvants*, which he had seen at the Venice carnival.

acted as a secret service agent, for which particular government, and on what particular political, military or diplomatic matters, was never entirely clear: perhaps not always to the governments themselves (he was rumoured in some quarters to be a double agent). Horne Tooke many years later was to recount the piquancy of sitting between this social oddity and the author of *Rights of Man*. There was also the Corsican, Paoli, Boswell's hero, who often dined at the Angelos with Wilkes and d'Eon. Grafton's well-meaning but desultory gesture of help to Corsican liberty from Genoese rule had come too late, and Paoli had been forced into exile in England, where he was much fêted by London ociety.

Wilkes took plays, players and playwrights in his stride alongside most of the notabilities of the day. The Garricks provided the bridge between theatrical and artistic bohemia and high society, which people like Wilkes, Joshua Reynolds and Sheridan (whom Wilkes, too, met) also spanned. It cannot be true, as Garrick's biographer, Carola Oman, claims, that Wilkes turned up with a party intent on wrecking Hugh Kelley's *A Word to the Wise* at Drury Lane on 3 March 1770 (Kelley, considered a government hireling and author of a previous play which attacked the Drury Lane company, was unpopular with the crowd and Garrick was forced to abandon the play after considerable barracking by the audience). Wilkes, as we know, was not released from the King's Bench until 17th April and there is no evidence at all to connect him with ill-mannered hustling of this kind, in the theatre or outside it. But he and the devotedly married, unraffish actor and ex-dancer sustained a pleasant occasional relationship, and Wilkes dined with them both at Garrick's splendid country mansion at Hampton (where Wilkes' old enemy Hogarth had painted them) and at their house in the superb new Adam terrace The Adelphi, built on the slopes between the Strand and the Thames. Here Wilkes could have admired the green drawing-room, with its chairs and sofa of japanned green and yellow and, probably very much to his taste, the ceiling painting by Zucchi of Venus adorned by the Graces, in a miasma of pink and blue clouds.

The Garricks had moved there from Southampton Street over a period of days in March 1772, accompanied by twenty-two horseloads of new furniture from the premises of Messrs Chippendale Haig in St Martin's Lane, to suit the room arrangements specifically designed by the architect, Robert Adam, himself. (Garrick, during this monolithic upheaval, had been left stranded in the old house, irritably searching for a chair, ink and paper in order to write a letter.)

On 22 May 1772 Wilkes also went to Sadler's Wells, recently given a new lease of fashionable life under the management of Mr King, who five years later joined Sheridan at Drury Lane to be the original Sir Peter Teazle in *The School for Scandal*. The Wells was no longer a spa: in 1764 the well had been covered over and the old wooden theatre pulled down and rebuilt at a cost of £4,225. (After a newer theatre still had been built on this site near the Angel, Islington, in 1931, under the management of Lilian Baylis which saw the birth of the Sadler's Wells Opera and Ballet, interested theatregoers were still sometimes shown the spot, under the floor at the back of the auditorium, where the old well still lurked and bubbled.)

The lowering of class contacts in the City, however, did not entirely rob Wilkes of a touch of snobbery, a consciousness of his own university-trained elegance. The manners of certain City aldermen at table irritated him, and he was not above reprimanding one Burnel (a bricklayer, who became Lord Mayor) of using his fork like a trowel. Nevertheless, he was not above, either, enjoying his position as Alderman, and it is often overlooked that many City merchants, like Beckford, had long been responsible Members of Parliament with friends in high places, while others (not always opposed to Wilkes politically) belonged to the nobility, even if often younger sons with their way to make in the world.

Class-consciousness as such was not a special feature of eighteenth-century life, although human nature being what it is it probably existed, as throughout history, to a greater extent than some modern social historians have been prepared to acknowledge. Sons of rich tradesmen, like Wilkes, bestrode the classes; but wealth, education and manners still set a man, in the world's eyes, above his fellows, and the resentment of those not admitted to the restricted franchise and education, or despised and feared as a 'mob' (an ambivalent and never accurate term) who might encroach on privilege and power, was probably not much different in its sense of social barriers from that felt by what we call the 'underprivileged' today. Wilkes made a few enemies among even those whose support he most needed in the City, although his infrequent odd remarks – thrown out mainly as 'bon mots' – suggesting social superiority have no doubt been exaggerated. The fact that he retained the support of the working classes to so remarkable a degree shows that his treatment of them generally must have been good-humoured and singularly lacking in condescension. Their common link was a sense of humour, a feature of the British working class which has been too often overlooked. Satire has always been one of its sharpest weapons, as writers from Dickens to G. K. Chesterton have realized. The ebullience, though feared by the upper classes, was often good-natured enough (like the burnings in effigy and obsession with the petticoats of the Princess-Dowager and the jackboots of her supposed lover). When the mob turned dangerous there were usually other elements in it than the more respectable citizens, and far more provoking social causes.

Polly, soon after their tour and his re-establishment in London society, had been sent again to Paris, and he wrote to her: 'I was sworn into office without any opposition; and all the Aldermen present took me by the hand and wished me joy with great *apparent* cordiality. I never heard such loud exclamations, nor so frequently repeated.' With memories of certain unhappy Channel crossings, he added a prayer to his 'dear daughter to drink plentifully of green tea, if she is sea-sick'. Where she was concerned, his generosity was always lavish: 'Whatever clothes you wish', he once wrote, 'desire Mme Carpentier to pay for. Any money you want, you may have . . . I beg you never to miss the Ambassador's chapel on Sunday. I wish you to inquire about the dancing master belonging to the Court: he is the only man for you to learn of.

I wish you would soon get the best music-master . . . Read the best books and they will be your pleasure thru' life. Desire Mme Carpentier to buy for you Boileau, Racine and Molière; you cannot read them, beside Shakespeare, Pope and Swift, too often . . .' She was told again not to spare any expense for her 'pleasure and enjoyment: I will contrive'. He recommended a good coiffeur by the week or the month. It was, especially in Paris, the age of the skyscraper wig, much adorned with birds, baubles and butterflies.

For private comfort, now Polly was gone, he still had Mrs Barnard, and with the continued support of the Society of the Bill of Rights he rented a house in Princes Court again, at No. 7, for a rent of 50 guineas a year, as he wrote to Polly. On the corner of Birdcage Walk, it was a supplement to the countryside at Fulham, with friends in the form of a cat, a canary, a linnet and a bullfinch to console him when human charms were not available.

In Parliament he was not forgotten, nor did he lack influential support. Chatham had failed, a month after his release, to get the Lords to pass a bill reversing his expulsion, as we have seen, but Burke in his pamphlet, *Thoughts on the Cause of the Present Discontents*, not only attacked the King's arbitrary form of government in which royal favour was the dominant factor, but expressed strong criticism of Wilkes' treatment. 'This gentleman, by setting himself strongly in opposition to the Court cabal, had become at once an object of their persecution and of the popular favour . . . A strenuous resistance to every appearance of lawless power; a spirit of independence carried to some degree of enthusiasm; an inquisitive character to discover, and a bold one to display, every corruption and every error of Government; these are the qualities which recommend a man to a seat in the House of Commons, in open and merely popular elections.'

By inference, if not by statement, Burke was referring here to Wilkes, and he drove in another nail of reproof when he stated: 'I will not believe, what no other man living believes, that Mr Wilkes was punished for the indecency of his publications or the impiety of his ransacked closet . . . I must conclude that Mr Wilkes is the object of persecution, not on account of what he has done in common with others who are objects of reward, but for that in which he differs from many of them; that he is pursued for the spirited dispositions which are blended with his vices; for his unconquerable firmness, for his resolute, indefatigable, strenuous resistance against oppression.'

On 23 May 1770 the City presented a second re-monstrance to the King, in person. 'I should ill deserve to be considered as the Father of my People', replied the King loftily, 'if I made such use of the Prerogative as I think dangerous to the Constitution.' This 'short, dry answer', which His Majesty had decided on in advance as the best way of dismissing the business, did not to His Majesty's astonishment end the matter. The Lord Mayor, Beckford, so far from retiring voiceless answered His Majesty back, and made, tradition insists, an impromptu speech sustaining his point. The King was speechless, and the City enraptured. The valiant Beckford was awarded with immortality in the form of a statue in the Guildhall, commemorating the event. His speech is engraved in gold on the black marble base.

It has been claimed that Beckford, primed by Horne Tooke, did not actually make, in his confusion, the actual speech attributed to him: that he remembered and spoke some part of it, or only a few words of it. Horne Tooke certainly afterwards claimed to have written the speech for recording in the newspapers. He may have done so, but on Beckford's by no means unvocal or negligible record in Parliament, where ready eloquence is of far greater value and effect than the ability to write speeches, it is necessary I think to question Tooke's claims more seriously than some historians have done. It may well have been true that Horne 'shaped' the speech for the press: but that so experienced a House of Commons debater as William Beckford should have been bereft of words when confronted with the King (to whose form of rule he was not specially deferent) is unlikely. Tooke, a man of frustrated ambition, was not above taking more credit than his due: he was to disclaim two allies later, both Wilkes himself and Thomas Paine. In any case, as

161

Wilkes' biographer Raymond Postgate has pointed out, the fact that Beckford made a speech of some effect is proved by the fact that, before the next interview of a City delegation with the King, the Chamberlain demanded an assurance that the Lord Mayor would not answer the King in this manner. [1]

Shortly afterwards, on 21st June, Beckford died. Wilkes recorded the fact on Friday, 22 June 1770, with genuine sorrow: 'Yesterday morning the Lord-Mayor died, to our great grief. He had of late behaved with spirit and honour in the cause of liberty; and was of singular service to what we all have most at heart.' There was no man remaining of the calibre of this West India merchant, with his knowledge also of East India Company affairs, who in spite of his vast sugar plantations and many slaves had managed to preserve the rôle, in Parliament and the City, of a staunch spokesman for freedom and reform (he was not alone among rich supporters of reform movements, then or later, to be in this rather ambivalent position with regard to slavery).

Wilkes did not yet press his hand, and the oddly-named Brass Crosby was the next Lord Mayor. Crosby stopped 'profiteering' by the posting at Mark Lane market of the prices and amounts of corn deals and the names of the dealers, and Wilkes as magistrate early made his reforming presence felt by proclaiming press-warrants for the Navy illegal, discharging John Shine, a barber pressed into service at sea. Wilkes' gesture, however, proved unavailing, as the Lord Mayor, after consulting three lawyers, was forced to admit the system was legal in time of war. In the autumn of 1770 England was in the midst of a quarrel with Spain, and the Admiralty had ordered the City authorities to impress for service 'strong bodies capable to serve His Majesty'. Wilkes was overruled, not without openly criticizing 'a suspension of Magna Charta in the City' and, with old wounds pricking, declaring Press Warrants as illegal as General Warrants, because the victims were unspecified. He also showed himself well aware of the conditions that bred the reluctance to serve in the forces, and need for impressment:

[1] *That Devil Wilkes* (revised edn, Dobson, 1956): *Annual Register*, 1770.

'If the Government offered £5 bounty, instead of the paltry sum of thirty shillings, and if we promised their discharge after a certain number of years, we should have enough sailors without the citizens of London being made the prey of lawless ruffians.'

Wilkes' next attempt at reform was once again in support of the liberty of the press. In March 1771 George Onslow, who had once been Wilkes' friend, denounced the printers of two papers, the *Gazetteer* and the *Middlesex Journal*, for publishing reports of debates in the House of Commons. The attack was supported by the King, who disliked newspapers on principle as checks upon governmental power, and referred to them to Lord North as 'daily productions of untruths'. 'It is highly necessary that this strange and lawless method of publishing debates in the papers should be put a stop to.' The two printers, Thompson and Wheble, were ordered to attend the House of Commons, and at the suggestion of Wilkes, through Brass Crosby and Alderman Richard Oliver, they went into hiding. On 15th March John Wheble was 'arrested' by his chief compositor, a man named Carpenter, who brought him to the Guildhall where Alderman Wilkes was officiating. There is small doubt that this was carefully arranged by Wilkes, who heard the case and ordered Wheble to be discharged. He bound over Carpenter on a charge of assault and then sent him to the Treasury to claim the £50 award the Government had offered for apprehension of each of the printers. Wilkes calmly wrote to Halifax, now once again Secretary of State, informing him what he had done, and that Wheble's arrest had been 'in direct violation of the rights of an Englishman and of the chartered privileges of a citizen of this metropolis'.

The comedy was not yet played out. The House of Commons, duly provoked, sent a messenger to seize the printers who had reported the debates and one of them, Miller of the *Evening Post*, let the messenger into his house. A constable, with aforethought placed on the spot, immediately the messenger touched Miller charged him with assaulting a freeman of the City of London and all three departed for the

Mansion House. Here Wilkes, Crosby and Oliver heard Miller's complaint and ordered the messenger to give bail. As he could not do so, the magistrates signed an order for his committal to jail. It was prevented only by a serjeant-at-arms, who provided bail.

This disrespectful treatment of their messenger, as doubtless intended, infuriated the House of Commons. Lord Mayor Crosby and the Aldermen Oliver and Wilkes were ordered to the House forthwith. Wilkes had the perfect reply. He was, he reminded the House (as if it could forget) Member of Parliament for Middlesex, and until invited to attend in that capacity he declined to enter the hallowed precincts. Brass Crosby and Richard Oliver attended (Crosby not failing, probably on Wilkes' coaching, to remind everyone present that he was chief magistrate of the City of London, and guardian of its charter which he considered violated by the messenger of the House). After a stormy passage both were committed to the Tower of London for contempt. Crosby's journey there was not unlike that of Wilkes to the King's Bench. The crowd unharnessed his horses and dragged the coach to Temple Bar. Crosby, rather the worse for wear and liquor (many healths were probably drunk en route), reached the Tower early the next morning.

He and Oliver were not forgotten in prison. The Common Council voted them 'tables' at the City's expense (although Crosby declined) and they were visited by an impressive and surprisingly aristocratic array of well-wishers including Lord Temple, the Marquis of Rockingham, the Dukes of Manchester and Portland, Earl Fitzwilliam, Admiral Keppel and Edmund Burke. There were popular demonstrations in their favour, including the beheading on Tower Hill of effigies of the Speaker of the House of Commons, Charles and Stephen Fox, and the much-harassed and inevitable Princess-Dowager and Lord Bute. Similar treatment of Lord Halifax, Colonel Luttrell, Lord Sandwich ('Jemmy Twitcher'), Onslow and others followed. When finally released from the Tower on 8th May, the two heroic magistrates were saluted by the firing of twenty-one guns and accompanied by a welcoming and indeed wildly triumphant procession.

Messages of congratulation reached them from major English cities, and London (so erroneously, it would often seem, described in the eighteenth century as a dark city at night) was once again illuminated.

It was over this episode that the King declared he would have nothing more to do with 'that devil Wilkes' and he was 'below the notice of the House'. The House, however, thought otherwise. It ordered Wilkes to the Bar of the House and this time Wilkes saw to it that he had everyone's attention. He pointed out that no notice was taken of him 'as a Member of the House' and he was not required to attend in that capacity. The House ordered him a second time, and again, for a third, on 8th April. On the 9th they were due to adjourn, and they thus evaded the whole issue.

The great issue of liberty of the press remained once again with Wilkes the victor, and the Court of Common Council of the City of London, on 24 January 1772, voted:

'That a silver cup valued £200 be presented to Brass Crosby, Esq., their late worthy Lord Mayor, and two others, value £100 each, to Mr Sheriff Wilkes and Mr Alderman Oliver, for the noble stand they made in the business of the printers against an arbitrary vote of the House of Commons, for the preservation of the rights and liberties of their fellow-subjects in general.'

Wilkes' cup was engraved with a picture of the murder of Julius Caesar and the lines of his friend Charles Churchill:

Let every tyrant feel
The keen, deep searchings of a Patriot's steel.[1]

The right to report debates was never again disputed.

Another good deed of Wilkes as Alderman was to try and ensure that there was better treatment of the animals at Smithfield Market and in the slaughterhouses. Few of his time gave a thought to cruelty to animals, even if they gave it

---

[1] Polly inherited Wilkes' cup, which at her death went by Will to her cousin Lady Baker. It was sold at Christie's among the effects of the late Duke of Sussex on 27th June, 1843. 'It excited considerable competition, and was ultimately secured by Mr Russell for £45.'

to cruelty to human beings. In this, as some other things, Wilkes anticipated a later popular hero, Tom Paine.

In 1771 he was elected Sheriff for London and Middlesex, and increased his popularity by stopping the practice of having the military attend executions, of taking money for admission to the Court of Old Bailey, and of trying prisoners in chains. On 16 October 1771 he and his fellow-Sheriff, Alderman Bull, wrote to the keeper of Newgate Prison:

'There are however two glaring abuses of Importance which we are determined to rectify at the ensuing Sessions on Wednesday next, and all the subsequent Sessions during our Shrievalty. The first is the prisoners remaining in irons at the time of arraignment and Trial – This we conceive to be equally repugnant to the Laws of England and of humanity, every person at so critical a moment ought to be without any bodily pain or restraint, that the mind may be perfectly free to deliberate on its most interesting and awful concerns in so alarming a situation. It is cruelty to aggravate the feelings of the unhappy in a state of such distraction . . . No man in England ought to be compelled to plead while in chains . . .

'The other abuse we are determined to reform is the taking of money for admission into the Court at the Old Bailey . . . It is one of the most glorious privileges of this nation that our Courts of Justice must always be open and free &c – We need not enumerate to you the constant complaints made on this subject every Session, and the tumults occasioned by the exactions of the Officers . . .'

At the end of their term Wilkes and Bull even made a move to redress the appalling number of crimes punishable by death under a legal system which had been crystallized in Blackstone's *Commentaries on the Laws of England* in 1765, and which was not to be seriously challenged until Jeremy Bentham published his *Fragment of Government* in 1776. The two Sheriffs recommended 'a revision of the laws which inflict capital punishment for so many inferior crimes'.

In 1772 and 1773, Wilkes was returned head of the poll for Lord Mayor, but rejected by the Court of Aldermen. It was

an awesome experience for the 1772 elected Mayor, who on
9th November, Lord Mayor's Day, had to endure a rioting
crowd of Wilkeites to the number, it was said (although it
was probably an exaggeration) of three thousand. Guests
arriving for the Lord Mayor's party were pressed for money
'to drink Mr Wilkes' health', and it was two in the morning
before the crowd dispersed. Seven were taken as prisoners,
three of them only were actually tried, and of these two were
acquitted and the third given a five-weeks' sentence. Perhaps
the magistrates were cowed; equally likely, they were
Wilkeites themselves.

Friendships and associations, however, soon began to suffer
from the human failing of conflicting personalities. One of
these now disputing friends was Laughlin Macleane, Under-
Secretary to Lord Shelburne. Macleane had first known
Wilkes in Paris, and Wilkes as already recounted had stayed
with him briefly in one of his illegal trips to England from
France. Apparently Macleane had lent Wilkes a sum of
money in their Paris days and, perhaps under financial
pressures himself, and aware of Wilkes' mounting City
success, he now reminded him of the debt. Whether in fact
Wilkes repaid him seems unclear, but the difference was soon
apparently overcome.

Horne Tooke's defection was a more prolonged, bitter and
public matter. The Bill of Rights Society had granted Wilkes
from its funds, collected on his behalf, £1,000 a year, and
Horne had recently tried in vain to get some of the Society's
funds diverted to aid a protégé of his own. This both the
Society and Wilkes had opposed as being outside its intended
scope. With the panache of a frustrated knight errant, and
stung also by press criticisms of himself, Horne now (January
1771) launched into a series of letters attacking Wilkes in the
Public Advertiser, concentrating much, and with surprising
pettiness, on Wilkes' supposedly luxurious way of life,
servants bedecked with gold lace, and cellars filled with
choice French wines.

There is no doubt Horne's own tastes, although he had
income enough to keep him (and his two natural daughters,
euphemistically known as the 'Misses Hart') in reasonable

comfort, were less socially elegant than Wilkes', but his mistakes about Wilkes' homes and spending seem to have been genuinely exaggerated, for Wilkes was provoked into public repudiation of Horne's assessment of his rent (confirmed by his letter to Polly) and use of various houses, one of which Wilkes maintained had been let to provide income. Wilkes in his replies kept his temper, reasonableness and good manners, which Horne did not, and Horne's accusations of graft in the election for Parliament of Wilkes' friend and lawyer Serjeant Glynn, and in Wilkes' obtaining of lucrative City posts for his friends and relatives (which in fact they did not obtain) seem to have been pure conjecture without substance. The correspondence in public reached its nadir when Horne brought up the matter of Wilkes' pasting of his (Horne's) letters of years before in an album to entertain his Paris friends (Wilkes replied that if so it was a compliment), and accused Wilkes of pawning, for his own resources, the unparsonly clothes he had left in his care in Paris! Wilkes had no difficulty in repudiating this and proving he had merely placed them for safety in the house of a friend, when he himself left. He characteristically and finally broke off the correspondence when Horne made a tactless reference to Polly's expensive visit to Paris to see the Dauphin's wedding.

The dispute was not without its entertained audience: 'Wilkes and Parson Horne have a civil war', wrote Horace Walpole.

The only interest in this long series of extraordinarily irrelevant public letters is in the strange psychological light they throw upon Horne Tooke, a man praised for his legal acumen (although he was debarred the profession, after full training, on a political/clerical quibble) and certainly often an advocate of genuine sincerity and distinction in the cause of political protest. Like Wilkes himself, however, he was late in life to dissociate himself from some of its more progressive aspects, and deny an attachment to the ideas of Thomas Paine which he had certainly (in active association with Paine) not maintained in 1791. He had, in fact, lent his signature to a specifically libertarian analysis of govern-

mental failure attributed to Paine in an *Address* at a meeting
of the Friends of Universal Peace and Liberty, held at
the Thatched House Tavern on 20 August 1791, and
subsequently published. In his trial for treason in 1794,
Tooke stated that his object 'did not go as far as Mr
Paine's'.[1] The trials of radical writers in 1794 came in the
wake of Paine's own trial for 'seditious libel' in 1792, and
Tooke was of course aware of the fact: hence perhaps the
disclaimer.

It is a not untypical indication of Wilkes' good nature and
failure to nurse resentments that twenty-five years later, when
Horne Tooke contested the election in Westminster, Wilkes,
now City Chamberlain, 'appeared in front of the hustings;
and, after an elegant compliment to the public virtues,
talents, and fortitude of Mr Horne Tooke, gave him his *sole*
vote'.[2] (Tooke, with 2,819 votes, lost the election to Fox,
3,961 votes. Sir Alan Gardner gained 3,884.) It is ironic to
note that by this time Tooke, earlier so stringent on Wilkes'
indebtedness to his admirers of the Society of the Bill of
Rights, was himself largely dependent on others for his
pecuniary support in the election. As Westminster was
allowed two Members of Parliament and the electors two
votes, Fox was of course the candidate with whom Tooke was
politically in alliance, and Wilkes' failure to use his second
vote indicates a long-standing difference with Fox on some
issues, and perhaps here at least a remembrance of Fox's
youthful support of Luttrell's being given his parliamentary
seat. This was, of course, before Fox's Whig conversion.
Tooke was not so ungenerous in one of his election speeches:

'Gentlemen, a nation that has been treated as this has
been, has a right to demand two things – security for the
future, and justice for the past!!! One of the candidates, Mr
Fox, by his declarations to you from the hustings, has given

---

[1] Melvin J. Lasky: 'The English Ideology' (*Encounter*, Dec. 1972). Mr Lasky's
series of articles in *Encounter* on this theme are a valuable contribution to studies
of the radical ideology and writers of this period and earlier. See *Bibliography*,
and Mr Lasky's book, *Utopia and Revolution* (Chicago University Press, 1974)
which incorporates the material.

[2] Alexander Stephens: *Memoirs of John Horne Tooke* vol. II (1813).

you full reason to be satisfied, that he will exert his utmost endeavours to obtain them both for you.'

Another dissension during Wilkes' years as an Alderman was with his City supporters, Sawbridge, Townsend and Oliver (Oliver at least owed his progress to Wilkes, but the young do not always wish to remember and acknowledge their first patrons). Sawbridge and Wilkes fell out at a meeting of Westminster electors, and the parties were probably not helped towards reconciliation when Horne took Sawbridge's part. When Wilkes stood for Sheriff, against Oliver, Horne had again thrown in his weight with his rival.

In the Sawbridge-Wilkes controversy there were again entertained onlookers. Lord Rockingham tended to favour Wilkes, not unshrewdly:

'In regard to the great quarrel now subsisting between Mr Wilkes and Mr Horne and James Townsend &c, I own my partiality is towards Mr Wilkes . . . If in the end Wilkes gets the better, he will be a great power but perhaps not so dangerous as the others would be if they get the rule, and probably too *Wilkes single* in the end would be easier to manage than a whole pandemonium.'[1]

Meanwhile, Wilkes continued his holiday tours, gathering support but complaining (at Swanage, 'a rascally dirty little town') that he was 'stunned with the ringing of bells'. He was certainly not intimidated into hyperbolic praise by the warmth of his reception: at Brixham he declared himself provoked to find no memorial to the historic landing of King William III, although he admitted the people were 'very staunch for liberty'. He himself seems to have had a particular predilection for Sussex. Never a gambler, he left Lewes to avoid the races (prominently posted in the Coffee House owned by Thomas Paine's friend, Henry Verral); but he admired the beauty of the downs at Eastbourne and the villages 'happily embosomed in the trees. But I prefer Brighthelmstone: the sea appears there with more majesty and dignity.' Always a hopeful connoisseur of painting, he

---

[1] Letter to Burke, 3 February 1771. *Burke Correspondence*, vol. ii.

paused to admire the Holbeins at Cowdray, and maintained his connection with the principal ornament of the English stage by taking a holiday in 1772 with Garrick, with whom he visited Lord Shelburne's brother.

In London, he had met an old friend. During the Wilkes agitations and his imprisonment in the King's Bench during 1768 and 1769, Boswell had thought it expedient not to renew his acquaintance; although Wilkes, when the publisher of one of the French translations of *An Account of Corsica*, not knowing Boswell's address, sent him a copy of the book care of the King's Bench Prison, had forwarded it with many compliments. 'I had a desire to visit the pleasant fellow' wrote Boswell, 'but thought it might hurt me essentially.' He had been confirmed in this attitude by hearing that Lord Mansfield (whom he visited on 29 March 1772) 'was so angry at me for having in some degree spoken well of Wilkes at his levée in spring 1768 . . . that he had declared he would never let me into his house again'. In a letter to Mansfield found among the Boswell papers at Yale University, dated 14 February 1783, he in fact brought up this matter of giving him offence 'by speaking too favourably in your presence of the gay and classical John Wilkes . . .'[1] Boswell certainly at times lived up to the description of him by Thomas Holcroft, the radical playwright, in his 1798 Diary as 'servile . . . defending and condemning, not according to any principles which his own experience and observation had taught, but in conformity to those opinions, whatever they might be, right or wrong, which might most probably ingratiate him with the powerful'.

On 20 April 1772, only three weeks after visiting Mansfield, Boswell attended a Mansion House dinner. 'Don't sit by me', said Wilkes drily, 'or it will be in *The Public Advertiser* tomorrow . . . You should have come and seen a friend in gaol.' Boswell replied 'I do assure you I am glad to meet you, but I cannot come to see you. I am a Scotch laird and a Scotch lawyer and a Scotch married man. It would not be decent.' After Wilkes became Lord Mayor,

[1] *Boswell for the Defence, 1769-1774* (Ed. W. K. Wimsatt Jr and F. A. Pottle: Yale University Press, 1959; Heinemann, 1960).

Boswell apparently thought it was once again a safe friendship.

Wilkes also engaged in an inquisitive correspondence with Junius, which makes it quite clear that Wilkes had no real idea of his carefully-concealed identity: he may have suspected Temple, with whose wife's handwriting experts have sometimes compared that of Junius. Did he suspect Macleane? It is impossible to say. He certainly did his best to lure the mysterious pamphleteer to reveal his identity by a meeting: 'Does Junius wish for any dinner or ball tickets for the Lord Mayor's Day? How happy should I be to see my Portia dance a minuet with Junius Brutus.' But Polly, the Portia alluded to, never had this golden opportunity to captivate the most talked-about journalist of the age. 'Alas, my age and figure would do but little credit to my partner', declined Junius. The description may have been deliberately misleading. He had ceased regular operations on 10 May 1772 and was to preserve his secret intact across two centuries.

In 1773 Wilkes stood for Mayor with Bull against Sawbridge and Oliver, who were now supported by the Shelburne faction. Wilkes headed the poll by 35 votes from Bull, but when James Townsend's casting vote in the Court of Aldermen gave Bull the election, Wilkes did not quibble, for Bull was a good Wilkes supporter. It was generally agreed that his own election as Lord Mayor was only a matter of time. On 8 October 1774, at the third attempt, he was elected, only Townsend and Oliver voting against him. The crown of his rehabilitation was at hand. Parliament had just dissolved, and in the General Election on 29th October he was returned, once again, for Middlesex.

It was, to some extent, the end of the great 'Wilkes and Liberty' phase. There were no more riots, which had always centred in the south, although Liverpool and Newcastle were northern cities which notably supported the movement and Norfolk was as always encouragingly radical in its sympathies. Lynn, Norwich and Swaffham were prominent in this support and King's Lynn, as we have seen, conferred the freedom of its city on Wilkes 'for his constitutional, spirited and uniform conduct in support of the Liberties of this country'. Wilkes' possessions in Norfolk encouraged him to visit the area; but he was also popular in Essex and perhaps most of all in the West Country: Somerset celebrated Wilkes' election victory over Luttrell with processions and illuminations, and Exeter and Bristol (the Bristol newspapers making much of Wilkes' visits to Bath) were equally enthusiastic. When Wilkes visited Bristol in 1772, a banquet was held in his honour.

On 2 December 1774, a month after his inauguration as Mayor, Wilkes took his seat in the House of Commons without opposition. Horace Walpole, as so often, provided the contemporary commentary: 'Thus after so much persecution of the Court, after so many attempts on his life, after a long imprisonment in a gaol, after all his own crimes and indiscretions, did this extraordinary man, of more extraordinary fortune, attain the highest office in so grave and important a city as the capital of England.'

Living in London near St Martin's Lane at the time was a young and much-travelled French physician, Jean Paul Marat. Already the author of a number of medical and scientific tracts, he had published in London that same year, 1774, a work called *The Chains of Slavery*, much concerned with the English General Election and the abuse of power by the King. This should, he thought, be curbed, but Marat was not yet a republican. He was, however, an enthusiastic Wilkeite, and took some of that enthusiasm back to France. To the end he maintained that, for all its Government's defects, the English nation had better conditions and a greater degree of freedom than could be found anywhere else in Europe. At the height of the French Revolution he was to fall out even with Thomas Paine in continuing to hold that opinion.

X

LORD MAYOR OF LONDON

Polly returned from Paris to share in her father's mayoral glory. She was now a young woman of twenty-four, and on her father's release from prison four years before she had delighted him with her elegance and capacity for companionship, as they gaily celebrated his freedom by touring Sussex and Kent. In France she had proved like himself an informative and entertaining letter writer; in particular her indulgent father had sent her there so she could enjoy the festivities at the marriage of the Dauphin to Marie Antoinette, and her description did not disappoint him. Such accounts today are overcast with a peculiar poignancy, but at the time only the raging storm which quenched the fireworks of the wedding night provided the superstitious with a fatalistic hint of tragedy to come. 'I gave the Dauphin joy of so handsome a wife', wrote Wilkes, the connoisseur; 'I have seen a monarch who had three kingdomes to give, matched with less beauty than generally falls to the lot of a common mechanic . . . I do not think it a reproach for the Dauphin to fall asleep twice at a French opera, provided that the Dauphiness was not present – unless, indeed, she was the occasion of it.' With Wilkes, a touch of cynical wit could never be long suppressed.

As Peter Quennell wittily put it, 'only a lingering odour of brimstone clung to the Lord Mayor's robes'. The Lord Mayor's Show on 9 November 1774 tried hard not to be eclipsed, in Polly's memory banks, by the royal festivities in France. It was said to be the grandest London had yet seen, and was watched by huge crowds, not only of established Wilkeites. On 5th November, 'His Lordship waited on the Lord Chancellor in a new black japan post-coach, with a box to take off, drawn by a pair of cream-coloured long-tail geldings about fourteen hands and a half high, decorated with blue and silver tassels', and a further record entitled

'History of the Lord Mayor's Day', in the Guildhall Library
of press cuttings, painted the full scene:

'Ever since the great patriot has been elected to his high
office, and approved of by the Lord Chancellor, every
evening's conversation has turned upon the grand day of
festivity, and the applause his Lordship would receive from
his friends by water, in the city, and at Westminster Hall,
the ladies in particular had long been pregnant with
curiosity. . . . About eight o'clock many smart lassies, neat
and trim, from head to toe, were tripping to some friendly
house in the city to see the grand procession. Early in the
morning preparations were made at Guildhall for the
reception of the company. The steps and railing were
covered with crimson bays. There were twelve large
chandeliers, each holding four dozen of wax candles. . . .
From a little after seven o'clock till near nine, three porters
were employed in carrying hampers of wine from carts to
the bar-room. . . . A vast profusion of edibles was provided,
the pastry was of various exquisite kinds, and the ornaments
in confectionery very elegant. Soon after ten o'clock
immense crowds of people were assembled at the Three
Cranes, hundreds of whom took possession of the lighters
and other vessels, one of which, having a large mast, about
thirty people hung to the shrouds, and one man sat on the
top of the mast, smoking his pipe. . . . Two women fell from
barges into the Thames, but were soon got out. . . . Two
barges, with about a hundred people on board, slipped from
their moorings, and drove towards London Bridge, and
about twenty boats put off to recover them. . . . As soon as
the city barge took off, a wag said, "This is Wilkes's naval
review". Vast crowds of people took possession of the
Surrey shore, and guns from each bank of the Thames were
repeatedly fired till the company landed at Westminster.
The river has not for many years been covered with such
numbers of cutters, and other small boats, gaily ornamented
with awnings, flags and streamers. Soon after the procession
of water was gone, the Companies began to parade the
streets as usual. The marrow bones and cleavers played in

Cheapside, etc., while a band of young chimney sweepers, dressed in blue paper sashes, danced in honour of the day. . . . It was full five o'clock before the company arrived at Guildhall, and it is supposed some part of the procession was seen by at least two hundred thousand people. The Lord Mayor's coach was drawn by six grey horses, beautiful and spirited animals.

'While the procession was passing up Ludgate Hill, a woman with a child in her arms was thrown down by the crowd at the end of Fleet Street, and both trampled upon by the mob. They were both taken up dead. The child was a shocking spectacle.

'. . . A man was run over by a coach at Queenhithe and killed. A boat was overset near Queenhithe stairs by the waterman attempting to row the passengers nigh enough to see the Lord Mayor take water, and, it is said, six people were drowned.'

Tragedy and pomp: it was perhaps an inevitable combination in a London in which the crowds were undisciplined and police supervision, or its equivalent, scarcely existed.

The coach used by the Lord Mayor had been built in 1757, with panels said to have been painted by Cipriani and heraldic devices attributed to Catton, one of the foundation members of the Royal Academy, who was also coach painter to George III. It is still in use. At the Lord Mayor's Banquet that night some invited political opponents were conspicuously missing. One of them was Dr Johnson, repudiating Mrs Thrale's attempt to justify the 'liberal fellow'. Johnson merely grumbled that it would be a triumph for Wilkes to show him 'that he is just where the King, Lords, Commons and myself, forsooth, have all endeavoured to prevent him being'.

Unfortunately the Mayor himself was one of the least happy diners. He was attacked by the ague, and spent the next week in bed, 'a lesson to humble vanity and ambition', duly pronounced his enemies. He had his own back less than two weeks later, when he and Glynn were returned as Members of Parliament for Middlesex unopposed. The scene for the Wilkeites, nevertheless, was not unclouded, for Westminster was lost to two Court candidates, a disaster which might not have occurred had Wilkes not broken a promise to support Burke, who had actually considered standing and would almost certainly have won the seat. Even in the City, his party pledged to support his programme was not entirely successful: Frederick Bull and Wilkes' brother-in-law George Hayley, husband of his trendy sister Mary, were elected, but Brass Crosby, an undaunted and undauntable Wilkes supporter, was defeated by Oliver. Even Cotes, in Westminster, helped to split the Patriot vote by standing as an independent, though still slanting towards the Wilkes programme. Wilkes owed him for a heavy amount of wine-bills, not on his own account (Wilkes remained a fairly abstemious drinker) but for his expensive habit of hospitality.

Bull, soon after Wilkes became Mayor, had made him a present of 'his handsome set of black horses, which his Lordship used in the state coach on Friday, the first time since his Mayoralty', reported a newspaper on 26th November. Wilkes characteristically named the twelve returned members who supported his programme his Twelve Apostles. Doubtless his mind was less on the New Testament than on Brother Francis of Medmenham Abbey and his inner circle of twelve.

His position in Parliament was never easy. Financially he was hampered by having no 'pocket boroughs' under his corruptive influence; he had irreversibly alienated the Scottish members; and he was soon to prove far too friendly to the Americans for the average member of the House or even the general public. His unsalubrious reputation, moreover, was a handicap not only with the King but with many of the more sober of his colleagues in Parliament. He was totally out of line with the general parliamentary thinking of his day in his preference for the more open kind of election and better representation, issues which were to be taken up increasingly as the century approached its end. Thomas Paine's chief opponent on the issue of the French Revolution, Edmund Burke, was also totally opposed to

Paine's ideas on democratic election which were to become the driving objective of the agitators for the Reform Bill, and which Wilkes anticipated in a more tenuous way. Burke's first election as member for Wendover had been purely the result of Lord Verney's orders to the freeholders of the district: the seat, like so many, was literally in the gift of the local peer. His idea of the Whigs' right as a dominant party was based on 'long possession of government; vast property; obligations of favour given and received; connections of office; ties of blood, of alliance, of friendship . . .' Wilkes with his attempt at a programme based on some form of liberal policy, supported by members who were in the small minority of having been elected to their seats on popular support and merit, could make little headway within a House of Commons still dominated by the crown and the King's party, headed by Lord North, on the one hand, and the long-established Whigs in Opposition on the other.

Also Wilkes, in spite of his charm of manner, was not a good public speaker. To fling out small brief brilliancies of witty repartee in conversation is one thing: to deliver extempory, or with a feeling of spontaneity, a long speech on complex political and controversial matters is quite another. Even as a journalist Wilkes had no outstanding claim to distinction of writing, other than the purely polemical: George Rudé has referred to his 'brilliantly polemical speeches, letters and addresses' but he never, like Paine or Burke, coined a memorable phrase. Nothing he wrote has come down, quotably, in history in the literary sense; only the principles in which he became (more by accident than design) involved. His speeches in Parliament and elsewhere had to be painstakingly written in advance, and when he read them his delivery (like Robespierre's) was notably poor. The loss of his front teeth had now incommoded him further in this respect. Fox's speeches were said to be unreadable, but he could toss off immediately impressive-sounding arguments in the hubbub of Commons affairs. Wilkes, on the other hand, and fully conscious of his principal defect, cannily developed the habit of sending advance copies of his speeches to the press, thus at least ensuring more respectful consideration of what he had to say. It was a practice, like others of Wilkes', which was to become more regular in the future.

Nevertheless he had his moments of genuine force. On 16 April 1777 he attacked the Civil List which he maintained had been deliberately made incomprehensible. 'The nation, sir, suspects that the regular ministerial majorities in Parliament are bought . . . and that the Crown has made a purchase of this House with the money of the people. Hence the ready, tame, and servile compliance to every royal verdict issued by the minister. . . . It is almost universally believed, sir, that this debt has been contracted in corrupting the representatives of the people.' It was a charge repeated on many sides and sustained by the King's correspondence and that of others; and in 1781 Burke (who at this time tended to liberalism in spite of his views on representation) introduced a Reform Bill which included a scheme for the Civil List restricting the King from spending large sums on Parliamentary corruption. Burke's Bill, which perhaps owed something to Wilkes' earlier protest, was rejected; but in the following year, 1782, when Rockingham was recalled to office and Burke became Paymaster of the Forces, it was successfully re-presented and passed.

Wilkes' first speech in the House, on 26 January 1775, ruffled some feathers even more. The Chaplain of the House had arranged to deliver a special sermon on 30th January, the anniversary of the execution of Charles I, and there was a motion before the House that the date should also be commemorated with a fast. Wilkes thereupon boldly asserted that it should be 'celebrated as a festival, as a day of triumph, not kept as a fast'. As the Hanoverian line, in spite of its heavy teutonic base, inherited the English throne through a princess of the Stuart dynasty, and King George's penchant for dictatorial government was well known, this remark did not increase Wilkes' popularity in many quarters. Nor did his firm independence of party line endear him even to the Whigs, although a number of them liked him personally and were attached to some of his more liberal ideas. It was an age in which allegiance to party or faction counted above most things, and neither Wilkes nor his twelve apostles could be relied on for their support in any Opposition emergency. Wilkes tended to think for himself: a quality in keeping with eighteenth-century enlightenment in matters of religion and the arts, but not yet at all welcome within Parliament.

His greatest sphere of influence was still within the City, and there his prestige and his publicity image were immense. Wilkes had the keenest possible eye for vote-catching entertainment, and the Lord Mayor's Feast on Easter Monday would have done credit to King Louis XIV and Renaissance Italy. The figures of 'Pleasure' and 'Freedom' were voluptuously presented with three little cupid-like genii as attendants. A painting of Bacchus and Ariadne, an aptly Wilkesian symbol of wine united with love, decorated the feast, and doubtless reminded Wilkes of the ceiling at West Wycombe Park. Mechanical elephants (even Wilkes, piling up his debts, could not run to the real thing) waved their trunks, jewelled flowers bloomed at table, and rhinoceroses, more static than the elephants, held up cabinets of agate and gold that chimed like clocks. The ballroom was dominated by a vast painting of a landscape inhabited by dancing nymphs and their lovers, almost in the Tudor poetic tradition, and the food, on a princely scale, 'was much warmer than is commonly the case at these great dinners'. It would appear that the Lady Mayoress's expensive education in the French ballrooms, banqueting halls and *salons* had not been in vain. As her father's hostess in office she was a radiant success, but not surprisingly in more homely housekeeping tended to be haphazard and to outrun her budget (it was Wilkes, who in spite of his debts had in mundane matters an economical side, who seems to have accepted main responsibility for the running of their joint private household).

Certainly Polly moved now in the highest circles: 'The company were as elegant and orderly as the decorations', reported a newspaper on 18th April of this expensive entertainment. 'The Duke of Leinster and the Lady Mayoress opened the ball; Lord Mahon danced another minuet with the accomplished daughter of the giver of the feast. . . . The dancing of minuets, cotillons, allemandes, and country dances continued till three in the morning. . . . The lamps were illuminated in a new taste, and by the variety of their colours, disposed in wreaths upon the pilasters in imitation of the orders of architecture, gave a most pleasing effect to the whole.'

Another 'Sketch of the Lady Mayoress's Rout' noted that the company departed 'full of the praises of the Lady Mayoress who for affability, ease, attention, and politeness perhaps is superior to most of her sex. Much vivacity and wit passed amongst the company, and some humorous strokes were produced by the ladies' feathers. One beautiful woman dropping the plumes of her head, a gentleman presented them to the lady again, with observing, "that he believed this was not the time for *molting*".' On the morning of 17th April, when the Lord Mayor and Aldermen went from the Mansion House to St Bride's Church, the Lady Mayoress 'was dressed in rich silk, a maiden's blush, trimmed with a bouquet of diamonds in her bosom'.

Wilkes certainly was proud of her, and at the same time treasured the occasional privacy of meals alone with her. 'Dined for the first time at Mansion House with Lady Mayoress, etc.' notes his Diary for 8 January 1775, and the 'etc.' makes clear his comparative value of the persons present. The Mansion House was fairly new: it had been built of Portland stone near the site of the old Stocks Market, where nearly all the City buildings, except only the Guildhall, had been destroyed in the Great Fire of 1666. The first Lord Mayor to occupy it was Sir Crisp Gascoyne in 1745. He was the father of Bamber Gascoyne, in Wilkes' time the Member of Parliament for Barking, who was a close friend of Mary Wollstonecraft's father during the few years, in the childhood of the author of *Vindication of the Rights of Woman*, when he pursued his desultory and unsuccessful career as a farmer in the Barking area. Previously to Gascoyne's mayoralty, the Lord Mayor's own home had been used for the functions now officially held in the new Mansion House, which was not in fact entirely completed until 1753.

In 1775, therefore, the year of Wilkes' mayoralty, it was still a comparatively new building and to be invited there was something to be sought after. Boswell certainly seized the opportunity, feeling it quite safe, socially, to be present at the Lady Mayoress's Rout. A few weeks later, on 9th May, Wilkes noted in his Diary: 'At Mansion House with Miss Wilkes and James Boswell.' He described Boswell's *Life of Johnson* as 'a wonderful book', and Boswell, that inveterate lion-hunter, wrote and asked him to put this down in writing, so that he might 'have your *testimonium* in my archieves at Auchinleck'.

Wilkes was a painstaking Alderman and Lord Mayor, sitting on many committees, attending them assiduously, and walking to the Guildhall from his home in all weathers (it was his special antidote to age and method of preserving his still slim and elegant figure). As a magistrate he heard many petty cases and judged them with careful fairness, showing some knowledge of the law: imprisoning a fortune-teller who defrauded a maid of fourteen pence, although reluctantly, owing to lack of legislation to meet the case; discharging a hopeful holder of a ticket in the State Lottery who had tried to bribe the Blue Coat School boys who drew the lottery tickets. (The State Lottery was a cherished feature of eighteenth-century London, not yet oppressed by the Wesleyan antipathy to gambling. The mysterious Count di Cagliostro, who with his beautiful young Roman-born wife Serafina had turned up in London in 1775, gained much helpful notoriety by reputedly giving the number of the winning ticket in advance, to a few lucky or carefully chosen intimates.)

Outside the petty cases of the magistrate's court, Wilkes (who ahead of his time was an advocate of wholemeal bread for health reasons) launched a campaign against bakers who sold adulterated loaves for profit (a baker caught with 120 lb. of alum in his house was fined £10), and in the summer, after a good harvest, he fixed a reduced price for a peck loaf. Under his successor as Mayor the bakers tried to raise the price again, but Wilkes, the son of a distiller, firmly advised the new Mayor that the best wheat was sent to the brewers, not to the millers, in any case, and the price he had fixed remained unchanged. He also tried to control tradesmen who persistently gave short weight, as well as attempting to prevent the ill-treatment of animals at market, as has been seen.

Another surprising and impermanent action was clearing the streets of prostitutes, a gesture repeated by the police in Soho nearly 200 years later. A more permanent one was moving the Court of Aldermen from the Corn Exchange to the Mansion House.

Personal happenings during his mayoralty were not entirely satisfying. Humphrey Cotes died in July, having refused an order for wine for the Mansion House, and his heir proved an implacable chaser after unpaid bills. Mrs Barnard, it is said following a nightmare in which a dead daughter appeared accusingly, confessed all to her husband, the Wilkesian Alderman. After an acrimonious correspondence with Wilkes, whose injured innocence seemed highly unconvincing (he accused Mrs Barnard of being neurotically unbalanced), and ineffectually demanding 'satisfaction', the betrayed husband sent Wilkes a copy of his Will, in which he had left the seducer a bequest of £8,000 and valuable library, and announced his intention of revoking it.

He could not have hit Wilkes in a tenderer spot, for Lord Mayor of London was and is notoriously a position which only a very wealthy man can sustain, and Wilkes was once again in debt up to the eyeballs. Comparatively with his immediate predecessors and successors as Mayor, Wilkes' expenditure did not exceed revenue by more than the average, the difference chargeable to his private fortune being in fact less than in the case of Townsend and Bull (the actual figures in Wilkes' case were Revenue £4,889, Expenditure £8,226, Difference £3,337);[1] but he was in no position to meet the personal deficit and in fact a wiser man would have rejected the mayoralty in the first place. 'I am

[1] Charles Chenevix Trench: *Portrait of a Patriot* (Blackwell, 1962). Trench prints a useful Appendix of comparative mayoral costs and expenditure over a number of years. Similar figures are also given by W. P. Treloar in *Wilkes in the City* (Murray, 1917).

steeped in poverty to the very lips', he wrote to a friend in 1778. His record in office was so good, however, that the vote of thanks to him by the Court of Aldermen at the end of his period was unanimous apart from one vote (Harley's):

> 'THIS Court doth return thanks to the Right Honourable John Wilkes, late Lord Mayor of this City, for his indefatigable attention to the several duties of that important Office; for the particular regard and politeness which he has been pleased at all times to shew the Members of this Court; for his wise, upright and impartial Administration of Public Justice; for his diligence on all occasions to promote the Welfare and true Interest of this City and for his unblemished Conduct and exemplary behaviour during the whole course of his Mayoralty.'

This was on 21 November 1775. A few days before, on the 17th, the Common Council voted similar thanks, including (perhaps with succulent memories of Wilkes' entertainments and dinners) a recognition of his 'Supporting the Honour and Dignity thereof [i.e. of his office], with Splendour and Hospitality'.

Not only Polly, but Jackie Smith, had come back from France to enjoy his prominence in the City; and Jackie was soon to prove a further expense, inheriting much of his father's love of pleasure without the capacity to sustain it by brains or hard work. It was, of course, a fair enough criticism of John Wilkes himself when young; but it was now obvious he had wasted a lot of his energy and ability and although his virility showed small signs of declining, he had learned to lavish his considerable extra vitality on the requirements of his office.

Although his main activity for a time had been diverted to City affairs, as soon as his mayoralty was over he did all he could for certain causes in Parliament too. As early as 21 March 1776, as he was to remind his constituents later, he put forward a motion for a more equal representation in Parliament. It was designed to give additional members to London, Middlesex, Yorkshire and other large counties, all grossly under-represented in comparison with quite tiny 'rotten boroughs'; to disenfranchise these 'rotten boroughs' and add their electors to the county constituencies; and to enfranchise Manchester, Leeds, Sheffield, Birmingham and other rich and populous trading and manufacturing towns (Manchester, when Paine wrote *Rights of Man* in 1791, still had no parliamentary representation, as he pointed out, in spite of a population of some 60,000). It was, in fact, more fully democratic in intention than any suggestion of the kind outside extreme radical circles towards the end of the century; it aimed to enfranchise 'the meanest mechanic, the poorest peasant and day labourer'. The Reform Bill of 1832 was certainly not to encompass suffrage on this scale. It cannot have been wholly insincere, for Wilkes' almost uncontested elections had demonstrated that he had no need of votes from such people to retain his own seat in Parliament. They had supported him in the streets, and it would seem this was one of his ways of expressing his gratitude. Along the same lines was his statement: 'I have a real pleasure in following the opinion of the people. I firmly and sincerely believe the *voice of the people* to be *the voice of God*.' Whether irony or not (some of the people had recently proved impatient of his lack of elocution) it was a bold phrase for his time and one that was to echo on many political platforms later, on both sides of the Atlantic.

In April 1777 he tried to secure further government funds for the British Museum, in particular in respect of a great free public library on the premises:

'This capital, after so many ages, remains without any considerable public library. Rome has the immense collection of the Vatican, and Paris scarcely yields to the mistress of the world by the greatness of the King's Library. They are both open at stated times, with every proper accommodation, to all strangers. London has no large public library. The best here is the Royal Society's; but even that is inconsiderable, neither is it open to the public, nor are the necessary conveniences afforded strangers for reading and transcribing. The British Museum, Sir, is rich in manuscripts, the Harleian Collection, the Cottonian

Library, the collection of Charles the First, and many others, especially of our own history; but it is wretchedly poor in printed books. I wish, Sir, a sum were allowed by Parliament for the purchase of the most valuable editions of the best authors, and an Act passed to oblige every printer, under a certain penalty, to send a copy bound of every publication he made to the British Museum.'

The British Museum Reading Room, one of the greatest sources of study for international scholars, and the assurance that every book published should be sent to it by the publisher, did not become available until after Wilkes' death, but his anticipation of scholars' needs, and perhaps remembrance of the disaster to classical scholarship of the destruction of the great library of Alexandria, shows how much Wilkes' public spirit was attuned not only to social reform but to the preservation of learning.

He supplemented his attempt to get better provision for the arts by suggesting also the formation of a National Gallery of painting:

'I understand that an application is intended to Parliament that one of the finest collections in Europe, that at Houghton, made by Sir Robert Walpole, of acknowledged superiority to most in Italy, and scarcely inferior even to the Duke of Orleans, in the Palais Royal at Paris, may be sold by the family. I hope it will not be dispersed, but purchased by Parliament and added to the British Museum. I wish, Sir, the eye of painting as fully gratified as the ear of music is in this island, which at last bids fair to become a favourite abode of the polite arts. A noble gallery ought to be built in the spacious garden of the British Museum for the reception of that invaluable treasure. Such an important acquisition as the Houghton Collection would, in some degree, alleviate the concern which every man of taste now feels at being deprived of viewing those prodigies of art, the cartoons of the divine Raphael.'

Edmund Burke moved that a grant to the trustees of the British Museum should be increased by £1,000, and was

seconded by Wilkes. It was opposed by Sir Grey Cooper on
behalf of the Government, and negatived without a division.
The Houghton Collection was allowed to go out of England:
two years later, it was bought by Catherine the Great,
Empress of Russia, for £40,555.

Music seems less to have aroused Wilkes' interest, in spite
of the fashionable fever for opera in the London of his day,
still steeped in the aftermath of the glories of Handel. In this
at least George III outstripped him: in 1764 he and his
Queen had acted as enraptured hosts to the child prodigy
Mozart, his father and sister, and the King had asked in
particular for the eight-year-old Mozart to play pieces by
Handel at sight. Wilkes seems, though, to have liked church
music and on one of his tours he made a point of attending
evensong at Trinity College, Cambridge, where the organ
and choir were accounted notably fine.

In 1775, during Wilkes' term as Lord Mayor, Joseph
Mallord Turner was born in Covent Garden: William Blake,
also London born in 1757, was eighteen years old. The
National Gallery of painting of which Wilkes dreamed was to
cover forms of art of which he, in the age of Royal Academy
portraiture, had little vision. The century of the enlightenment was soon to take new pathways, bearing its artists and
musicians, as well as its philosophers and social reformers,
along revolutionary streams. Soon he himself was to be
outpaced, letting the stream flow past him. But he was
striking a chord that was to reverberate, and herald a new
public spirit towards the arts.

In Parliament Wilkes also became conspicuous in
advocating religious tolerance, an outlook which was to cost
him dear later. On 3 March 1779, he supported measures
suggested for the relief of dissenting ministers and
schoolmasters. 'There were not', he said, 'in Europe men of
more liberal ideas, more general knowledge, more cultivated
understandings, and in all respects better calculated to form
the rising generation, to give the state wise and virtuous
citizens, than the Doctors Price, Priestley, and Kippis. Yet
the rod of persecution hangs over them by a single thread, if
they do not subscribe thirty-five articles and a half of our

Church. A mercenary informer or a blind zealot may bring under the lash of the law men who do honour to the age in which we live, and the most abandoned of our species have it now in their power to persecute virtue and genius, when exerted for the benefit of mankind.'

Dr Richard Price, author of *Observations on the Nature of Civil Liberty* (1776), and campaigner for Old Age Pensions and a sinking fund for the National Debt, was prominent also as a Unitarian, as was Dr Joseph Priestley, the theologian chemist. Both, with Benjamin Franklin, the Duke of Grafton and Thomas Hollis, had attended the opening of Theophilus Lindsey's Unitarian Chapel in September 1774, just over a month before Wilkes took office as Mayor. In America, Price was honoured by Yale University at the same ceremony as George Washington, and Priestley, long a friend of Franklin, was eventually to seek asylum in the United States after persecution for his radical views. Hollis also had longstanding American connections.

Twelve days after his parliamentary appeal on behalf of such dissenters as these, Wilkes switched his good offices to the Roman Catholics, who were now being abandoned by Henry Dundas because of some riots in Glasgow and Edinburgh. Dundas had promised to bring in a Scottish Relief Bill. 'I would not', said Wilkes, 'persecute even the atheist.'

In the age of enlightenment it was still not wise to admit to atheism, although deism was respectably established through the English deists and their more influential disciple, Voltaire, at least among a certain section of the community. A compromise had long been reached with dissenting churches throughout the country, although their members had restricted civil rights which disturbed Wilkes as a magistrate. No civil magistrate, he contended, had the right to interfere in matters of conscience. Outwardly, at any rate, Wilkes conformed to the outlook of his age, 'to my good orthodox mother the Church of England' as he wrote to Polly. Whatever his private views on the after-life, he went on his cheerfully profligate way. The hell fire of the Calvinists and Wesleyans held no terrors, to the end, for the ex-member of the Hell-Fire Club. It is possible he was more completely rationalist than he cared openly to admit.

His greatest test in Parliament was sparked off by the rebellion of the colonists in America, and more than anything except the Gordon Riots of 1780 it was to undermine his political position.

XI
THE AMERICAN REVOLUTION

Wilkes was a figure early seized on by American radicals as a possible battering-ram for their own political aims. The anger and discontent over the Stamp Act had only subsided with its repeal, and it burst out again with renewed violence when the Government, forgetting the lessons of the past, tried to meet the expenses of providing a frontier army by imposing a tea tax on those who were said to benefit by it, the American colonists. But long before the War of Independence broke out certain American 'sons of liberty' had sensed in Wilkes' own struggles against authority a reflection of their own growing grievances. The prisoner in the King's Bench was flooded with goods and good wishes not only from admirers in England but across the Atlantic.

'Virginia sent tobacco, and Boston turtles, to John Wilkes in prison. South Carolina voted him £1,500 to pay his debts. The Sons of Liberty sent him a formal address from Boston and Wilkes acknowledged their identity of interest. Many believed that the fate of Wilkes and America must stand, or fall, together. Americans and Englishmen felt themselves to be the victim of the same wanton prejudice, the same blind insistence on the letter of constitutional rights, the same ignorance of the broader principles of justice and humanity. And it was to the immense advantage of America that so many Englishmen were sympathetic to their struggles.'[1]

To all this Wilkes had been quick to respond: neither he nor his Atlantic allies lacked anything in opportunism. He did not even flicker when his Atlantic radical followers wrote to him and sought his commiseration when they were condemned for tarring and feathering their opponents: an

[1] J. H. Plumb: *England in the Eighteenth Century* (Pelican, 1950–69).

American custom, when faced with actions that displeased them but which were outside the law, that Thomas Paine was strongly to condemn even among his supporters. Wilkes' conscience was not so queasy: he wrote back blandly giving the requested commiseration.

On 6 June 1768 the 'Committee of the Sons of Liberty in the Town of Boston' had written him a long letter which began 'Illustrious Patriot' and ended with five signatures, including that of John Adams, later second President of the United States. It informed him that 'The friends of Liberty, Wilkes, Peace and good order to the number of forty-five assembled at the Whig Tavern, Boston, New England', took this first opportunity of congratulating his country, the British colonies and himself on his happy return to the land 'alone worthy such an Inhabitant'. They suggested he was '*one* of those incorruptible *honest men* reserved by heaven to bless and perhaps save a tottering Empire' and added that 'nothing but a common interest, and absolute confidence in an impartial and general protection, can combine so many Millions of Men, born to make laws for themselves; conscious and invincibly tenacious of their Rights'.

'That the British constitution still exists is our glory: feeble and infirm as it is, we will not despair of it – To a Wilkes much is already due for his strenuous efforts to preserve it. Those generous and inflexible principles which have rendered you so greatly eminent, support our claim to your esteem and assistance . . .'

Wilkes replied to the effect that he promised 'always to give a particular attention to whatever respects the interests of America', and a special meeting of the committee of the Sons of Liberty was called to hear his letter read out loud. They asked, and received, permission to publish it. A lively correspondence followed between the prospective saviour of a tottering Empire and various Bostonian admirers and in February 1769 William Palfrey (whose signature had appeared attached to the gift of turtles) wrote and heavily underscored the general conviction: '*The fate of Wilkes and America must stand or fall together.*'

Three of the names attached to letters to Wilkes were to be of particular prominence at the outbreak, several years later, of the War of Independence: James Otis, Samuel Adams and John Hancock (who was to write his signature particularly large on the Declaration of Independence, so that King George III, he said, could read it without spectacles). In America today they figure far more prominently in the public mind than John Wilkes, who is to a large extent forgotten. But at the time they were almost unknown citizens with a penchant for freedom, humble admirers of a great man whose fame and fight for individual liberty had resounded across the Atlantic. The great man was to keep his word, he never forgot 'the interests of America'.

Nor did the Americans forget Wilkes. 'It is significant that between 1768 and 1771, though Wilkes was out of office', wrote the historians Nye and Morpurgo, 'his activities received more press comment in North America than in Britain and were certainly more fully reported than those of any other British political figure. The articles of some of the small London political societies which were formed to stand by Wilkes in his "martyrdom", were drafted in almost identical terms with those of the North and South Carolina Regulators; one of these London groups actually borrowed Sam Adams' name for his own group and called them "Sons of Liberty".' By 1771, they add, 'it was almost possible to regard the English and American radical movements as one'. [1]

By 1774 the situation with America was so deteriorating that Benjamin Franklin, representative in London of Pennsylvania and other colonies, was invited by Lord Chatham to Burton Pynsent to discuss the whole problem and means of conciliation, which they did over a period of many hours: even Dashwood, Lord Le Despencer, earnestly engaged Franklin at West Wycombe Park on the same subject.

The imposition of a sparking point of confrontation, the Tea Act, was merely a symbol in the struggle between the English Parliament (meaning the Government in power) and the American colonists. 'Whoever would govern a country

[1] R. B. Nye and J. E. Morpurgo: *The Birth of the USA* (Pelican, 1955–1970).

6. The Adelphi from the River. Print by Thomas Molton, 1796.

7. Sandham Cottage, Isle of Wight. 1798 print.

18. 'News from America' or 'The Patriots in the Dumps'. *London Magazine*,
November 1776. Lord North waving despatch signed 'How' on capture of
New York by the British. Behind him, Lord Mansfield. *L.* foreground,
Wilkes. *R.* Lord Bute, Lord Sandwich and the King.

without its consent', declared Charles James Fox in 1774, 'endured resistance.' Fox, at twenty-five years old, had at last started thinking for himself along liberal lines, outside family influence, and he had voted with the Rockingham Whigs for the repeal of the tea duty. One major resentment of the Americans, as his remark indicated, was that they were being taxed without being allowed representation in Parliament. They were being governed from a distance of two thousand miles, in an age of painfully slow sea travel, and they had no rights of commerce for their growing imports and exports except through England itself. This meant they paid inflated prices for imports, especially from the European continent, and received reduced ones for their own goods: all to the enrichment of the English middleman. When a party of Wilkes' Bostonian followers dressed themselves up as Indians, boarded the ships in Boston Harbour, and threw the taxed tea overboard, it was a gesture of defiance not so much at the threepenny tea tax itself as against the whole question of tax and subservience without representation in Parliament. The gesture took place in 1773; the next year Wilkes was back in Parliament; and in 1775 the War of Independence had begun.

During the next few years not only Wilkes but most of the leaders of the Whig party, including Pitt, Fox, Grafton and Burke, resisted the idea of the American War. Grafton, in fact, in November 1775 resigned his seals and broke his always uneasy alliance with the Government, and joined the Opposition with whose general views, in spite of his loyalty to the King, he had always been in sympathy. The upholder of Wilkes' liberty, Grafton's old friend Charles Pratt, Lord Camden, wrote letters in strong but sometimes pessimistic support: 'Who could have imagined, that the Ministry could have become popular by forcing this country into a destructive war, and advancing the power of the Crown to a state of despotism? And yet, that is the fact; and we of the minority suffer under the odium, due only to the ministers, without the consolation either of pay or power.' (Camden was no longer Lord Chancellor.)

Perhaps it was partly in revulsion to the Unitarians among

the American sympathizers, as well as his natural Toryism and resistance to any form of secular reform, that projected John Wesley in the opposite direction with his pamphlet, *Calm Address to the American colonies*, which he defended in a letter to *Lloyd's Evening Post* on 29 November 1775 with a further attack on the Americans as the whole cause of the situation. ('Now there is no possible way to put out this flame, or hinder its rising higher and higher, but to show that the Americans are not injured at all, seeing they are not contending for liberty; (this they had even in its full extent, both civil and religious) . . . what they contend for is, the illegal privilege of being exempt from parliamentary taxation. . . . This being the real state of the question, without any colouring or aggravation, what impartial man can either blame the King, or commend the Americans?') Wesley's influence on the poorer classes with his firebrand form of methodism was growing. It was a force used to instil into the lower classes a total acceptance of their lot, as the special design of providence, and his influence may partly account for the apathy of portions of the working people to resisting the War. Only when the pinch was felt in their pockets did the public begin to stir on a large scale. It was the professional classes that sometimes resisted. Major John Cartwright, a major figure in the radical movement for reform over the next fifty years, ruined his earlier naval prospects by refusing to serve against the Americans.

Within Parliament, the resistance did not lessen. When early in 1775 General Gage, the new Governor of Massachusetts, sent an army of occupation into restive Boston (not without protest and misgiving), Wilkes denounced the action as 'unfounded and sanguinary. It draws the sword unjustly against America.' He showed in his speech of February a full grasp of the roots of the problem, taxation and lack of representation, and an unexpected delving into history to find a comparable situation:

'The business before the House, in its full extent and respecting the British Colonies in America, is of as great importance as was ever debated in Parliament.

'The assumed right of taxation without the consent of the subject is plainly the primary cause of the present quarrel. If we can tax the Americans without their consent they have no property, for we might by violence take the whole as well as a part.

'If gentlemen will search the Records in the Tower and the Chapel of the Rolls they will find that the Town of Calais in France, when it belonged to the imperial Crown of this realm, was not taxed until it sent a representative to Parliament; a Thomas Fowler actually sat for and voted in this House as a burgess of the town of Calais; from that period and not till then was Calais taxed.'

He added: 'This I know, a successful resistance is a *revolution*, not a *rebellion*. Who knows whether in consequence of this day's violent and mad address – whether in a few years the *independent* Americans may not celebrate the glorious era of the revolution of 1775 as we do that of 1688?' No one believed the prophecy; and everyone except Wilkes was wrong.

In October he called the War which had broken out 'unjust, felonious and murderous', and claimed that the greater part of America was lost and could not be reconquered. Unfortunately for Wilkes and the colonists this was not yet true; a savage winter bogged down Washington and his tattered army in Valley Forge, and although Paine's widely read and publicized *Common Sense* put heart into the depressed Washington and his soldiers, the militia had a tendency to scatter back to its villages and farms and under General Howe the British army pushed forward into New York and beyond. The English knew nothing of the rallying of the American defence and the growing mastery of guerilla fighting: as with most people fighting a war at long distance they heard mainly their Government's publicity of the 'successful' campaign, and as yet prices had not risen, nor was their trade directly threatened. Wilkes and the rest campaigned on, but in increasing isolation. The Americans, declared Wilkes, would dispute 'every Thermopylae, every Bunker's Hill', and after the Declaration of Independence he saluted 'the free and independent States of America'. (It was Thomas Paine who coined the phrase 'The United States of America'.)

'An honourable gentleman near me, sir', he declared on 31 October 1776, 'attacks the American Declaration of Independency in a very peculiar manner. He pronounces it a wretched composition, very ill-written, drawn up only with the view to *captivate the people. That*, sir, is the very reason why I approve it most as a composition as well as a wise political measure; for the *people* are to decide this great controversy. If they are *captivated* by it, the end is attained.' In fact the Declaration, largely ascribed to Thomas Jefferson, although not now without scholastic dispute, was to transform democratic history with its ringing phrasing. 'We hold these truths to be self-evident, that all men are created equal . . .' It is doubtful if many, even Wilkes, seriously believed this at the time; but two great revolutions were to be built on the assumption within the next 150 years.

It was only after 1777, and General Burgoyne's surrender at Saratoga, that the tide began to turn, and something of Wilkes' prophecy begin to become apparent. Earlier in the year he had spoken against the suspension of Habeas Corpus and the common law in America, supported by a petition from the City; but the news of Saratoga was slow in coming through and even then, at first, not fully believed, and with the King's fanatical obstinacy and refusal to compromise the War dragged on into the 1780s. Lord North followed the King, though not without an occasional air of dragging his feet. 'Lord North in private life', wrote the kindly, uncensorious Duke of Grafton, 'was an upright, honorable man; and his talents were unquestioned: but he neither had the peculiar talent himself of conducting extensive war operations; nor was the ability and judgment of his co-adjutors sufficient to make up the deficiency.' Both Sandwich at the Admiralty and Lord George Germain as War Minister were, according to Grafton, a part of this general deficiency, and Germain, indeed, had been to a large extent responsible for Burgoyne's defeat: in the first place for giving him no discretionary power of strategic decision, and in the second, and most vitally in the matter of Saratoga, failing to sign the despatches addressed to General Howe, requesting him to effect a junction with Burgoyne's forces at Albany. Germain had not wanted to delay his trip to the country, to wait for the despatches to be fair copied; and on his return forgot them. [1] Burgoyne, who had struggled through a difficult terrain all the way from Canada, was left alone, hopelessly outnumbered, and with no recourse but to surrender. The British soldier, as Bernard Shaw made him remark in his play on the American War, *The Devil's Disciple*, 'can stand up to anything except the British War Office'.

When Burgoyne returned home – released by the Americans, who without Government ratification of the terms of surrender refused to send his army back with him – Wilkes mercilessly cross-examined him on his use of savage Indians among his army. The British Army certainly used Indians and the bribery of them to fight on the British side was one of Paine's own most bitter complaints. The army in fact was also fortified with Hessians from one of the original Hanoverian possessions in Germany, and its reputation for burning and outrage was not unlike that of most historic armies of occupation. This was particularly resented by the Americans, many of them English-born or English by descent, and there were loud cries that King George was attempting to suppress the Englishmen's own kith and kin with foreign troops. Most of the atrocities however were attributed to Howe's army which had taken over or was disputing the inhabited areas in New York and Pennsylvania, or further in the south: Burgoyne's army had marched south on the long journey from Canada along the shores of Lake Champlain, Indian country but largely uninhabited.

The actual composition of Burgoyne's army shows the Indians, in fact, to be in a minority, and he found them more of a hindrance than a help, being unreliable in their support. As against 503 Indians and 148 Canadian militia, he had 4,135 British and 3,116 German troops, and it was the Germans who created the problems.

[1] Lord E. Fitzmaurice: *Life of Lord Shelburne* (Macmillan, 1875).

'. . . there can be no doubt but that they were frequently enlisted and transported across the Atlantic much against their will. The extravagant sums paid by the British Government in the shape of levy money and bounty was a powerful incentive to the avarice of the despotic petty princes, whose unscrupulous barter of their subjects created indignation throughout Germany. The King of Prussia denounced the practice, and actually made the legionaries, whenever, on their way to embarkation, they had to pass through his dominions, pay toll as "cattle exported for foreign shambles".'[1]

The situation, in fact, was notorious in Germany and was mentioned bitterly by Schiller in *Kabale und Liebe*.

Whatever the excesses of a few of his Indians, Burgoyne, a soldier conspicuously humane for his time, would not willingly have countenanced them. 'My advice to General Gage,' he wrote in a letter, 'has been to treat the prisoners taken in the late action, most of whom are wounded, with all possible kindness, and to dismiss them without terms.' In Parliament, in 1772, he had been foremost in moving for an enquiry into the affairs of the East India Company and the abuses of power of its officials, and when the report was brought up on 3 May 1773 he had maintained in a vigorous House of Commons attack that 'it contained the recital of crimes which it shocked human nature even to conceive'. Among the crimes he specified was the execution of native rebels by blowing them to pieces at the mouths of the British army's cannons; a method still notorious in the Indian Mutiny the following century. Paine, no friend to the British army in its imperial wars, was to point out to the Americans the humanity of this speech of Burgoyne's after the General's surrender at Saratoga.

Burgoyne's attachment to the Crown led him in some ways into a curious ambivalence. 'There is a charm in the very wanderings and dreams of liberty that disarms an Englishman', he had said in the House on the eve of his

[1] Edward Barrington de Fonblanque: *Life and Correspondence of the Rt Hon John Burgoyne* (Macmillan, 1876).

embarkation for America: but he had added, 'but while we remember that we are contending against brothers and fellow subjects, we must also remember that we are contending in this crisis for the fate of the British Empire'. He had also voted against the repeal of the duty on tea, in condescending terms ('I look upon America as our child, which we have already spoilt by too much indulgence') which would hardly have conciliated his antagonists, although he had added shrewdly enough that the matter was not really one of tea: 'it is the right of taxation which they dispute, and not the tax. It is the independence of that country upon the legislation of this for which they contend.' He had voted meekly enough also for the Royal Marriage Bill, demanded by the King as the result of a royal misalliance, and giving the monarch full future control of veto over the choice of partner of his kinsmen. (It is typical of George III's conviction of his right to sway Parliament that he told Lord North that had Burgoyne not done so he would 'have felt myself obliged to name a new Governor for Fort William'. This was Burgoyne's official position at the time.)

On the question of his treatment before and after Saratoga, however, Burgoyne was far from meek. He had complained continually in letters home of the restrictions on his personal strategic authority and the parsimony of the Treasury towards his army, and had early realized, partly from correspondence with Charles Lee, once his colleague in the British army and now a General on the American side, that the War Office could have 'no probable prospect of bringing the war to a speedy conclusion with any force that Great Britain and Ireland can supply'. Hence his recourse to Canadians (he wished for many more) and Indians. It was 'at best a necessary evil', he stated later in the House of Commons. Lee's own faith in the outcome was in January 1776 stimulated to enthusiasm by Paine's *Common Sense*. 'I never saw such a masterly irresistible performance', he wrote to Washington. 'It will, if I mistake not, give the coup de grâce to Great Britain.' Time proved him right. Paine's pamphlet provided what Washington described as the 'unanswerable reasoning' that propelled the wavering

Americans not only to resistance but thoughts of independence. In a sense the colonies were lost a full year before the
surrender at Saratoga.

Burgoyne seems early to have realized that his position and
defeat were made inevitable by War Office incompetence,
but tried in vain to get an investigation and the clearing of
his name. The failure of Howe to send or bring troops to his
aid had, indeed, been so conspicuous that even Washington,
writing from Delaware on 30 July 1777, had shown
disbelief: 'Howe's in a manner abandoning Burgoyne is so
unaccountable a matter, that till I am fully assured of it I
cannot help casting my eyes continually behind me.' The
decision of the Government, however, was to try to cover up
the blunder, and leave Burgoyne the scapegoat. Germain,
when he resigned at the end of the War, was raised by the
King to the peerage as Viscount Sackville: Burgoyne, on his
return to England, was refused both an audience with the
King and the court-martial he demanded to clear his name,
its being ruled by a piece of characteristic eighteenth-century
chicanery that as he was still officially a prisoner of war this
could not be allowed. When he prepared to appeal in
Parliament an effort was again made to silence him, on the
grounds that he was a 'prisoner on parole' and could not
take his seat. This echo back to his own past predicament
should have disposed Wilkes in his favour. Burgoyne
nevertheless appeared and made his speech, and Shelburne,
Fox and others made clear they fully understood the
position: 'a gallant officer', declared Fox, 'sent like a victim
to be slaughtered where his own stock of personal bravery
would have earned him laurels if he had not been under the
direction of blunderers'.

It was of little help to Burgoyne. A handsome man of wit,
distinction, varied talents and irresistible charm, he had
made a romantic marriage with the Earl of Derby's daughter
by elopement and later proceeded to captivate his reluctant
in-laws. His appeal to an even greater wit, Bernard Shaw, was
to immortalize him. Failing to clear his name officially, he
resigned his commission, returned to playwriting at which he
had dabbled earlier in his career, and in 1786 produced one

of London's brightest theatrical successes, a comedy entitled *The Heiress*. Horne Tooke in *Diversions of Purley* was to describe it as 'the most perfect and meritorious comedy of any on our stage'. Another act of Burgoyne's late in life Wilkes himself would surely have appreciated. In 1782, at the age of fifty-nine, 'Gentlemanly Johnny' created something more substantial and lasting than his play: a hearty natural son, who as Sir John Fox Burgoyne carved out a successful career as an officer of the Royal Engineers, spanning a whole military era which included serving under Wellington in the Peninsular War and the Crimea at Sebastopol, down to his death as a Field-Marshal in 1871.

In the American issue at least Wilkes remained throughout the War a staunch supporter of the colonists and the attitude of Fox, whose conversion to the Whig cause he seems otherwise sometimes to have looked on with a distrustful eye. He made a number of speeches on the issue and always with a shrewd evaluation of the position. It is often forgotten that in Parliament Wilkes abandoned the polemical excesses of *The North Briton* and became a remarkably balanced and even penetrating political commentator. In 1775 he proclaimed:

'I speak, Sir, as a firm friend to England and America, but still more to universal liberty and the rights of all mankind. I trust no part of the subjects of this vast empire will ever submit to be slaves. I am sure the Americans are too high-spirited to brook the idea . . . England was never engaged in a contest of such importance to our most valuable concerns and possessions. We are fighting for the subjection – the unconditional submission of a country infinitely more extended than our own, of which every day increases the wealth, the national strength, the population. . . . The idea of the conquest of that immense continent is as romantic as it is unjust.'

In the same year he described Samuel Adams and John Hancock as not only 'worthy gentlemen' but 'true patriots', and anticipated Paine's *Rights of Man* in pulverizing the Government on the matter of the National Debt and the useless and corrupt expenditure on 'placemen and pensioners' for political support (Dr Johnson, with a series of pamphlets attacking the Americans, was among the pensioners):

'The Congress, Sir, have not the monstrous load of a debt of about one hundred and forty millions, like our Parliament, to struggle with, the interest of which would swallow up all their taxes! nor a numerous and hungry band of useless placemen and pensioners to provide for. . . . Every shilling which they raise will go to the man who fights the battles of his country.'

On the Declaration of Independence he not only defended its phrasing but counselled the withdrawal of British armed forces from the country and the negotiation of peace on 'just, fair, and equal terms, without the idea of compulsion'. He added: 'We know that there is no more *love of liberty* in the French Court than in our own; but I rejoice that *liberty* will have a resting-place, a sure asylum, in America, from the persecution of almost all the princes of the earth.' For the moment, at least, Wilkes was coming dangerously near to a republican sentiment he had always scrupulously avoided in *The North Briton*.

In December 1777, hard upon the news of Saratoga, France recognized the independence of America and in February 1778 she declared war on England. She had already been secretly supplying arms to America through a specially-formed merchant company known as Hortalez and Company, of which the main architect was Beaumarchais, author of *The Marriage of Figaro* (a comedy of revolutionary social tendencies, attacking the infamous *droit de seigneur*). He and the American agent Silas Deane, both deeply involved in the scheme, were sent over to London to meet Arthur Lee, then representative of the American colonies in London, and they met at a dinner given by the Lord Mayor. The year was 1775, and the Mayor John Wilkes. In view of his pro-American views, it would be interesting to know if he were in any way concerned in the plot, or had any suspicions of it. The following year, on 25 June 1776, Wilkes certainly dined 'at Mr Dilly's in the Poultry' with Arthur Lee.

The renewed war with France, now an open ally of America, did not improve Wilkes' position as an opponent of the American War, although he remained in distinguished company among the Opposition. Lord Chatham died in 1778, still bitterly castigating the North Government for its refusal to negotiate. 'The constitutions which the colonists had devised for their own government must be accepted', he had maintained, and the Congress to which thirteen states had sent representatives at Philadelphia was 'representative of American opinion, an institution, in fact, of enduring worth'. [1] Although Shelburne and others supported him, the majority were against him, notwithstanding that Chatham's friend, Thomas Brand Hollis, had managed through his wide American connections to obtain reports of the Congress debates as well as first-hand information from Massachusetts, New York and Maryland.

Hollis was a benefactor of Harvard University (one of its halls bears his name) and later one of the few English parliamentarians to become a radical supporter of Thomas Paine in England. During the early years of the American War, he had commissioned a portrait of Paine by the American artist in Philadelphia, Charles Willson Peale. [2] The fame of *Common Sense* and indeed the book itself had very quickly crossed the Atlantic. Hollis' internal knowledge probably in fact stimulated Chatham's own acute awareness of the hopelessness of the War, as well as its general inexcusability.

In 1780 there was a rally of popular feeling against the War, now weighing more heavily on the populace and City merchants, and its corollary, the increasing power of the Crown, which was questioned in Parliament. The freeholders of Yorkshire met and petitioned for a redress of grievancies and parliamentary reform, and their example was followed in Sussex, Hertfordshire, Cheshire, Devonshire, Essex, Bedfordshire, Dorsetshire and Buckinghamshire. [3] On 2nd February the same year the electors of the City of Westminster held a

[1] J. H. Plumb: *Chatham* (Collins, 1953; 'Makers of History' series, 1965).
[2] Moncure D. Conway: *The Life of Thomas Paine* (New York, 1892).
[3] Horace Walpole: *Memoirs of the Reign of George III*, vol. ii.

great meeting of similar protest at Westminster Hall. Wilkes, Temple, Burgoyne and Burke were all present to support the motions, and Fox, 'the Man of the People' was proposed as one of the future candidates for Westminster. Wilkes, recorded Walpole in a letter, 'was his zealous advocate', adding with a touch of irony, 'How few years since a public breakfast was given at Holland House to support Col. Luttrell against Wilkes!' When Parliament was dissolved on 1st September, the same year, Fox won the Westminster seat despite the Government's payment of £8,000 out of the notorious Civil List to try and secure the victory of its own candidate, Lord Lincoln.

The same year, 1780, Wilkes opposed a vote of thanks proposed to General Clinton and Lord Cornwallis for their services in America: 'Every part of it conveys an approbation of the American War – a war unfounded in principle and fatal in its consequences to this country . . . a war of glaring injustice and wretched policy.' Wilkes in his turn was openly thanked by the Westminster Committee of Association, under the chairmanship of Fox, for his opposition 'on the ground that success in the American war would be the ruin of the liberties both of America and England'. That despotic government in one country would lead to further despotism in the other was one of the generally expressed fears of those with misgivings about the War.

It was April 1783 before the War ended. By then everyone in England knew that enough was enough. Lord North was forced to resign in 1782, to the grief and humiliation of the King, and a Whig cabinet under Lord Rockingham was formed to arrange the peace. Fox and Lord Shelburne were the two Secretaries of State, Fox spectacularly turning over a new leaf and giving up his passion for the gaming table, in order to set a good example. As Walpole wrote to Sir Horace Mann: 'Mr Fox already shines as greatly in place as he did in Opposition, though infinitely more difficult a task. He is now as indefatigable as he was idle. He has perfect temper, and not only good humour but good nature . . .' As in most Whig cabinets, however, there were conflicts of personality. Fox resigned when outvoted on the question of recognizing at once and unconditionally the independence of the United States, and it was Shelburne who, after the sudden death of Rockingham on 1 July 1782, took nominal charge. He was, however, both disliked and distrusted by his colleagues and with some difficulty was forced to resign in favour of a party coalition (strongly opposed by Grafton who refused to act with it) headed by North and Fox. (This alliance with North, temporary though it was, was one of the things for which Wilkes never forgave Fox.) These personal dissensions undoubtedly delayed the peace, which at last came in 1783.

The tragedy of the American War was that even the American leaders had not originally intended to break completely from Britain: they were forced into revolution and republicanism by the refusal of the King, and the Government largely concurring with him, to compromise. King George III never again had such influence over events, and his recurring mental illness was to ravage any future opportunities to regain it. But the damage was done: England had lost what was to prove potentially her richest and most exciting colony.

Lingering Wilkes connections in America are traditionally the towns of Wilkesboro in North Carolina and Wilkesbarre (named jointly after Wilkes and Colonel Isaac Barré, another American sympathizer),[1] the capital of Luzerne county in Pennsylvania; but Wilkes Land in Antarctica certainly did not derive its name from John Wilkes but from Lieutenant Charles Wilkes of the US Navy, who discovered it on Antarctic exploration in 1840. Born in 1798, he was said to be the son of Wilkes' elder brother Israel but on the date, unless Israel exceeded even his younger brother in virility, this seems unlikely, and grandson is a more sensible conjecture. He lived until 1877, having published two travel books, become a Rear Admiral in 1866, and a few years before this, at the beginning of the American Civil War, caused much consternation to the British Government and fleet by intercepting, as captain of the US ship *San Jacinto*, Her

---

[1] Barré, whose opposition to Grenville's American Stamp Bill has been noted, became Treasurer of the Navy in the Rockingham Ministry and both Grafton and Camden thought highly of his character.

Majesty's ship *Trent* off the coast of Cuba and removing two
Confederate envoys who were held on board. [1] His uncle (or
great-uncle), who had been so staunch an advocate of
American independence, could hardly have complained.

[1] This engagement and its implications are described by Jasper Ridley in his
monumental biography of *Lord Palmerston* (Constable, London; Dutton, New
York, 1970).

XII

ROMANCE AND THE GORDON RIOTS

The aged William Pitt, Lord Chatham, died on 11 May 1778. Histrionic to the last, he had come to the House of Lords enwrapped in flannel to urge reconciliation with America. We must not fight our own kith and kin, he passionately declared, but must seek peace with them, and turn our forces against our foreign foes. Once again he and Wilkes were fighting on the same side, but the alliance was ephemeral. After his powerful harangue the invalid collapsed and fainted in his seat, and was carried from the House home to die. The War went on as before, and soon after it ended another William Pitt was to become Prime Minister, the youngest man, at twenty-four, ever to achieve that office.

Early the following year, on 20 January 1779, Garrick also died. He had retired from the stage in 1776, amid farewells and acclamations that spanned the Channel. The French minister Necker and his wife (the parents of Madame de Staël) headed a contingent from Paris who came to see the great actor's last performances, and they dined with Garrick at both the Adelphi and Hampton as well as with Wilkes at Thomas Walpole's house in Lincoln's Inn Fields. Wilkes was a visitor to Hampton not long before the actor's death. His funeral at Westminster Abbey on 1st February was almost as splendid in its processional pomp as that of the kings he had so often portrayed on the stage, and he was buried under the pavement of Poets' Corner, at the foot of Shakespeare's monument. The Adelphi was hung with black, and Dr Johnson proclaimed his death had eclipsed the gaiety of nations. If it did not eclipse Wilkes' own mercurial gaiety, he must still have been conscious that time, inexorable, was beginning to make inroads on his friends. Two years later his mother died, leaving him property at Enfield, and soon afterwards his long-forgotten wife. Polly, who inherited her fortune, was now a rich woman but there is no indication that Wilkes himself ever touched her money.

Meanwhile, as the War dragged on, Wilkes did not neglect his private affairs. In May 1777 he finally parted with Mlle Carpentier, who had managed to retain the position of mistress-in-chief ever since she had attracted Wilkes' attention in Paris as Polly's governess. The parting was not in sweet sorrow, but a crackling burst of gunfire. '*Monsieur, vous m'êtes devenu aussi odieux que ma mère*' ('Sir, you have become even more hateful to me than my mother') was her parting shot. Wilkes was not slow to fill the gap, and formed what was to be the most staid (if such a word could ever be used of Wilkes) and lasting association of the kind. Amelia Arnold was the daughter of a Wiltshire farmer: solidly built, reasonably handsome, affectionate and quite without jealousy. She was not uneducated and apparently ready to welcome being set up in a home by Wilkes, and to give him genuine and untroubled affection. She was exactly suited to his temperament, which had always been surprisingly domesticated at home, especially now he had reached middle age.

The liaison was, of course, soon a subject of newspaper comment (then as now the gutter press lived and thrived on such stories, without at that time the restrictions of a workable law of libel) and Wilkes found her in tears after reading a paragraph suggesting that her looks were not quite up to his usual mark. He consoled her (if it were consolation) with the kindly-meant comment: 'You see, my dear, there is *no difference* between us.' Her daughter, Harriet, was born in October 1778 and her father was devoted to her. This was for Wilkes a happy second home for the rest of his life, where he could go at any time and watch proudly the progress of his second daughter, and make a fuss of the horde of pet animals – dogs, cats and birds – Harriet and her mother delighted in. There is no evidence that Polly and Harriet ever met, but as Harriet grew older they corresponded, and Polly sent little gifts to her sister. She could afford not to be jealous. By now

Thomas Paine. Engraving by Sharp from
ait by Romney.

20. General John Burgoyne ('Gentlemanly
Johnny').

John Hancock.

22. John Horne Tooke.

23. The Gordon Riots, 1780. 'The Burning and Plundering of Newgate and Setting the Felons at Liberty.'

she knew full well she would always come first in her father's life, and would always remain mistress of his principal home.

Wilkes' love-life was, however, by no means finished. Within a few months of establishing Millie Arnold in a house, the gallant MP fell in love again, this time with overtones of seriousness. Her name was Maria Stafford, and her husband was temporarily separated from her. 'I passionately desire', wrote Wilkes, 'to be employed in your service. . . . Will you permit me to present Miss Wilkes to you, as something resembling yourself in goodness?'

It looks very much as if Wilkes was contemplating introducing his daughter as a preliminary to serious intentions, in spite of the absent husband. The attractive Maria resisted, but not in the way of one unflattered by the attentions of so famous a connoisseur. 'Why will you oblige me to be angry with you? I have more than once entreated you would send me neither letters nor presents. I must now *insist*. . . . Death has deprived me of my natural protectors and advisers, infidelity of my legal one. Therefore the slightest deviation from Prudence must inevitably ruin me.' 'Make me your *protector*, I shall have a happier lot than Cromwell', replied her besieger, unabashedly drawing a parallel of which Cromwell would greatly have disapproved.

The fact that she was attracted is shown by the way she continued to correspond, often through letters of some length. Wilkes' glamour as a famous fighter for freedom and ladies' man had long obliterated his face. By walking and riding he continued to take pride in his figure and his manners, all are agreed, were impeccable. He continued to shower gifts, and on her bringing up the sensitive matter of their respective marriages, from which death at present seemed unlikely to release them, he made a gallant attempt to explain away his own:

'In my nonage, to please an indulgent father, I married a woman half as old again as myself, of a very large fortune; my own that of a gentleman. It was a sacrifice to Plutus, not to Venus. I never lived with her in the strict sense of the

209

word, [1] nor have I seen her near twenty years. I stumbled at
the very threshold of the temple of Hymen.

> The god of love was not a bidden guest
> Nor present at his own mysterious feast.

Are such ties at such a time of life binding, and are
schoolboys to be dragged to the altar? I have since often
sacrificed to beauty, but I never gave my heart except to
you . . .'

It may have been true, it may not: moving along the less
primrosy paths of middle age, Wilkes may certainly have
persuaded himself it was true. 'You are the only person of
your sex, either at home or abroad, who has inspired me with
the wish even of an honourable and indissoluble union for
life' he affirmed, and called her 'the most faultless woman in
face, in form, in soul'. She was certainly a woman, by birth,
whom a gentleman of that time could be accepted as
marrying without question. The association with Millie
Arnold, placidly accepted by her, proves that Wilkes,
whatever his support of 'the voice of the people' in
Parliament, was far too much a victim of his social education
and surroundings even to contemplate marriage with the
tincture of misalliance.

It is even possible he may have succeeded with Maria
Stafford, had not the traditional interfering woman friend,
noticing flowers on the hall table, taxed Maria about her
admirer and remonstrated with her on even contemplating
such a match. 'I will own to you', wrote Maria tearfully,
'that she has made me see it in a very different light from
what I have hitherto viewed it, and I now wonder at my
own want of discretion.' He had delivered the flowers with
a concert ticket on Saturday 18 April 1778, four months
after he first met her, and left them when he found her out.
She now returned the ticket, and told him to 'shake off this
idle fancy'. She refused, after that, to see him alone, but
apparently found the correspondence too enlivening (and

---

[1] A curious impression seems here conveyed that Polly was born of an
Immaculate Conception: a most unlikely event for Wilkes to be involved in.

perhaps secretly daring) to drop. The friendship continued for at least six years, and did not cease when Maria Stafford was reconciled to her errant husband. Wilkes then had the opportunity to visit the lady again, fully protected, and predictably informed Polly that the husband was 'a puppy', although, as it amusingly turned out, in politics a 'Wilkeite'.

The exchange not only of letters but of small gifts continued. Wilkes sent books, franked envelopes (which surely suggests the pleasure her letters still gave him) and venison. In return Maria knitted purses for him. It had all the air of a genuine, if blighted, romance. If so, it was the only one of Wilkes' by no means womanless life: perhaps, with growing age, he really was becoming a little sentimental, and wistful about the kind of marriage he had missed. 'Marriage is an excellent fruit when ripe. You have been unlucky enough to eat it green', Boswell had once written to him. Perhaps he was now prepared to think that 'ripeness is all'. If so, it was rather a sad little incident – and not even 'little' by Wilkesian standards of romantic time. He was not the man, however, to relinquish his compensations. Harriet must have been conceived around the month of February 1778, a month after her father's siege of the heart of Maria Stafford began. It is doubtful if the besieged lady ever knew of her birth that October, or indeed of her existence.

In 1779 Wilkes had a consolation of another kind. Ever since 1776 he had been trying to get election for the lucrative post of City Chamberlain, as a way to help meet some of his debts incurred as Lord Mayor. The City, however, not unwisely decided (helped by some spirited jogging by Wilkes' opponents) that the hazard of appointing, as guardian of their finances, a man so incapable of handling his own, was too great, and Wilkes was defeated by Benjamin Hopkins, who polled a majority of 177 votes. Hopkins, the Court candidate, was responsible for reverberations in the theatre: when the following year *The School for Scandal* came up for licensce it was very nearly banned, and only saved for the stage by Sheridan's personal appeal to Lord Hertford, the Lord Chamberlain. The reason for this surprising sensitivity on the part of the Court was that

Hopkins had been charged with practices similar to those of Moses the Jew – i.e. lending money at interest to young men under age – and Sheridan's character was taken to be a deliberate reference to this. Sheridan, in 1795, the year of the repeal of Habeas Corpus, made the story the basis of a speech against censorship in the House of Commons.

Annoyed, for this was an unexpected City setback, Wilkes continued annually to fight for the position, ignoring an unwritten law by which the holder held it until his death. But in 1779 Hopkins died, and Wilkes obtained the election by a large majority. It helped him a great deal financially, and doubtless provided the wherewithal for even more gifts to the besieged Maria.

By an irony of fate, political life was to arrange a reversal for him from which his career never recovered. In 1778 he had enthusiastically supported the passing of a Catholic Relief Bill, unaware of the disastrous chain of events that this tolerant measure would set in motion. In Scotland, particularly, over whose inhabitants the shadow of the kirk and the ghost of John Knox still loomed, there was widespread unrest; and more pertinent to Wilkes, and apparently overlooked by him, the unrest spread to the working classes who had been his most loyal supporters.

The fact is that the pressure behind the passing of the Catholic Relief Bill was not only religious. Less admirably, it was military. Ever since Burgoyne's defeat at Saratoga the English armies in America had continued to be hard pressed, and impressment (still legal in times of war) and publicity had failed to raise sufficient recruits. The Catholics were exempt from military service, because they had no legal rights in the State; and one result of the Catholic Relief Bill was to release them from that embargo, and to enable them to be recruited in the army. It is strange that Wilkes, so opposed to the American War, does not seem to have been disturbed by this aspect of the Bill, or even particularly aware of it. It was not so with some of his humbler followers. They were beginning at last to suffer from the new course of the War, as the poor are always the first to suffer in a national crisis; and, most of them Protestants in any case, they bitterly resented a measure which meant the sharing of some of their state advantages (which were small enough) and which also could ensure that the War continued to drag on with a new influx of recruits.

There was also another fear, among the working class, that of loss of work through cheap Irish labour, and the Irish were virtually all Catholics. There had been serious anti-Irish riots in July 1736, and again at Covent Garden in 1763. Although the most extensive, they were not the only examples of anti-Irish unrest. The Gordon Riots of 1780 were specifically concerned with the protest of the Protestant Association at the Catholic Relief Bill, but the fact that they became so widespread can only be attributed to the joining in of other elements with other major grievances, and the analysis of buildings destroyed or damaged, their owners and the varied nature of the rioters, from the records of convictions and damages awarded in the Courts, confirms this.

It was doubtless the religious element that lit the first fuse, and to understand this in the twentieth century it is necessary to remember, too, that ever since the reign of Mary Tudor the English had had cause to be nervous of their recently-won freedom from Catholic and Papal domination. The lessons of the Spanish Armada, and the appalling atrocities committed on the population by the Spanish Catholic armies under the Duke of Alva in the Netherlands, were still only a century and a half away; and it was one of the special indictments against Mary, Queen of Scots, and her followers, in the public remembrance, that they had sought the Duke's support in an invasion and therefore risked letting loose this form of suppression-by-atrocity in England. It does much to explain the extraordinary pressure put on Queen Elizabeth by Parliament both in dealing with the Babington plot (the last of a long series) and the execution of the Queen of Scots. Men did not forget that it was only in 1688, ninety years before, that the Catholic-minded Stuart dynasty had been expelled in the 'Glorious' Revolution, and fewer years still since Bonnie Prince Charlie's march south had spread fear and financial chaos in London. In addition, England was now

Wilkes

at war not only with America but, far more popularly, with the Catholic powers of France and Spain, against whom there was a longstanding national hatred. Although to the more balanced modern mind most of these prejudices seem irrational, they cannot be left out of account.

The English Catholics were tolerated, as long as their claws were drawn and they had no state rights or influence; but religious intolerance, fermented by new evangelical movements, still lay but a few inches below the surface. It needed only a leader to ignite it, and unfortunately the leader was present.

Lord George Gordon – one of the family of which Lord Byron was a member – was a Member of Parliament by no means untalented in debate but a young man with a grievance. Lord North, who sometimes more by ill luck than ill judgment set the world falling about his ears, had arranged with the Duke of Gordon, in 1778, to make Lord William Gordon Lord Admiral of Scotland. In gratitude for this, the Duke as head of the Gordon family was expected to make Lord George Gordon, third son of the third Duke, resign the pocket borough of Ludgershall in Wiltshire, which provided his seat in Parliament, in order to free it for one of North's friends.

Lord George Gordon was righteously indignant, and the grievance was supplemented by a dispute with the Admiralty during the American War, as a result of which he left the service. The Protestant cause became his vanguard to fame, and on 2 June 1780, on behalf of the Protestant Association, he headed a contingent of sympathizers in a petition to the House of Commons, requesting the repeal of the Roman Catholic Relief Act. Significantly, and to the Member for Middlesex's embarrassment, the large crowd that came with Lord George Gordon wore the Wilkeite blue cockade: it had become the Protestant as well as radical colour, in part perhaps because the supporters overlapped. Nor was the crowd inactive. After ten in the morning no Member was allowed to enter the House without crying 'No popery!' and a few were further mishandled. The Bishop of Lincoln escaped only by taking flight into a private house, changing his clothes and escaping over the roof: not the first time, perhaps, that an ecclesiastic in the free-and-easy eighteenth century could be said to be out on the tiles.

The crowd were not discouraged by Lord George Gordon himself, who appeared frequently at the head of the gallery stairs, elevating the spirits of his followers with anti-papal harangues, and denouncing by name members he believed were betraying the Protestant cause, notably 'Mr Burke, the member for Bristol'. He obstinately resisted all attempts to dissuade him, and when a small force of soldiers eventually dispersed the crowd from Old Palace Yard, it went away and pillaged a number of Roman Catholic chapels, principally the two attached to the Bavarian and Sardinian embassies.

Two days later, on Sunday, 4th June, riots broke out in good earnest, and the reassembling of Parliament, on Tuesday, 6th June, was the signal for more demonstrations, the reading of the Riot Act, and the dispersal of the crowd to various districts and more mischief. Watched by the young engraver, poet and radical sympathizer, William Blake, a crowd set fire to Newgate Prison and released the prisoners, much as nine years later a Paris mob was to release the prisoners of the Bastille. (Newgate's total of over 300 released, however, far exceeded the Bastille's seven; but Newgate, too, held political prisoners, not only those who would be criminals in our legal sense, and the basic resentments behind the attacks were not dissimilar.) A separate crowd wrecked the Catholic quarter near Red Lion Square (which is still a centre, at Conway Hall, named after Thomas Paine's American biographer, for radical and rationalist meetings). Both the good magistrate, Sir John Fielding, and Wilkes' enemy, Lord Chief Justice Mansfield, lost their houses. Neither was a Catholic.

The Government inaction was marked, but Wilkes as Alderman was one of those responsible for the maintenance of law and order in the City. He must have known that old allies like Bull and Sawbridge were among the chief supporters of Lord George Gordon, and that many of the crowd were former members of the Wilkeite mob. The Court of Common Council of the City, two days before the riots, had supported the demand for the repeal of the Catholic Relief Act and on 7th June, at the height of the disturbances, presented a petition to Parliament on the matter. For Wilkes it was a question of staying neutral, or taking action before the City itself was, if not destroyed, at least heavily damaged. By 7th June thirty-six fires were already raging. He made his choice, the choice perhaps of the good magistrate he had been so long, as well as the advocate of religious tolerance; and after failing to gain immediate support from the Lord Mayor in ordering the sheriffs to call out the *posse comitatus*, he collected what armed force he could and set out determined to use it.

From the City's point of view the situation was already desperate and out of hand. Wilkes' old home, the King's Bench Prison, and also the Fleet Prison were in flames; houses, shops and factories had been partially destroyed or looted; and at the Holborn distillery of Thomas Langdale, a Roman Catholic distiller, the vats had been pierced and a drunken crowd was wallowing in a flow of raw spirits. It was the scene of an appalling tragedy when the liquor caught fire and many of the crowd were burned to death, or severely burned or trampled on in the ensuing panic. Langdale received compensation of nearly £19,000 for damage by fire to his premises at Nos 26 and 81 Holborn.

That night the danger shifted to the Bank of England. 'Attack near the Bank between 11 and 12 at night,' records Wilkes' laconic Diary; 'fired 6 or 7 times on the rioters at the end of the Bank towards Austin Friars and towards the middle of the Bank. Killed two rioters directly opposite the great gate of the Bank, several others in Pig Street and Cheapside.' Did any memories of the massacre of St George's Fields echo in the remoter cells of his mind?

Next day the Mayor at last gave him an official draft for troops, and the Government, too, took action. Wilkes and the King together were in a large part responsible for the belated show of courage and decision: it was always a quality which had linked them, irreconcilable as their other characteristics were. On 10th June Wilkes recorded dispersing 'a great mob in Fleet Street', seizing several treasonable papers at the printing shop of one William Moore, where the mob was congregating, and committing Moore to prison. The last actions show how long a road he had travelled since the days of 'Wilkes and Liberty'. Moore had been a printer of *The North Briton*.

By 14th June the riots were over. But in the clearing-up process in the Courts it became evident that a large proportion of buildings destroyed did not belong to Catholics, although a considerable proportion belonged to the rich. 'Of 136 claimants for damages whose occupation or status is given, there were one peer; two ambassadors; two doctors; two priests; three magistrates, five schoolteachers; thirty gentlemen; twenty-nine publicans, distillers, brewers and brandy-merchants; nine other merchants and dealers; ten manufacturers; twenty-four shopkeepers; fifteen independent craftsmen (or persons appearing to be such); and four wage-earners. That the victims of the riots were, on the whole, persons of substance is further confirmed by a study of the Rate Books and Land Tax registers for the period . . .' [1] Magistrates, justices, constables and prison keepers were also among those whose property was damaged. Nor were the areas of most Catholic occupation the ones with the highest figures for damage: some were hardly touched, in particular those where the poorer class of Catholic worker resided.

The rioters were not mainly from the unemployed or criminal classes but wage-earners such as journeymen, weavers and artisans of all kinds, as well as apprentices, small shopkeepers and sailors on shore leave from the War. As Rudé points out, Dickens' description of them in *Barnaby Rudge* as comprising a fair proportion of 'sober workmen' proves, on examination of the records of the Courts throughout London, to be true. The burnings of the prisons, and release of the prisoners, suggested quite different motives from the religious. Prisoners in those days were often political as well as criminal, and the laws were savage against theft

[1] George Rudé: *Paris and London in the Eighteenth Century. Studies in Popular Protest* (Collins, 1952–1970). Rudé's painstaking analysis of the records is the most valuable yet made and forms the basis of many of the figures and observations given here. Further comments are my own.

even when the thief was driven by the only-too-prevalent poverty. Of this the 'sober workmen' would be only too bitterly aware. It is notable that although 458 persons were killed or wounded by the Volunteers or military, and twenty-five subsequently hanged, no one was killed by the mob: only property was attacked. It was a pent-up lava of social unrest from a multitude of causes, which suddenly, on a given excuse, burst from the top of a volcano which had been simmering, on and off, for some time. Many old scores were settled, not only general but also, in some cases, individual. In one sense, it was an explosion of frustration, the protest of a whole body of people who felt themselves excluded from political action and the victims of an unequal system under which they could only toil in poverty while wealth and opulence flourished, like orchids, all round them. 'Protestant or not', as a Bermondsey barge-builder remarked when told one of the victims, a prosperous iron merchant, was no Papist, 'no gentleman need be possessed of more than £1,000 a year: that is enough for any gentleman to live upon'. The sense of social justice was stirring, but as yet there was no means of directing it, except in isolated sections of the community (as early as 1719 the tailors formed their own committees, followed by the sailors and weavers when conducting their strikes in 1768 and 1769).

Wilkes spent the next two weeks seizing arms, visiting the volunteers of Farringdon Without who had helped quell the riots, attending the Court of Aldermen and examining 'rogues and vagabonds' seized by special warrant. 'Sent some to Bridewell, and discharged others', he notes in his Diary on Saturday, 18th June. On the 28th, his entry, 'Romish schoolmasters' petition not received', suggests he was trying to strike a balance and not stir up further trouble by seeming to favour the Catholics. The harm, however, was done. By ordering his troops to fire on the crowd Wilkes had placed himself in exactly the same position as the supporter of the French Revolution, General Lafayette, scarcely a decade later, when the National Guard under his command fired, killing a number of people, in the 'Massacre of the Champ-de-Mars'. It is true that the crowd in the Champ-de-

Mars was said to be peacefully demonstrating, while the crowd in the City of London was destructively out of hand. But the effect was the same: followers of Wilkes and the General had been killed, and neither was ever trusted again. Wilkes' defence was obvious, and patently he was not responsible for the larger proportion of those killed, by troops under other command; but inevitably he was blamed. It was virtually the end of the 'Wilkeite' movement.

It may be significant that the same year, 1780, saw the formation of the Society for Promoting Constitutional Information, more popularly known as the Constitutional Society. With Horne Tooke as one of its most prominent members, it was to become one of the largest, most active and influential of the English radical societies in the next decade, when the French Revolution was to stimulate the growth of such societies in Britain. One of them, the London Corresponding Society founded by a shoemaker, Thomas Hardy, brought together for the first time sections of the working class, as compared with Tooke's middle- and upper-class associates, and paved the way for more peaceable and organized unions of workers in the future. The societies marked a new onward direction of radicalism in which Wilkes was to have no share. The Wilkeite movement had served its purpose, which was the promotion of liberty of the individual and the press. Its influence was to live on through the pursuit of other, more widely democratic, ideals, although the matter of the suppression of free press comment was by no means finally settled.

Nevertheless the Gordon Riots, too, had served a purpose: the alarm they had spread in the Government had bred a permanent fear of revolution, and the repressive measures meted out to the more literate radicals in the future, including the trial of Thomas Paine for 'seditious libel' and the 1794 treason trials of Horne Tooke, Hardy and others, were all rooted to some extent in the reactions to the Gordon Riots of 1780. Wilkes' fight for the freedom of the writer, and against condemnations for 'seditious libel', was only partially successful: the matter was to recur several times before the end of the century and well on into the following one.

Lord George Gordon, who quite obviously lost control of his followers at an early stage in the riots, faced a trial for high treason before the King's Bench on 5 February 1781, and was acquitted. His defending counsel was Thomas Erskine, a son of the Earl of Buchan, a brilliant lawyer and later a Whig Lord Chancellor, often seen in radical circles. In 1792, he was unsuccessfully to defend Thomas Paine in his trial, and two years later he offered his services free to Thomas Holcroft, one of the radical writers imprisoned for treason by the Government in 1794 but eventually released without trial.

The charge that the Gordon Riots were prearranged for a sinister political purpose by either Gordon or the Opposition (another accusation made, greatly to Grafton's indignation) seems untenable, but Gordon was neither so stupid nor so demented as accounts of the riots often suggest. His stance on the American War had been a liberal one: only two years before, in a parliamentary debate on 26 May 1778, he had stated that it was clear 'that the most accomplished General at the head of the completest army was impotent when employed by arbitrary power to reduce mankind to unconditional submission'. Wilkes himself could hardly have opposed such a sentiment, even though the speaker of it was indubitably a Scotsman. Gordon, in fact, 'displayed considerable talent in debate, and no deficiency of wit or argument', as one historian has admitted.[1] It is certainly untrue, as often misreported, that he died in an asylum. In 1787 he was convicted for writing and publishing a pamphlet criticizing the laws and criminal justice of the country, and also for publishing a libel on Marie Antoinette and the French Ambassador to London. He escaped to Holland, but on his return was apprehended, and he died in Newgate of fever on 1 November 1793. On religious matters, he certainly wavered mentally. At the time of his death he was a convert to Judaism.

[1] *Chambers's Encyclopaedia* (1908).

It was an odd footnote to the 1780 riots that when Wilkes' brother-in-law, George Hayley, died in August 1781, Lord George Gordon offered himself as candidate for his position as Alderman of the Ward of Cordwainer. Perhaps wisely, he retired before the day of the election.

XIII

'THAT WAS ALL OVER LONG AGO'

If Wilkes' political influence was in decline, he showed no indication as yet of accepting the fact. When the American War, which seemed on the point of being lost, flared up again with victories at Charlestown and Camden, and the Government moved their vote of thanks to the Generals concerned, they indicated they expected the vote to be unanimous. After a dramatic pause, Wilkes was on his feet, declaring he had no intention of thanking generals for killing his fellow-subjects, and prolonging a War about to lead to fresh slaughter and humiliation. He wanted peace, and peace at any price. The refusal to concede the Americans independence, he added, was merely an amusing theme of speculation among a set of 'idle, listless, loitering, lounging, ill-informed gentlemen at Westminster'. After this spirited hurling of a weapon of alliteration, he deeply lamented that 'the lustre of such splendid victories is obscured and darkened by the want of a good cause, without which no war, in the eye of truth and reason, before God or man, can be justified'.

Wilkes' speech revived a little of his sagging popularity. Westminster's vote of thanks to him was followed by Yorkshire in the New Year, 1781. In February Burke gingerly renewed his Bill for reducing the Civil List, but he made as yet little headway and the second reading was deferred in order that the members could attend the benefit performance for the great male dancer Vestris, as famous and adulated in London as in Paris (it is a curious instance of the flexible eighteenth-century attitude to the arts and politics).

Washington's decisive victory at Yorktown, in which his young French recruit the Marquis de Lafayette particularly distinguished himself, virtually if not actually marked the end of the American War. When the peace negotiations were completed, Parliament, heaving sighs of relief as well as groans of humiliation, turned its mind to other matters. On 3 May 1782, after several attempts, Wilkes had at last succeeded in getting his expulsions expunged from the records of the House of Commons. The vote was 115 to 47, and Wilkes at once issued a manifesto to his constituents, informing them of the event and adding that a bill of reform in the matter of representation was about to be put before the House by 'a gentleman of as great abilities, matured even in youth, as this country has at any time produced'. He reminded them that following their instructions he had himself, as long ago as March 1776, tried to bring in a Bill 'for a just and equal representation of the people of England in Parliament', but without success.

The young gentleman of great and matured abilities, Lord Chatham's son William Pitt the younger, proved, however, to be as unsuccessful as Wilkes himself in promoting a committee to consider such a Bill. A few days after his first defeat on the issue, on 18 May 1782, Wilkes attended a meeting of protest at the Thatched House Tavern, at which Pitt himself, the Duke of Richmond, Lord Mahon, the Earl of Surrey, the well-known radical writers, Dr John Jebb and Major John Cartwright, and other supporters of Pitt's Bill were present. Under the chairmanship of the Lord Mayor, they resolved that 'it is become indispensably necessary that application should be made to Parliament by Petition, from the Collective Body of the People', suggesting a reform of the House of Commons. [1] Pitt presented the Bill a second time the following year, without success, and as the years passed he was to move to the Right and leave his original more liberal-minded colleagues – Grafton, Fox, Sheridan and others – in helpless and infuriated Opposition. Fox's brief alliance with North and his followers, so deplored by Grafton and Camden at the time, seems never quite to have been forgiven by Wilkes, whose attitude to him thereafter was ambivalent. Wilkes was almost alone among the more liberal members to oppose Fox's East India Bill, a measure put before the House on 8 December 1783 and designed to reform the

[1] P. A. Brown: *The French Revolution in English History* (Allen & Unwin, 1918; Frank Cass, 1965).

government of India with a lessening of oppression towards the native population. Although it failed to gain a majority, it was highly praised by the Scot, Adam Smith, whose *Wealth of Nations* had appeared in 1776, giving political economy a new forward emphasis.

Pitt became Prime Minister on 23 December 1783 (he was the first actually to bear such a title and incontestably head the Government). In 1785 he once again made a gesture towards reform, and was once again defeated. He did not try again. Soon the outburst of the French Revolution was to turn his mind to other matters, and his sympathies in another direction, in which Burke in particular followed him. In the meantime, in 1788, the public and official mind was more engrossed with India. Robert Clive, who had made an immense fortune there, had been arraigned before Parliament and rebuked in 1772; now it was the turn of Warren Hastings, the present Governor. Sheridan in 1787 started the attack with a dazzling display of elocutionary fireworks (he had not been an actor and dramatist in vain), and Burke in 1788 opened the actual trial which was to drag on for seven years.

Wilkes, once again, went against the Opposition, and supported Hastings in a speech of some eloquence: he was, he maintained, a consummate statesman and the saviour of India. There is no doubt Hastings was to some extent a scapegoat, but Wilkes' attitude seems based on a personal friendship. Mr and Mrs Warren Hastings are recorded at dinner at Princes Court, along with that unlikely character 'Mlle D'Eon' whom Wilkes had known ever since his exile in Paris. There was also the question of Jackie Smith involved. Wilkes' son had become a squadron officer in the Bengal cavalry through Warren Hastings' influence, even though Hastings, by ill luck, fell into disgrace by the time Jackie reached India. As a result, promotion did not come quickly, but apparently Jackie had at last found his niche. 'I assure you there is not a happier man in India than I am', he announced joyously in his last extant letter home.

In other ways, Wilkes was gradually moving into more orthodox channels. Heading a City delegation, years before, he had forced the reluctant King George III to meet him personally and had surprised the King by his good manners. The King grudgingly admitted he had never known so well-bred a Mayor. Now he could even be seen at levées. Unlike the leading Whigs, particularly Fox, he never made overtures to the Prince of Wales, who was known to be bitterly antagonistic to his father. When the Prince advertised his racing stud and horses for sale, to meet his crushing load of debts, Wilkes proclaimed the stud should indeed be given up: 'I would not tax the people £30,000 a year to divide among the blacklegs of Newmarket.' The statement probably did not endear him to Grafton any more than to the Prince.

When the French Revolution broke out he at first gave it his approval. To him it seemed an extension not only of the American Revolution he had so arduously supported, but also of the 'Glorious' Revolution of 1688. The teachings of his friends, the French *philosophes*, were no doubt still treasured in his mind. In August 1791 he saw the French adoption of a limited monarchy, such as that of England, as a political innovation only for the good. Only later, as the Terror spread, did he refer to 'this nation of monkeys and tigers'.

In 1792, in a speech to his constituents in the Ward of Farringdon Without and in the wake of more republican developments in the French Revolution, he stated he was 'a firm friend to a limited monarchy, as a government founded on laws – a government which does not depend on the will or caprice of an individual, but rests on known and written laws. Such a government best answers the great end designed by it – to give security and safety to persons and to property . . .' He had added that in a republican government 'there is a continual struggle who shall be the greatest', a statement only too prophetic of the coming National Assembly conflicts across the Channel. 'On these principles it is that I profess my regard for limited monarchy – a monarchy which is not above law, but is founded upon law, and secures freedom to the subject.' He even declared some enthusiasm for the Hanoverian dynasty, certainly a diplomatic *volte face* in comparison with earlier sentiments. Not an enthusiastic card player, he had once let drop the witticism that he was so ignorant of the game that 'I cannot tell the difference between a king and a knave.'

Nevertheless, when in the wake of government panic about Paine's *Rights of Man*, a mob wrecked the Birmingham house and laboratory of his radical friend Dr Priestley, Wilkes was, he wrote to his daughter, 'shocked to read of the savage, cruel, and persecuting spirit of the mechanics at Birmingham; and I trust the Government will exert itself in the punishment of so vile and wicked a crew'. The Government, which was probably behind the wrecking, did of course nothing of the kind, and the King himself was smugly triumphant: 'As the mischief did occur, it was impossible not to feel pleased at its having fallen on Priestley rather than another, that he might *feel* the wickedness of the doctrines of democracy which he was propagating.'

By this time Wilkes had left Parliament, and he was therefore not present when Fox, in his Libel Bill, referred to the improvements now gained from the liberty of the press, for which Wilkes had been so much responsible; nor when, in the debate on the treason and sedition bills, which helped to destroy all the liberties gained, Fox directly compared what the consequences might have been had these bills become law when Wilkes was tried for libel:

'I have not the honour of that gentleman's acquaintance, nor have I, in the course of our political lives frequently agreed with him in opinion; but now that the intemperance of the time is past, I submit to the House what must be the feeling of every liberal heart at the idea of condemning a person of such high attainments, so dear to the society in which he lives, so exemplary as a magistrate, and who has shown himself to be so zealous a defender of the prerogatives of the Crown, to a punishment so degrading.' [1]

The lack of actual acquaintance shows, among other things, how completely Wilkes had kept his independence from

[1] *Fox's Speeches*, vol. vi.

party factions within Parliament. But he could have relished no more than the liberal Whigs the new encroachments on the freedom of the writer, the acquisition of what, as Fox wrote to Grafton a few months after Wilkes' death, they 'used to call the *exploded* principles of tyranny'.

Wilkes' retirement from Parliament had been voluntary. On 11 June 1790 Parliament dissolved and he failed to stand as a candidate in the General Election. He had represented Middlesex throughout his parliamentary career, once readmitted to the House.

Perhaps he was tiring. It had been a long, tough battle, simultaneously fought with more agreeable but no less athletic battles in the sex war, in which (with one exception) he had been the invariable victor. He remained tolerant of his old, humbler supporters, and when a mob broke his windows (in mistake for those of someone else) in 1794 he refused to prosecute. 'They are only some of my old pupils', he said indulgently, 'now set up for themselves.' But it was no longer wise, in his new guise of sedate retired country gentleman, to be associated with the old, flame-tossing Wilkes of 'Wilkes and Liberty!': it might have involved him in further political effort, and Wilkes had become too old, in his opinion, for that. When an aged countrywoman recognized him in his coach, driving along a rural lane, [1] and called after him the old slogan, he silenced her. 'Be quiet, you old fool', he said, not unkindly, perhaps a little wistfully: 'That was all over long ago.'

He had leased a small house which he called his 'villakin' on Sandown Bay in the Isle of Wight. Formerly occupied by the Earl of Winchelsea, it was named Sandham Cottage and situated on Sandown Bay, overlooking the sea. Here he pottered happily in his garden when not in London attending assiduously, still, to his work as City Chamberlain. He also turned to scholastic work. In 1788 he published a de luxe edition of Catullus, consisting of 300 copies on vellum, 100 on fine paper, quarto. Catullus was not in fashion in the eighteenth century, and it was supposed Wilkes had been

[1] The actual geography of the scene differs with the reports: some place it in the City.

attracted by the similarity of the tempestuous careers of the two men. In 1790 he added the first complete edition of the *Characters* of Theophrastus: three copies on vellum, 100 on fine paper, quarto. He was criticized for omitting the Greek accents and breathings from the texts, but the accents in any case are a scholastically controversial matter, as they are Alexandrine not classical in date. If Wilkes' Leyden education was too interrupted for classical erudition to take a completely accurate hold (the Latin in his letter in verse to Sir Francis Dashwood had either been faulty or part of an acknowledged secret code), these later printed studies had some contemporary and posthumous success. He also made some progress with a translation of Anacreon, which was admired by Joseph Warton but unpublished.

Perhaps partly in reaction to his own unprepossessing physical traits, he had a genuine love of beautiful things. He had written to Polly in Paris for Sèvres china, he continued to haunt art exhibitions and was an admiring friend of Sir Joshua Reynolds, first President of the Royal Academy. His taste was conservative but solid: he remarked on the vanity of the English in its almost exclusive passion for portraiture and neglect of 'historical paintings', but the grandiose scenes of history were forerunners of the popular taste of the Victorians for pictures with a moral story. He remained an active member of the Royal Society, and was concerned in the striking of a medal by the Society to commemorate a voyage of Captain Cook. He was also one of the Governors of St Thomas' Hospital and dined with them at the London Tavern on 31 July 1778. In spite of past enmities, he had a room full of Hogarth prints, and had no inhibitions at all about sitting for his portrait, of which there are several, including one, full-length, with his rather stiff-looking daughter Polly, whose hand he holds in fatherly appreciation. Wilkes, either with the blindness of fond devotion or the kindness of fatherly encouragement, had written of his 'pretty daughter' but it seems to have been an exaggeration. 'Accomplished' was a more usual descriptive term used of Polly.

His love of dress continued, even in age, nor did he neglect

Bath and the ballroom. His scarlet and green coats with gold lace were now supplemented by fancy waistcoats, bright with embroidery but otherwise 'grave enough for an Alderman'. He now had two town houses, in May 1789 leasing one at the corner of Grosvenor Square and South Audley Street. And suddenly he began to age, and to show nostalgia for the past. In 1794, the Doric pillar inscribed with the Latin verse commemorating Churchill was put at the end of his Isle of Wight garden, in a cypress grove, and he described its pastoral setting with affection and a touch of sentimentality:

'It is in the middle of the grove, and backed with weeping willows, cypresses, yews, etc. Laurels grow out of the column as from Virgil's tomb at Naples, and come down nearly to the tablet, on the *pillar*, which is fluted and seems in some parts already injured by Time. On the fore-ground are large myrtles, bays, laburnums, etc. The *pillar* is broken, about nine feet high, and five feet diameter.'

A friend after visiting him described his dress, 'excepting one instance', as 'perfectly Arcadian; instead of a crook, he walked about his grounds with a hoe, raking up weeds, and destroying vipers'. Still a fastidious diner, he kept his pond well-stocked with carp, tench, perch and eels 'because fish is almost the only rare article by the seaside'.

He encouraged visitors, although preferring them in small doses: 'a dinner party, to be comfortable, should never consist of more than the number of the Muses, nor of less than that of the Graces'. He also enjoyed the sailing still associated with the island. 'If you can come by the 30th', he wrote to one of his Ward Deputies, John Nichols, 'you will be amused, as I believe, by a grand *sailing match* round the Isle of Wight, by about 50 vessels, carvel-built, not exceeding 30 tons. You will add greatly to your stock of nautical ideas, in which I suspect you are very poor; and at Christmas Wardmote, we will compel the Common Council of Farringdon Without to admire the profoundness of our Naval skill, so necessary for every true-born Briton.' That his eye for graceful objects other than sailing vessels had not dimmed was, however, shown when he praised Newport market and commented that his *glance* had done great execution with the farmers' pretty daughters.

He developed a tendency to begin anecdotes with the words: 'Now I'll tell you something that happened in the days of the late Jack Wilkes.' The anecdotes were as racy as ever about his profligate adventures, as well as his political battles; but when asked if he would like to live these events over again he commented 'Not at all': 'Adversity may be a good thing to breakfast on; nay, a man may dine on it. But, believe me, it makes a confoundedly bad supper.' Byegones, in other ways, were byegones. He dined in company with Boswell with the eldest son of his old target, Lord Bute, and while still in the House actually applauded his speech there. Without always being fully conscious of it, he was also sometimes touching the hem of England's future history. Among his last City speeches was one to Admiral Nelson, wishing him joy when (as was customary with military and naval heroes) he received the freedom of the City for his victory at Cape St Vincent, on 28 November 1797. Many years before he had also presided at the ceremony when William Pitt the younger was made a freeman.

At the age of seventy he was reported in the gossip-columns to be making 'a last Essay on Woman in the neighbourhood of Soho'. It may well have been true. But Millie Arnold and Harriet now saw much of him, and often had happy seaside holidays at the cottage overlooking Sandown Bay, attending Shanklin Fair and (Harriet in particular) eating the strawberries in the garden. He corrected Harriet's letters with admonitions on spelling, bred pigeons, and roamed the countryside on his Welsh pony with his dog, Trusty, at his side. In London, Millie's house at Kensington Gore was a haven even from Grosvenor Square. He died at Grosvenor Square on 26 December 1797, quite peacefully and without pain. Christmas had never been one of his most fortunate periods.

His Will dated 1795 left £100 to 'Mr John Smith now an officer in the service of the East India Company formerly educated under Mr Lauchoix at Paris'; to Mrs Amelia Arnold the lease of the house at 2 Kensington Gore with its contents plus £1,000; to Harriet the lease of the house at Sandham with the contents and the sum of £2,000 at the age of twenty-one; and to Polly the house in Grosvenor Square with its contents and all real estates, etc. But in fact, and not unexpectedly, he died insolvent, and Polly to her credit from her own fortune discharged the legacies her father had wished. She survived him only just over four years, dying suddenly (and rather characteristically) after a party, in the middle of the night. A great deal of her fortune went to charity, including a City annuity for the relief of widows and children of freemen. Harriet eventually married Sir William Rough, a rising young lawyer who afterwards wrote some interesting commentary on his father-in-law.

Wilkes was buried in Grosvenor Chapel, where he had regularly worshipped. It was very close to his house, and as he had directed, his coffin was carried by six poor men of the parish, who were given a guinea each and a suit of clothes for their trouble. A plaque on the coffin gave simply his name, the dates, and the description 'A friend to Liberty'. A plain marble tablet in the North Gallery commemorates him in similar terms.

In 1927 the Rev. Francis Underhill, later Bishop of Bath and Wells, and his assistant priest at the Chapel, maintained they 'felt' a supernatural presence in a corner close to Wilkes' memorial tablet. 'A lady with psychic powers' was called in and, after vigils in the Chapel, told of a figure she had seen which, after research, seemed to correspond with John Wilkes. She spoke of 'two horns growing back from his head, like a devil'. Various pictures of Wilkes, especially Hogarth's, show that his wig was gathered into rolls which could possibly be said to resemble two short horns. Tom Harrison also felt the presence of Wilkes in the house adjoining the Chapel, and wrote an account of it in *The Listener* of 20 December 1956. Whether prior knowledge (especially of the Hogarth print) set imaginations working in this matter, it is for the reader to decide.

Wilkes' real contribution to society is of a different nature, and more valuable. His supporters were not, as sometimes erroneously stated, only working class but a disparate body of what might today be called the lower middle classes, the middle rank of merchants, craftsmen and traders. Well-dressed people were often seen in Wilkeite crowds. The aristocracy and politicians where they supported him did so for the furtherance of their own policies and ambitions: they never seriously considered absorbing him into their own hierarchy, but this was partly Wilkes' own choice. The Whigs, which would have been his natural party, were themselves split into warring factions and Wilkes by nature was independent and could never be relied upon not to vote the other way when his conscience dictated it. He thought for himself, and if his conclusions seemed sometimes the wrong ones they were at least his own. Once in Parliament he was singularly incorruptible.

There is every evidence that the public at large saw in him a spokesman for their own political needs, including a widened franchise and more equable social order. Beckford in Parliament had himself long centralized this need. The fluctuating cost of bread, both in London and the provinces, and the miseries in the country districts caused by this and 'enclosures' of the common lands, provoked resentments and sometimes riots on their own account. In 1787 the first convicts were sent to Australia. It was an eight months' journey and conditions were such that in 1791, 183 men and twelve women died in one cargo. These brutalities, the slave trade, the exploitation of Africans and Indians (as is shown by his opposition to Fox's East India Bill) seem to have come outside the range of Wilkes' reforming zeal, nor was he deeply concerned with workers' wages and conditions of work. Probably this was lack of imagination rather than inhumanity: his social vision had limitations. But whatever was brought to his notice as a magistrate found him compassionate and often practical in reforming suggestions, consistently fair-minded, and urgent in his recommendations for alleviation of the harshness of the laws, as in the matter of the offences punishable by death. In issues such as the widening of the franchise he was among the most advanced parliamentary leaders of his day and in some ways ahead even of a radical such as William Godwin, who felt strongly the nation was not ready for universal suffrage.

On Wilkes' relationship with the 'mob' it is too often
overlooked that only two generations back his family was
working class; it gave him an instinctive rapport with the
lower or 'middling' classes of people and this mutual
response was particularly expressed, as I have earlier
suggested, by their common bond of satiric humour. Wilkes
was a London Cockney, and Cockney humour takes in its
stride quips against itself and relishes in ironic inversion. It is
a vein of national humour 'which can be traced through
English literature', as I once wrote, 'to the sardonic thrust
of Cockney speech. It is the vein of Henry Fielding, whose
Jonathan Wild is written in a style of irony which applies to
that squalid rogue throughout the appellation of a "great
gentleman"; and it is the vein of Charles Dickens, whose
reference to "Golden Balls" gives a sardonic double-meaning
to the "distinguished" activities of a Chuzzlewit ancestor. . . .
It was G. K. Chesterton, himself only too delighted to devise
"a paradox, a paradox, a most ingenious paradox", who in
an essay on *Pickwick Papers* pointed out that ironic humour is
a peculiar and distinctive attribute of the English poor:
"The phrase that leaps to their lips is the ironical phrase. I
remember once being driven in a hansom cab down a street
that turned out to be a cul-de-sac, and brought us bang up
against a wall. The driver and I simultaneously said
something. But I said: 'This'll never do!' and he said: 'This
is all right!' Even in the act of pulling back his horse's nose
from a brick wall, that confirmed satirist thought in terms of
his highly trained and traditional satire: while I, belonging
to a duller and simpler class, expressed my feelings in words
as innocent and literal as those of a rustic or a child." '[1] The
attachment of the 'mob' to Wilkes was the attachment to a
popular comedian: his quips even against themselves would
be taken in good part, and he knew it.

Although it would be true to say that Wilkes' cause had
begun by being John Wilkes, where he found himself drawn
into issues that spread, like the effect of a stone thrown in a
pond, into widening circles, he had the humanity and sense

[1] Audrey Williamson: *Gilbert and Sullivan Opera: A New Assessment* (Rockliff,
1953).

233

of justice to recognize the broader applications and quite sincerely, on the whole, he clung to them. He was never, *au fond*, a revolutionist, although perhaps, as Franklin sensed, the only man in England who could have led one, had he had the mind. (The remark was a tribute to his hold over the English people.) He settled back into apparent conservatism in old age; but never of the Burke kind, reversing former standards and in suspected government pay. It certainly does not mean that he abandoned the stand of his younger days. Given his time again, and the same provocations and problems, he had no doubt, he once declared, that he would have gone the same way.

'But the fear of innovation, in this country', wrote Mary Wollstonecraft in 1792, 'extends to everything'.[1] It was a perspicacious remark, and it is still true. Wilkes was not by natural English instinct an innovator, or a political 'original': he had none of Tom Paine's breathtaking internationalist foresight and economic and scientific vision. Indeed, in spite of his friendship with Priestley, he seems surprisingly free from the questing scientific experiments and changing industrial technologies of his age, in which so many contemporary radicals and dissenters were actively involved. Even his art enthusiasms overlooked Joseph Wright, the great painter of the iron processes and industrial scenes of the North, whose 'Experiment with the Air Pump' was exhibited in London in 1768, the year of Wilkes' Middlesex election. But unlike Godwin, who wrote 'I am bold and adventurous in opinions, not in life', he had immense courage in the battles outside the printed page and this too was a quality which appealed to the London 'mob', already infused with the British characteristic of resistance to anything like tyranny.

Fate threw him into the cauldron of politics and controversy, and he played it 'by ear'. But he played it also with superb instinct and charm, and thus imprinted his personality on the history of the English people, and the new thrusting quests for liberty that marked his age. Nearly a

[1] *Vindication of the Rights of Woman.*

century later a great Prime Minister, William Gladstone, crystallized his democratic position. 'Judged by his achievements he must be enrolled among the great champions of English freedom.'

His own favourite quotation was from Swift:

'Might the whole world be placed within my span
I would not be that thing a prudent man.'

———

BIBLIOGRAPHY
(including MSS and Collections)

ALMON, JOHN: *History of the Late Minority*
ALMON, JOHN: *Letters of John Wilkes* (1805, 5 vols)
ALMON, JOHN: *Annual Register, The*, 1763–1787

Battle of the Quills (1768)
BLEACKLEY, H. W.: *Life of John Wilkes* (1917)
BRITISH MUSEUM:
    ADD MSS. 30865 onwards: 30887 (false *Essay on Woman*);
    30865A and B (fragments of autobiography);
    30878 (Churchill's letters); 30886 (Phillips' letters);
    30888 (Kensingtoniana, by Wilkes).
    PC. 31, k. 7 (true *Essay on Woman*); PC. 31, f. 30 (false *Essay*)
BROWN, P. A.: *The French Revolution in English History* (Allen & Unwin, 1918; Frank Cass, 1965)
BURKE, EDMUND: *Correspondence*
BURKE, EDMUND: *Reflections on the Revolution in France* (1790)
BURKE, EDMUND: *Thoughts on the Cause of the Present Discontents* (1770)
BYRON, LORD: *The Vision of Judgement*

CARLYLE, THE REV. DR. ALEXANDER: *Autobiography* (1860)
CHURCHILL, CHARLES: *The Candidate* (1764)
CHURCHILL, CHARLES: *The Duellist* (1764)
CHURCHILL, CHARLES: *The Rosciad* (1761)
CONWAY, MONCURE D.: *Life of Thomas Paine* (New York ,1892)

DICKENS, CHARLES: *Barnaby Rudge* (1841)
DIDEROT, DENIS: *Les Pensées sur l'interprétation de la nature* (1753)
DILKE, C. W.: *Papers of a Critic*, vol II (Murray, 1875)

FAGG, EDWIN: *Old Sadler's Wells* (Vic-Wells Association, 1935)
FIELDING, HENRY: *The Enquiry*
FIELDING, HENRY: *Jonathan Wild*
FITZMAURICE, LORD E.: *Life of Lord Shelburne* (Macmillan, 1875)
FONBLANQUE, EDWARD BARRINGTON DE: *Life and Correspondence of the Rt. Hon. John Burgoyne* (Macmillan, 1876)
FOX, CHARLES JAMES: *Speeches*

GODWIN, WILLIAM: *Political Justice* (1793)
GOOCH, G. P.: *French Profiles* (Longmans, 1961)
GOTTSCHALK, LOUIS R.: *Jean Paul Marat: a Study in Radicalism* (University of Chicago Press, 1927, new edn 1967)
GRAFTON, AUGUSTUS HENRY FITZROY, 3RD DUKE OF: *Memoirs with Political Correspondence* (Ed. Sir William Anson: John Murray, 1898)
GRENVILLE CORRESPONDENCE

GUILDHALL MSS:
Papers of Crown Solicitor in *North Briton* and *Essay of Woman* cases. MS Journals of City Proceedings, JOR.66 and 179 Rep. Collections dealing with City elections, petitions and addresses (1778) and Acts of Common Council (1790) Sandwich-Webb correspondence (13 letters), 22 Oct. to 14 Nov. 1763 (214/1)

HALL-STEVENSON, JOHN: *Confessions of Sir F . . . . . of Medmenham*
HALL-STEVENSON, JOHN: *The Works of* (1795, 3 vols)
HART, ROGER: *English Life in the Eighteenth Century* (Wayland, 1970)

HAZLITT, WILLIAM: *The Life of Thomas Holcroft*, including Holcroft's *Memories* of hisearly life (Ed. E. Colby, Constable, 1925)

JOHNSTONE, CHARLES: *Chrysal* (1760–5)
JUNIUS, LETTERS OF (1772)

KEGAN PAUL, C.: *William Godwin, His Friends and Contemporaries* (1876, 2 vols)
KEMP, BETTY: *Sir Francis Dashwood* (Macmillan, London; St Martin's Press, New York, 1967)
KEMP, BETTY: *Some Letters of Sir Francis Dashwood, Baron Le Despencer, as Joint Postmaster General, 1766–81* (Manchester University Press, reprinted from 'Bulletin of the John Rylands Library', Vol 37, No. 1, Sept. 1954)

LA METTRIE, JULIEN OFFRAY DE: *L'Homme Machine* (1748)
LASKY, MELVIN J.: 'The Prometheans: Fire and Revolution' (*Encounter*, Oct. 1968)
LASKY, MELVIN J.: 'The Metaphysics of Doomsday' (*Encounter*, Jan. 1969)
LASKY, MELVIN J.: 'The Sweet Dream' (*Encounter*, Oct. 1969)
LASKY, MELVIN J.: 'The Novelty of Revolution' (*Encounter*, Nov. 1971)
LASKY, MELVIN J.: 'The English Ideology' (*Encounter*, Dec. 1972 and Jan. 1973)
LASKY, MELVIN J.: 'The Recantation of Henry Redhead Yorke' (*Encounter*, Oct. 1973)
LASKY, MELVIN J.: *Utopia and Revolution* (Chicago University Press, 1974)
Letters of John Wilkes to his Daughter (Ed. Sir William Rough, 1804, 4 vols)

MCCORMICK, DONALD: *The Hell-Fire Club* (Jarrolds, 1958; paperback reprint, West Wycombe Caves Ltd, 1964)

NAMIER, SIR LEWIS and JOHN BROOKE: *Charles Townshend* (Macmillan, 1964)
New Foundling Hospital for Wit
North Briton, The, 1762–3
NYE, R. B. and MORPURGO, J. E.: *The Birth of the USA* (Pelican, 1955–70)

OMAN, CAROLA: *David Garrick* (Hodder & Stoughton, 1958)
OMAN, CHARLES: *A History of England* (1895)

PAINE, THOMAS: *The Age of Reason* (1794)

PAINE, THOMAS: *Rights of Man* (1791 and 1792)

PARLIAMENTARY HISTORY, vol. xv, xvi, xviii–xxvi

PLUMB, J. H.: *Chatham* (Collins, 1953; 'Makers of History' series, 1965)

PLUMB, J. H.: *England in the Eighteenth Century* (Pelican, 1950–69)

POSTGATE, RAYMOND: *That Devil Wilkes* (Constable, 1930: revised edn, Dobson, 1956)

POTTLE, F. A.: *James Boswell: The Earlier Years, 1756–62* (Heinemann, London; McGraw Hill, New York, 1966)

PRIESTLEY, HAROLD: *Voice of Protest: A History of Civil Unrest in Great Britain* (Frewin, 1968)

QUENNELL, PETER: *Four Portraits. Studies of the Eighteenth Century* (Collins, 1945)

RAE, W. FRASER: *Wilkes, Sheridan, Fox: The Opposition under George the Third* (1874)

RHODES, H. T. F.: *The Satanic Mass* (Rider, 1954; Arrow paperback, 1964–73)

RIDLEY, JASPER: *Lord Palmerston* (Constable, London; Dutton, New York, 1970)

RUDÉ, GEORGE: *Paris and London in the Eighteenth Century: Studies in Popular Protest* (Collins Fontana Library, 1970 edn)

RUDÉ, GEORGE: *Wilkes and Liberty: A Social Study of 1763 to 1774* (Clarendon Press, 1962)

SHAW, G. BERNARD: *Man and Superman* (1903) and *Saint Joan* (1924)

SHERRARD, O. A.: *Life of Wilkes* (1930)

SMITH, J. T.: *Nollekens and His Times*

STEPHENS, ALEXANDER: *Memoirs of John Horne Tooke* (1813)

STEPHENS, ALEXANDER: *Sussex Weekly Advertiser or Lewes Journal* (1770–8)

SUTHERLAND, LUCY S.: *The City of London and the Opposition to Government, 1768–1774* (University of London, Athlone Press, 1959)

THOMPSON, E. P.: *The Making of the English Working Class* (Gollancz, 1963; (Pelican, 1968–72)

TOOKE, JOHN HORNE: *Diversions of Purley*

TRELOAR, WILLIAM PURDIE: *Wilkes and the City* (Murray, 1917)

TRENCH, CHARLES CHENEVIX: *Portrait of a Patriot* (Blackwell, 1962)

TREVELYAN, G. M.: *Illustrated English Social History* (Vol. 3, *The Eighteenth Century*), (Pelican, 1964)

WALDEGRAVE, LORD: *Memoirs*

WALPOLE, HORACE: *Journal*

WALPOLE, HORACE: *Letters*

WALPOLE, HORACE: *Memoirs of the Reign of George III*

WHITE, R. J.: *The Anti-Philosophers* (Macmillan, London; St Martin's Press, New York 1970)

WILKES, JOHN: *A Letter to the Rt. Hon. George Grenville, M.P.* (1769)

WILKES, JOHN: *The Speeches of Mr Wilkes* (1786)

WILLIAMSON, AUDREY: *Gilbert and Sullivan Opera:* a New Assessment (Rockliff, London; Macmillan, New York, 1953)

WILLIAMSON, AUDREY: *Thomas Paine: His Life, Work and Times* (Allen & Unwin, London; St Martin's Press, New York, 1973)

WIMSATT, WILLIAM K. JR. and POTTLE, FREDERICK A. (Eds): *Boswell for the Defence* (Yale University, 1959; Heinemann, London, 1960)

WOLLSTONECRAFT, MARY: *A Vindication of the Rights of Woman* (1792)

YOUNG, ARTHUR: *Travels in France during the years 1787, 1788 and 1789* (Ed. Constantia Maxwell: Cambridge University Press, 1950)

INDEX

INDEX

Rudé, George 28n, 76, 140n, 178, 217, 217n.
Rumbold, Thomas, M.P. 143–5

Sackville, George. *See* Germain, Lord George
Sadler's Wells Ballet 158
Sadler's Wells Opera 158
Sadler's Wells Theatre 27, 158
'Saint Agnes' 142
Saint Joan (Shaw) 115n
St James's Chronicle 136
Sandwich, 4th Earl of (1718–92) 23, 39, 40, 55, 77, 82, 90, 91, 92, 95, 103, 164, 196
Satanic Mass, The (Rhodes) 35n
Sawbridge, John 137, 151, 153, 155, 170, 172, 215
Schiller, Johann Christoph Friedrich 198
School for Scandal, The (Sheridan) 158, 211
Selwyn, George 129
Seven Years' War 27, 43–4, 47, 65
    Peace of Paris 51–2, 60, 73, 79, 96
Shakespeare Jubilee (1769) 39, 121
Shakespeare, William 39, 55, 60, 83, 102, 160, 207
Shaw, George Bernard 15, 80n, 111, 115, 197, 200
Shelburne, Lord 51, 119, 123, 167, 171, 172, 197n, 200, 203, 204, 205
Shelley, Percy Bysshe 42
Sheridan, Richard Brinsley 157, 158, 211, 212, 223, 224
Sheriff, Henry 21
Sidney, Sir Philip 120
Silva, Isaac Fernandez 23
Sir Francis Dashwood (Kemp) 30n
Smith, Adam 224
Smith, Jackie (Wilkes' natural son) 45–6, 101, 103, 184, 224, 230
Smith, J. T. 71

Smollett, Tobias 52, 54, 56
Social Contract (Rousseau) 112
Society of Antiquaries 32
Society of Dilettanti 32
Society for Promoting Constitutional Information. *See* Constitutional Society
Society of Supporters of the Bill of Rights 146, 147, 160, 167, 169
Staël, Mme de 207
Stafford, Maria 209–11, 212
Stapelton, Sir Thomas 33
Star Chamber 154n
Stephen, Leslie 54
Stephen, Alexander 169n
Sterne, Laurence 37, 53, 79, 102
Stevens, John 21
Stuart, Charles Edward ('The Young Pretender') 53, 56, 109, 213
Surrey, Earl of 223
Sussex Weekly Advertiser or Lewes Journal, The 143–4, 151, 153, 154
Sutherland, Lucy S. 76n, 152n, 153
Swift, Jonathan 160, 235
Système de la Nature (d'Holbach) 79

Talbot, Lord 57, 63, 78
Temple, Richard Grenville, Lord (1711–79) 23, 44, 56, 58, 62, 63, 65, 66, 71, 73, 74, 75, 77, 86, 91, 100, 103, 105, 106, 118, 123, 128, 142, 164, 172, 204
Terry, Edward and Richard 21
That Devil Wilkes (Postgate) 38n, 162n
Thelwall, John 146
Theophrastus 228
Thompson (printer) 163
Thoughts on the Cause of the Present Discontent (Burke) 160
Thrale, Mrs 176
Townsend, James 137, 151, 170, 172, 183

251